Cover:
Rembrandt, *The Anatomy Lesson of Dr. Nicolaes Tulp* (detail),
1632, oil on canvas, 169.5 x 216.5 cm,
Mauritshuis website, The Hague

TLC

2018 The Low Countries

ARTS AND SOCIETY IN FLANDERS AND THE NETHERLANDS

26

**Published by
the Flemish-Dutch
cultural institution**
Ons Erfdeel vzw

Contents

'About suffering they were never wrong,
The old Masters'
Dutch and Flemish Artists Around the Globe

Chronicle

Next page:
Caravaggio, *The Sacrifice of Isaac*, 1603,
oil on canvas, 104 x 135 cm, Uffizi Gallery, Florence

Anonymous artist,
Barthélémylaan / Boulevard Barthélémy,
Brussels

'About suffering they were never wrong, The old Masters'

Dutch and Flemish Artists Around the Globe

On 20 January 2017 a mural appeared on Barthélémylaan/Boulevard Barthélémy on the canal in Brussels, of an imminent beheading. The knife and the fear on the face of a child in the depicted scene raised a furore. People thought of IS executions, and panicked.

Until it transpired that the anonymous street artist responsible had copied a section from a Caravaggio painting, *The Sacrifice of Isaac* (1603). The hand with the knife belongs to Abraham, a father who is about to murder his son. The hand on Abraham's arm, holding him back, belongs to the angel, to whom Abraham surrenders at the last moment. But the anonymous imitator has expertly severed the image: we only see the child whose mouth hangs wide open in fear, a hand with a knife, another hand on an arm, a third hand holding the child's neck. Knife and jaw attract the most attention.

A few days later, the bloody figure of a man with his stomach cut open hanging upside-down by a rope materialised on a facade on Brigitinnenstraat/rue des Brigittines. Here the painter had been inspired by *The Corpses of the De Witt Brother*s, a work attributed to the seventeenth-century Dutch painter Jan de Baen (see page 107).

As if to say – since an understanding of traditions, in this instance of painting, the Bible, and the crisis of 1672, the 'disaster year' of the Dutch Republic, radically changes both perception and experience of the image –, *it's all about the context, stupid*. Panic and indignation give way to uncertainty and hesitation. The complexity of the images invites us to think. Our judgement no longer comes down like an axe, but is suspended.

Art, like everything really, exists in context: every thing refers to other things, from the past or from elsewhere. Artists always build on the work of their predecessors. That network provides a frame of reference.

It is therefore worth our while to keep learning more about the canon, traditions, the history of Christianity and the history of art, for example. Because the Old Masters were never wrong about suffering... nor about so much else. It was about time we paid tribute to our Flemish and Dutch Masters in this yearbook. They are renowned worldwide, and appreciated for their masterly use of light, colour and detail.

The theme of this yearbook was developed jointly with CODART, the international network of curators of Dutch and Flemish art which this year celebrates its twentieth year. At present, CODART connects almost 700 curators from more than 300 museums in almost fifty countries. The fact that works of art from the Low Countries of the fifteenth through to the nineteenth century are widely disseminated means that CODART's network is extensive and unique.

This twenty-sixth edition of the yearbook *The Low Countries* will be the last ever in print. With pride – and a little melancholy – the editorial board looks back on those twenty-six volumes: 'It has not gone unnoticed.' But don't worry. From next year you can find us at www.thelowcountries.eu where we will continue with the same fervour and depth to publish information, comment and essays about the Low Countries. For more people. We still have a lot more to tell about 'this undigested vomit of the sea'.

LUC DEVOLDERE | *Chief Editor*

HIDDEN
GEMS

BY 5 CURATORS

CURATOR
Anja K. Sevcik

An Enigmatic Laugh in Cologne

Oh, that laugh! No less mysterious than the secretive smile of the Mona Lisa, it has preoccupied art historians for decades and never fails to fascinate the viewer. Rembrandt's self-portrait is one of the best-known paintings in the Wallraf-Richartz-Museum in Cologne. And at the same time it is one of the most enigmatic. I return to it again and again, wondering, marvelling, admiring.

Another Cologne icon, the contemporary artist Gerhard Richter, once said: 'To me, pictures which I understand, are bad.'[1] That explains, conversely, my fascination. In a masterly way, Rembrandt does not make it easy for us to understand his work.

How should we interpret the old man, portrayed with such humility, who stands out brightly against the darkness? Is the artist striving for that 'one' interpretation anyway? Is Rembrandt alluding to the philosopher Democritus laughing at the world? Is he depicting himself cynically scorning death? Or, mahlstick in hand, does he step into the role of the classical painter Zeuxis, who notoriously laughed himself to death painting the portrait of an ugly old woman? Could she be the grotesque profile on the left-hand edge of the picture?[2]

Rembrandt, *Self-Portrait*, c. 1662/1663, oil on canvas, 82.5 x 65 cm,
Wallraf-Richartz-Museum & Fondation Corboud, Cologne
© Rheinisches Bildarchiv Köln, Britta Schlier

On closer inspection the comedy is also art historical drama, because that forthright laugh, like the raised eyebrows, was the result of overpainting. Many comprehensive technological studies have been carried out, yielding numerous discoveries regarding the possible original state of the painting and its current precarious condition, which further lessens its readability.[3]

The indiscernibility, the 'great blackness' that dominates many of Rembrandt's works, 'because one must often do without three-quarters of a work for a stirring section gleaming with light,'[4] already irritated the connoisseur Gerhard Morell in 1767. No, Rembrandt was never easy to digest. His grasp of painting, the virtuoso mountain of layers that unite to form an ecstasy of brown and gold tones, challenges the viewer. The comparison of his art, in a play in 1648,[5] with haptically gleaming gold embroidery is apposite. Nonetheless, in Rembrandt's work it is the grand gesture rather than painstaking handwork that dominates, that conceals his art – real dissimulatio artis. John Elsum describes it congenially in 1704 in his epigram to 'an Old Man's head, by Rembrant':

'What a *coarse rugged* Way of Painting's here, / *Stroake* upon *Stroake*, *Dabbs* upon *Dabbs* appear. / The Work you'd think was huddled up in haste, / But mark how truly ev'ry Colour's plac'd, / With such *Oeconomy* in such a sort, / That they each other mutually support. / *Rembrant*! Thy Pencil plays a subtil Part / This *Roughness* is contriv'd to hide thy Art.'[6]

With laughter in my eyes, I draw on this wonderful ekphrasis for the old man of Cologne.

Translated by Lindsay Edwards

NOTES

1   Quoted by Christoph Menke in *Die Kraft der Kunst*, Berlin, 2013, p. 77.

2   See for further explanation: Jürgen Müller, *Der sokratische Künstler. Studien zu Rembrandts Nachtwache*, Leiden/Boston, 2015, pp. 102-109.

3   Iris Schaefer, Kathrin Pilz, Caroline von Saint-George, 'Rembrandts Selbstbildnis als Zeuxis. Neues zum Original, zur Erhaltung und zur Frage der Restaurierung', in: *Zeitschrift für Kunsttechnologie und Konservierung*, 25/2011, pp. 285-323.

4   Gerhard Morell, *Beurtheilendes Verzeichniß aller in der Neuen Gallerie befindlichen kostbahren Malereyen* […], Copenhagen 1767, cited in Michael North, *Gerhard Morell und die Entstehung einer Sammlungskultur im Ostseeraum des 18. Jahrhunderts*, Greifswald, 2012, p. 143.

5   Jan Zoet, *Zabynaja of vermomde loosheid*, cf. Cornelis Hofstede de Groot, *Die Urkunden über Rembrandt*, The Hague, 1906, no. 112a.

6   John Elsum, *A Description of the Celebrated Pieces of Paintings of the most Eminent Masters, Ancient and Modern* […], London, 1704, p. 92, CXIX.

CURATOR
Irina Sokolova

The Bon Vivant Back in the Hermitage

The life of the painting *The Bon Vivant* (*De vrolijke drinker*), by Louis de Moni (1698-1771), has been quite eventful. During the lifetime of the Dutch master, at the start of the 1760s this work in cabinet format was purchased for the collection of Catherine the Great along with its pendant *A Fish-Woman* (*Verkoopster van zeevis en garnalen*). For a century and a half, these two paintings hung in the gallery at the Hermitage, an extension of the Winter Palace, which was not open to the public. The Russian Revolution of 1917, which brought radical change to the rule of the land and in all segments of society, however, saw their fate shift dramatically. In 1930, together with many other art objects, both paintings were moved from the Hermitage into storage at the Antiquariat,[1] then sold in a Soviet-organised auction of museum pieces to art dealers mainly in Western Europe. For a long time, every trace of both paintings appeared to be lost. It seemed as if they had left Russia forever. But almost a hundred years later one of them was to return to the banks of the Neva. In 2015, *The Bon Vivant* emerged at the Rafael Valls art gallery and dealers in London. Not long after, the painting was bought by the State Hermitage Museum from a Russian art dealer.

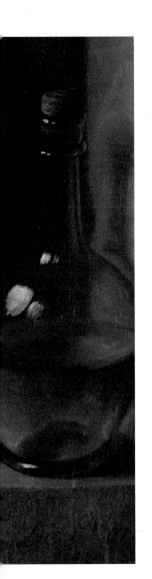

Until the present day the panel has been mounted in the gilt frame, with characteristic scroll-type cartouche, with which all paintings in the Hermitage galleries were 'uniformly' displayed in the mid-nineteenth century, in the preferred style of Tsar Nicholas I. This fact testifies that the work was once in the possession of the Imperial Hermitage Collection.[2]

Russian sources from the eighteenth and nineteenth centuries name the panel differently: 'The bon-vivant', 'Un homme faisant collation', 'The merry drinker', 'The enjoyer of life', 'The reveller'. A wax seal on the back of the painting and its old inventory number 40 on the front indicate a connection to the renowned collection of Johann Ernst Gotzkowsky in Berlin.[3] The acquisition of this collection by Russian Empress Catherine the Great in 1764 formed the basis of the picture gallery at the Hermitage. According to the archives, *The Bon Vivant* and its pendant *A Fish-Woman* did not go for a small sum: Gotzkowsky was paid 500 Reichstaler for them.[4] In the mid-eighteenth century, there was much demand for De Moni's genre paintings.[5] At the auctions of the famous collections of Gerrit Braamcamp (1771) and Johan van der Marck (1773), for example, his paintings once fetched high prices: at the latter, two kitchen scenes sold for 825 guilders.[6]

'The merry drinker', a smiling man sitting at the window with a glass of wine in his hand, is painted in the tradition of the 'fijnschilders' from Leiden and at first glance brings to mind the work of Golden Age masters: many familiar elements appear in this scene. The still life painted with elegance and painstaking detail – herring on a tin plate, a carafe of wine and a piece of bread on a stone windowsill, on which the signature and the date are inscribed: L. de Moni, 174[3] – bears a striking resemblance to the oeuvre of Frans van Mieris, the elder (1635-1681) in particular. The light, refined colour palette and the nonchalant pose of the protagonist, however, belong more to the eighteenth century: the 'galant era'. The arched window which gives the composition a trompe-l'œil effect not only demonstrates the virtuosity of the rendition, but also draws the viewer unwittingly into a dialogue with the painted figure, who merrily raises his goblet to the viewer of the panel.

That *The Bon Vivant* by De Moni was known in Russia is clear from the engraving made after the work by S.M. Vasilev,[7] which was part of a particularly popular series of prints about the paintings of the Flemish School published in St. Petersburg between 1826 and 1832.[8] In the State Hermitage Museum, photographs of both paintings by De Moni – taken by court photographer F. Nikolaevski in 1904 and 1917 – have been preserved in which we can see that they were excellently preserved.

As is well known, the year 2017 saw the commemoration of the 100th anniversary of the Russian Revolution, which so dramatically determined the course of history in Russia, and with it that of Russia's art treasures. How extraordinary the story of a painting can therefore be, is demonstrated by the singular fate of the small panel, *The Bon Vivant*, by Louis de Moni. We may still hope that at some point the whereabouts of its pendant, *A Fish-Woman*, will become known.

Translated by Elisabeth Salverda

NOTES

1   According to the deed of 27.06.1930, the Antiquariat agency of the USSR (1925-1937) was tasked with the sale of valuable artworks (paintings, drawings, sculptures, silverwork, porcelain, and so on), in order to finance accelerated agricultural and industrialisation plans.

2   While no longer visible today, on the auction photograph from the Rafael Valls gallery, the name of the artist 'De Moni' is still legible on the cartouche of the frame, in Russian and in French.

3   Out of the three wax seals on the back of the panel, one can be identified as the seal of Prince V.S. Dolgoroekov, Russian envoy in Prussia, who brokered the purchase of Gotzkowsky's collection, and another as the seal of Tsar Paul I, whose paintings were all numbered in the 1797 inventory of his collection. Of the inventory numbers on the front: number 40 at bottom right, painted white, is from the Gotzkowsky collection; on the bottom left are traces of the number from the Hermitage catalogue of 1797 (no. 2140).

4   Malinovski, K. V., *Istoria kollektsionirovaniya zjivopisi v Sankt Peterburge v XVIII veke* (The History of Collecting Paintings in St. Petersburg in the Eighteenth Century), St. Petersburg, 2012, p. 440.

5   See: P. Terwesten, *Catalogus, of Naamlyst van schilderyen, met derzelver prysen, zedert den 22. Augusti 1752 tot den 21. November 1768, zo in Holland, als Braband en andere plaatzen, in het openbaar verkogt, dienende tot een vervolg of derde deel op de twee deelen der uitgegeeve cataloguen door wylen de ... Gerard Hoet ; zynde hier agter gevoegt: Catalogus van een gedeelte van't vorstelyk kabinet schilderyen van ... den ... prince van Orange en Nassau.* The Hague, 1770, pp. 85, 267, 325, 531, 589-590, 599, 668, 679.

6   A. J. van der Aa, *Biographisch woordenboek der Nederlanden, Gorinchem 1852-1878*, volume 12 out of 21. Part II. 1869, p. 982.

7   Vasilev Sakerdon Mihaylovich (1793-?) was a painter and lithographer who started his studies at the Imperial Academy of Arts in 1803, graduating in 1818 with the title: 'Portrait painter, first class'.

8   G. Mirolubova, *Ruskaya litografia 1810-e – 1890-e.* (Russian Lithography in the Years 1810-1890), Moscow, 2006, pp. 212-215.

CURATOR
Alejandro Vergara

An Explosive Struggle in the Prado

Rubens's *Hercules and Cerberus* from 1636-37 is a small picture (28 x 31.6 cm) bursting with formal power. The sense of compressed energy is palpable – handling the painting at the Prado feels like holding an explosive.

We usually think of Rubens as an artist who favoured large-scale work, but approximately one third of his paintings are small. Most of them are sketches, as is the case here. This type of picture, made in preparation for a larger work, offers us visible traces of the creative process, and a sense of privileged access. In *Hercules and Cerberus*, the brown tone of the oak support glows through the overlapping translucent layers. Two lines drawn in black mark two axes of the composition: one runs through the head of Hercules, the other, to the left, through the head of one of the Furies and the hindquarters of the three-headed dog. Strokes of paint pile over each other as traces of the painter's evolving thoughts.

Peter Paul Rubens, *Hercules and Cerberus*, c. 1636-1637,
oil on panel, 28 x 31.6 cm, Museo Nacional del Prado

In spite of the dazzling show of craftsmanship, the painting is not boastful. The perfect fusion of content and form is characteristic of Rubens, and key to understanding his art. His goal is to activate empathy, to make us feel the emotions involved in the stories that he paints as if they were lived experience. Virginia Woolf, talking about her writing, once explained that words lead people to think and feel, but 'to think and to feel not about them, but about something different' (in the BBC radio recording *Craftsmanship*, 1937). Rubens shares this approach to art-making. His painterly skills, the qualities and powers that he brings to bear in his art, are never self-serving.

Hercules and Cerberus illustrates an episode from Ovid's *Metamorphoses* (VII, 409-419): 'There is a dark cavern with a gaping mouth, and a path into the depths, up which Hercules, hero of Tiryns, dragged the dog, tied with steel chains, resisting and twisting its eyes away from the daylight and the shining rays'. Rubens's telling of the story in this sketch exemplifies how he translates meaning into form. The impressions left by the vigorous strokes of the brush over the surface animate the scene. Dynamic forms and lines create an impression of ebb and flow, pulling us into the contest of strength taking place before the gates of Hell. Because of how they are characterised, the figures appear as if engaged in an exalted moment, yet they also seem close and real, as if directly witnessed. Rubens makes the struggle between the youthful hero and the forces of the underworld feel as an event where great things are at stake.

CURATOR
Adriaan Waiboer

Double Dutch in Dublin

'Oh ... I thought they were by Vermeer!' This comment is frequently expressed by visitors to the National Gallery of Ireland upon seeing the wall text next to Gabriel Metsu's *Man Writing a Letter* and *Woman Reading a Letter*. Personally, I do not blame people for misidentifying the artist of these pendants, as they look more Vermeer-like than any other work by contemporary artists. In fact, I have sometimes wondered myself whether Metsu deliberately painted works that might be mistaken for Vermeer's.

The celebrated companion pieces have fascinated me ever since I started my Ph.D. dissertation on Metsu's work in 1999. Five years later, I was fortunate to take up a curatorial position at the museum that owns these works. Seeing them on a daily basis gave me ample opportunity to ponder what Metsu tried to achieve. It became clear to me that he combined several of what he considered to be signature elements of Vermeer's repertoire, including the division of the composition in geometrical shapes, the shallow interior, the checkered marble-tiled floor, and the natural daylight reflecting off a white plastered back wall. Metsu even painted some of Vermeer's typical *pointillés* on the lady's shoe in the foreground. Towards the end of the painting process, he made one change that encapsulates his strategy: he changed the colour of the lady's jacket from red (his favourite colour of such garments in the mid-1660s) to bright yellow. By doing so, Metsu replicated what he saw as a trademark of Vermeer's work.

Gabriel Metsu, *Man Writing a Letter*, c. 1664-1666, oil on panel, 52.5 x 40.2 cm,
National Gallery of Ireland, Dublin, Sir Alfred and Lady Beit, 1987 (Beit Collection)

Gabriel Metsu, *Woman Reading a Letter*, c. 1664-1666, oil on panel, 52.5 x 40.2 cm,
National Gallery of Ireland, Dublin, Sir Alfred and Lady Beit, 1987 (Beit Collection)

As I kept looking at the pendants, I realised however that Metsu did not copy or imitate, but merely approached Vermeer's style: his colouring is brighter, his natural light has fewer tonal values and his spatial relations are poorly defined; moreover, Metsu's superb brushwork aimed at carefully describing textures and surfaces bears little relationship to Vermeer's work. Furthermore, I should admit that after all these years I still cannot identify with certainty which of Vermeer's individual paintings served as direct sources of inspiration to Metsu. He certainly did not study Vermeer's *Astronomer*, now in the Louvre, in preparation of *Man Writing a Letter*, and *The Love Letter*, currently at the Rijksmuseum, to arrive at *Woman Reading a Letter*, as scholars have argued in the past. True, Metsu's and Vermeer's two pensive men seated at a carpeted table near a window and a globe look very much alike; and both other paintings depict ladies in fur-trimmed jackets, seated next to a sewing basket, having received letters from a maid standing in front of a marine painting. These similarities are hardly coincidental. Yet, Metsu completed the works two to four years before Vermeer finished his. It is far more likely that the Delft artist saw Metsu's pendants, which, although inspired by his own earlier works, provided him with ideas that he had not previously explored. Intriguing as this scenario may sound, I am afraid we are still a long time away from museum visitors in Paris and Amsterdam mistaking Vermeer's *Astronomer* and *Love-Letter* for works by Metsu...

CURATOR
Yao-Fen You

A Miniature Netherlandish Treasure in Detroit

Among the many treasures in the encyclopaedic collection of the Detroit Institute of Arts is a miniature Netherlandish altarpiece deftly executed in boxwood – a hardwood favoured by carvers for its fine grain and remarkable density. Measuring no more than nine inches high, the altarpiece comprises three principal components: a triptych body, a circular winged predella, and an openwork tracery foot. The altarpiece's exterior is exceedingly plain. It hardly prepares the viewer for the hypertechnical virtuosity of a world rendered in miniature that waits inside.

When the triptych wings are open, one finds a central scene of the Nativity combined with the Annunciation to the Shepherds. The Nativity is prominently depicted in the lower half, in the foreground, and the Annunciation to the Shepherds in the upper half, but in the background and on a slightly smaller scale. The brick ruins help to separate as well as to connect the two chronologically distinct episodes. This spatial arrangement contributes to the remarkable illusion of pictorial depth in an otherwise shallow space that measures no more than an inch deep. The interior of the left wing bears the Annunciation and that of the right, the Presentation in the Temple. Both are carved in very low relief. In the predella below is an Adoration of the Magi that displays many compositional similarities to the Nativity.

The first half of Matthew 2:6 is inscribed along the bottom edge of the triptych body: ET TV BETHLE[hem] / TERRA•IV[da] NEQVAQVAM MIN[im]A / ES I[n] PRI[n]CIPIB[u]S (But you, Bethlehem, in the land of Judah, are by no means least among the rulers of Judah). The words appear cramped towards the end of the inscription, with some of the letters carved into the moulding. This suggests that the sculptor might not have planned accordingly. I find this endearing, for it is the plight of the sculptor to carry on, knowing that such oversights cannot be reversed in the art of the carving.

Unknown (Netherlandish), *Miniature Altarpiece with the Nativity and the Annunciation to the Shepherds*, c. 1520,
boxwood, dimensions (open): 22.9 x 13.7 x 3.2 cm, (closed): 22.9 x 8.6 x 3.2 cm
Detroit Institute of Arts, Founders Society Purchase, Robert H. Tannahill Foundation Fund, Benson Ford Fund, and Henry Ford II Fund

This altarpiece exemplifies the late medieval tradition of microscopic box-wood carving for which the Duchy of Brabant served as a major centre of pro-duction. Having written my dissertation on another popular Brabantine carved form, namely, that of large-scale carved oak retables with painted wings – many of which still adorn the high altars and side chapels of churches scat-tered throughout the Rhineland, Sweden, and Belgium – I cannot but marvel at this portable miniaturised version. It is small enough for me to cradle with my two hands. Not only can I open and close the wings with just the slightest touch, I can fully rotate the object to examine all sides. The triptych's back-side is slightly chamfered, not flat – a feature that we sometimes encounter in large-scale winged retables – and on the reverse of the winged predella is a hinged circular door that reveals a relic cavity when opened. Such intimacy of handling is almost impossible with larger altarpieces, making me cherish even more this miniature boxwood one in the DIA's collection.

In Careful Hands

Exceptional Private Collectors

[ERIC RINCKHOUT]

Since the start of the nineteenth century, private collectors all over the world have greedily sought out the old masters of the Low Countries. Painters such as Jan van Eyck and Pieter Bruegel were rediscovered thanks to tireless research on the part of private collectors who worked their way up to become true connoisseurs. Other painters, such as the ever-popular Rubens and Rembrandt, were bought by fabulously wealthy collectors who acquired an ensemble the likes of which museums could only dream of having.

Fritz Mayer van den Bergh, Henry Clay Frick and the married couple Nélie Jacquemart and Edouard André still welcome visitors into their private collections in Antwerp, New York and Paris respectively. The collectors themselves may be long dead, but their spirits still inhabit their houses: a cosy patrician's house, an elegant city palace and a luxurious *bonbonnière*. Visiting their collections is always a true pleasure, as the visitor is confronted with their personal, generally exquisite taste. The art collections reflect their characters, knowledge and, yes, identity.

Collectors such as the Anglo-Austrian Count Antoine Seilern and the Antwerp ex-mayor Florent van Ertborn chose to donate their phenomenal art collections to the community on their deaths: Seilern's staggering ensemble of works by Rubens can now be viewed at the Courtauld Gallery in London, while Van Ertborn's invaluable collection by Van Eyck, Van der Weyden and Fouquet contributed to the foundation of the Royal Museum of Fine Arts in Antwerp.

Each of these collectors harboured the express wish to develop, and, yes, to elevate, the cultural knowledge and aesthetic taste of their contemporaries and subsequent generations through their collections.

Mad Meg for under 500 francs

Fritz Mayer van den Bergh (1858-1901) was one of Antwerp's most exceptional late nineteenth-century collectors. In the city so closely associated with Rubens, he resolutely avoided baroque art. Fritz Mayer's father Emil Mayer came from Cologne and in 1849 set up a family business in Antwerp to import spices and pharmaceutical products. He married Henriëtte van den Bergh, the

daughter of a brewer and shipbroker from Antwerp. Fritz Mayer, who studied literature, philosophy and law at Ghent University, seemed destined for the diplomatic service, but after his father's death he devoted himself exclusively to his great passion, collecting art. The family was sufficiently well off to make that possible. Fritz worked with his beloved mother to expand his collection. She was so dear to him that he even changed his name to Fritz Mayer van den Bergh.

After what he himself termed his 'trial period', he sold off his antiques to 'begin again' and from 1891 focussed resolutely on the art of the medieval period and the renaissance. A year earlier, Fritz Mayer had already bought his first Bruegel print, a remarkable *démarche*, as at the end of the nineteenth century Pieter Bruegel the Elder had only a modest reputation. The wider public had barely heard of him but presumably Fritz Mayer had studied the authentic Bruegel paintings during his many trips to Vienna and found himself captivated by the sixteenth-century master, who was glaringly absent from Belgian museums and collections.

In 1893 he bought as many as twenty-two Bruegel prints from an antiquarian in Brussels. He also collected paintings by the son, Pieter Brueghel the Younger, who copied his father's work: *Winter Landscape with Bird Trap and Flight into Egypt* and *The Census at Bethlehem*. Fritz also owned work by Jan Brueghel, Bruegel's second painter son and a good friend to Rubens.

In her book *Pieter Bruegel. De biografie*, Leen Huet calls Fritz Mayer's interest in Bruegel 'original and eccentric': 'most collectors at the time, after all, were after classic art or variants on that theme from the sixteenth to the nineteenth century.' Huet moreover attributes Bruegel's rediscovery entirely to Fritz Mayer, the 'shrewd young collector from Bruegel's home city of Antwerp'.

Mayer's 'tour de force' was yet to come. On 5 October 1894 a strange painting belonging to a jeweller in Stockholm was auctioned in Cologne. The catalogue described it as a 'fantastic depiction', 'a landscape with a crowd of ghostly figures'. On the viewing days the auctioneer hung the peculiar work high

Rogier van der Weyden, *The Seven Sacraments Altarpiece*, 1445-1450, oil on panel, 200 x 223 cm, Royal Museum of Fine Arts Antwerp © KMSKA-Lukas-Art in Flanders vzw. Photo: Hugo Maertens (Van Ertborn Bequest)

up. It was not worth much, after all. The young art historian Max Friedländer, working in the Wallraf-Richartz Museum, climbed a ladder to inspect the piece but was unable to convince his director. In a letter he tipped off Mayer, whom he called 'the specialist when it came to Brueghel' – Brueghel with an 'h', because at that point it was still thought that the painting was the work of Pieter Brueghel the Younger, alias 'Hell Brueghel'. Fritz Mayer bought the painting through an agent for 390 marks, less than 500 francs. By way of comparison, in the same year a sum of 45,000 francs was paid for Rubens's *Prodigal Son*. Fritz Mayer studied the work thoroughly as soon as it arrived in Antwerp. After a few days he was certain of it: it was the *Mad Meg* described by Karel van Mander in 1604 in his *Schilder-Boeck* (Book of Painting), a painting thought to have been lost. Leen Huet writes, 'His purchase was the clarion call with which research on Bruegel, which has since filled an entire library, began in Belgium.' She also liberally praises Mayer for his thorough interpretation of the piece, some of whose many elements are yet to be elaborated in the art history literature.

Following the acquisition of *Mad Meg*, Fritz Mayer bought his second Bruegel at an auction in Paris in 1899: a panel consisting of twelve separate wooden plates with depictions of proverbs. Unfortunately he had little time to enjoy his purchases or study them further, as he died at the age of forty-three from complications of a fractured skull after falling from his horse. He was unable to complete his research into the mysterious Flemish painter Hugo van der Goes. His mother honoured him by housing his magnificent collection – including Master Heinrich of Constance's thirteenth-century *Group of Christ and St John* and a fifteenth-century manuscript, the Mayer van den Bergh Breviary – in a museum which she had built in late gothic style beside her own house on Lange Gasthuisstraat in Antwerp. The museum opened its doors in December 1904.

A unique gesture

Leen Huet calls Fritz Mayer the spiritual son of Florent van Ertborn (1784-1840), who was mayor of Antwerp from 1817 to 1828 – under the United Kingdom of the Netherlands – and a gifted collector of antique art. Van Ertborn was born into a family who belonged to Antwerp's financial elite. Art collecting was in their blood. He was five years old when the French Revolution broke out. As a child he fled with his family to Bremen, fearing the French invaders. In Germany he heard stories of raided churches, disbanded monastic orders and works of art carried off by the French troops to Paris. As the Musée Napoleon, the Louvre was intended to exhibit an overview of European art history, but it was really Rubens first and foremost who triumphed here: he was viewed as the highlight of Flemish art. The French had no interest in 'old-fashioned' masters, even when the pieces in question were the central panels of Van Eyck's *Adoration of the Mystic Lamb* and a triptych by Hans Memling.

The old masters also piqued the curiosity of two young brothers from Cologne: Sulpiz and Melchior Boisserée. They were interested in the medieval architecture of the cities of Flanders and Brabant, and in the early nineteenth century they succeeded in purchasing works of art to match their architectural tastes. The second-hand dealerships were pleased to be relieved of their 'old junk'. The brothers thus laid the foundation for the Alte Pinakothek in Munich

Hans Memling, *Man with a Roman Coin*, oil on panel, 30.7 x 23.2 cm,
Royal Museum of Fine Arts Antwerp © KMSKA-Lukas-Art in Flanders vzw.
Photo: Hugo Maertens (Van Ertborn Bequest)

with work by Rogier van der Weyden, Hans Memling and Dirk Bouts. They made
their acquisitions known to a broader circle and in so doing influenced the taste
of Florent van Ertborn, who met them in 1824 in Antwerp. Van Ertborn had in
fact already purchased a work by Hans Memling, even before 1818, having re-
putedly spotted it under a layer of dirt and having it restored. Van Ertborn con-
sciously sought out late medieval art: in his view that was the 'missing link' in
art history. He even exchanged seventeenth-century paintings for older work:
that is how Antonello da Messina's *Calvary* (1475) is thought to have come into
his possession.

Van Ertborn travelled a great deal and conducted thorough research, but he
was not the only private collector in search of (late) medieval art. The company
in which he found himself was that of a relatively small but wealthy group of
English and German romantics. The German philosopher Friedrich Schlegel,
with whom Van Ertborn maintained close contact, was also a proponent of this
early romantic trend. Although Van Ertborn often complained that German
collectors had beaten him to it, he did succeed in purchasing Rogier van der

Weyden's *Seven Sacraments* in 1826 from a family in Dijon. He is said to have paid the modest sum of 300 guilders, evidence of the scant appreciation for late medieval art at the time. Four years later he acquired the small panel *Saint Barbara* (1437) by Jan van Eyck and five years after that he added *Madonna at the Fountain*, also by Van Eyck. The signed and dated (1439) panel had long been hidden away in a sacristy and came from the village of Dikkelvenne in East Flanders. He further enriched his collection with Rogier van der Weyden's *Portrait of Philip de Croÿ* and Jean Fouquet's *Madonna* among others. As to the purchase price, the collector unfortunately offers no information in the catalogue he drew up in 1828.

Jan van Eyck, *Saint Barbara*, 1437, oak panel, 18 x 31 cm,
Royal Museum of Fine Arts Antwerp © KMSKA-Lukas-Art in Flanders vzw.
Photo: Hugo Maertens (Van Ertborn Bequest)

At that point Van Ertborn's collection was renowned among art lovers all over Europe. The German novelist Johanna Schopenhauer, mother of philosopher Arthur Schopenhauer, visited the collection during her journey through the Netherlands. In *Ausflug an den Niederrhein und nach Belgien im Jahr 1828* (Tour of the Niederrhein and Belgium in the year 1828) she writes, 'The collection is not particularly large, really only filling the walls of a rather large chamber, but outside of the former collections of Boisserée and Solly, which are now in the museum in Berlin, there are none more interesting for the history of antique art. Here one finds very rare works by masters about whom all but their names have been forgotten for some time.'

After his stint as mayor and once Belgium had gained independence, Van Ertborn moved to Utrecht as a staunch Orangist, where he took the office of provincial governor, but he maintained his connections with Antwerp, continuing to play a part in managing the academy there. In his collection catalogue he exhaustively compared the use of colour, perspective and composition by the baroque painters and Flemish Primitives, arguing that Van Eyck and Van der Weyden should be seen as a step in the evolution towards the baroque. He emphasised the importance of the study of so-called primitive painters, offered a nuanced perspective on the exceptional position of Rubens, legitimised his own art collection and prepared the way for his endowment.

In 1840 Van Ertborn died of an eye tumour, which had gradually blinded him – a terrible fate for an art lover. In 1832 he had written a will leaving 115 works to the city of Antwerp, specifically to the academy museum, a unique gesture. Initially, however, the academy was at a loss as to what to do with the gift, simply because it lacked the expertise to estimate the value of the pieces. The Van Ertborn Bequest has since become a benchmark for the sector and the works of Van Eyck, David, Van der Weyden, Memling, Fouquet, Martini and Da Messina are now seen as masterpieces of the Royal Museum of Fine Arts in Antwerp.

A public monument

At the end of the nineteenth century prices for antique art began to increase rapidly, due to the ever-greedier American collectors. One of them was Henry Frick, a coal magnate from New York. Henry Clay Frick (1849-1919) was the embodiment of the American Dream, rising from a modest background to become one of the most powerful American industrialists. He spent his fortune on European fine arts and built a house, now The Frick Collection, a gallery in a prime New York location, opposite Central Park on the corner of Fifth Avenue and East 70th Street. It is one of the world's best private art collections in a magnificent city palace, built in French neoclassical style.

As an industrialist Henry Frick happened to be in the right place at the right time. He realised that the rapidly rising iron and steel industry in the United States would require a great deal of coke. Steel was used among other things for the railways, which were fast being laid in a country constantly shifting its border westwards. Frick bought up coalfields and in 1871 he built fifty coke ovens, making him a millionaire by the time he turned thirty. From a young age he had been fascinated by art. His office was full of prints and drawings, some

Anthony van Dyck, *Frans Snyders*, c. 1620, oil on canvas, 142.6 x 105.4 cm,
© The Frick Collection, New York

by his own hand. In 1880 he travelled to Europe and his visit to the Wallace Collection in London convinced him to expand his art collection.

Frick, however, was not the only one with such plans. In the Gilded Age, the industrial 'golden age' of the US between 1875 and 1914, various private fortunes came into being. Carnegie, Rockefeller, Pierpont Morgan and Mellon all followed the example of European aristocracy and bourgeoisie, and were keen to build art collections to confirm their status and prestige, or if necessary to boost it. Their intentions were facilitated by a fiscal reform in the British inheritance system, which caused a number of aristocrats to put their art collections on the market. Those works of art were immediately snapped up by the wealthy Americans.

At the end of the nineteenth century Frick dedicated himself entirely to art. He was well assisted, largely by European advisers, but he had a good nose for art himself, generally purchasing individual pieces rather than buying in bulk. Frick also bought old masters from the Low Countries. Although he had little affinity for religious art, in 1915 he acquired Gerard David's *Descent from the Cross* (c. 1495), a painting which had once been the property of William II of Orange. Frick in fact was most interested in portraits. In that respect the pur-

Johannes Vermeer, *Officer and Laughing Girl*, c. 1657, oil on canvas, 50.5 x 46 cm,
© The Frick Collection, New York

chase of Anthony van Dyck's double portrait of Frans Snyders, painter of animals and still life, and his wife was a major success. Frick succeeded in unit-
ing the once separated, life-sized, realistic images in 1909. He subsequently
bought six more portraits by Van Dyck, whom he greatly admired.

Opposite the Snyders in New York hangs Rembrandt's largest self-portrait,
purchased in 1906 in Dorset from the Earl of Ilchester. The fifty-two-year-old
Rembrandt depicts himself with a staff in his left hand and is further dressed in
an imaginative oriental costume. But the real cherry on the cake was no fewer
than three Vermeers, bought in 1901, 1911 and 1919, the year Frick died, representing true luxury to the collector. For *Officer and Laughing Girl* he had to sell
two of his Rembrandts. Vermeer had only come back into fashion since 1860
due to the French critic William Bürger, while Rembrandt had always remained
a favourite with the public, but prices for Vermeers sky-rocketed.

From 1914 Frick lived amidst his art. After his death in 1919 the house was
extended and in 1935 the museum opened its doors, still breathing the personal atmosphere of days gone by. Frick wanted his collection to be a 'monument',
a 'public gallery to which the entire public shall forever have access'.

Edouard André and Nélie Jacquemart started their collection a little earlier. In their Parisian city palace, surrounded by Italian, French and English opulence, they brought together an essential core of Flemish and Dutch masters. Despite only having been built around 1870, the Hôtel Jacquemart-André is eighteenth-century through and through. It was commissioned by Edouard André, who was descended from a Protestant banker's family and wanted to house his art collection at the luxurious residence on Boulevard Haussmann. In 1881 he married Nélie Jacquemart, a portrait painter with a completely different background, rooted in Catholicism and the royalist petite bourgeoisie. Fortunately they shared the same taste, both operating as keen art collectors and generous patrons.

In the library a few Flemish and Dutch seventeenth-century works hang together, very appropriately in *clair-obscur*: a small but dramatic Rembrandt (*The Supper at Emmaus*, bought in 1891), a view of Haarlem with menacing storm clouds by Jacob van Ruisdael and a large, unusual mythological scene with vivid brush strokes by Van Dyck, *Time Clipping the Wings of Love*, acquired in 1899. Those works are surrounded by a few portraits by Rembrandt, Frans

Rembrandt, *The Supper at Emmaus*, c.1629, oil on paper mounted on panel, 37.4 x 42.3 cm, Musée Jacquemart-André-Institut de France, Paris © Studio Sébert Photographes

Anthony van Dyck, *Time Clipping the Wings of Love*, c. 1627, oil on canvas, 175 x 110 cm,
Musée Jacquemart-André-Institut de France, Paris © Studio Sébert Photographes

Hals and another piece by Van Dyck: a corpulent, ruddy Antwerp magistrate, bought in 1890, when it was still attributed to Jordaens. Edouard André hung these works alongside a portrait of a man by Philippe de Champagne, to highlight the extent of the influence of seventeenth-century masters from the North on subsequent generations of French painters.

A recluse in a gloomy house

The final salvo is released by an Anglo-Austrian private collector, who had maintained a passion for Peter Paul Rubens almost all his life: Count Antoine Seilern (1901-1978) owned thirty-two paintings and twenty-three drawings by Rubens – enough to turn many a museum green with envy. 'Everything connected with Rubens interests me,' was his motto. Seilern's father was Austrian. His mother was born in 1875 in New York as Antoinette Woerishoffer and it was from her side of the family that Antoine Seilern received a substantial inheritance.

Seilern began studying philosophy, Freudian psychology and art history at the University of Vienna as late as 1933, having previously been occupied with travel, hunting and reading. In 1939 he graduated with a dissertation on the Venetian influences on Rubens's oeuvre. Shortly afterwards, when World War II broke out, Seilern fled to England, where he had been born. At that point he had already acquired his first works by Rubens, including the legendary *Landscape by Moonlight*, once part of the collection of British painter Joshua Reynolds, two panels from the Achilles series, and designs for the side panels of the

Peter Paul Rubens, *Landscape by Moonlight*, 1635-1640, oil on panel, 64 x 90 cm,
© The Samuel Courtauld Trust, The Courtauld Gallery, London (Collection Antoine Seilern)

Peter Paul Rubens, *The Entombment*, 1615-1616, oil on panel, 83.1 x 65.1 cm,
© The Samuel Courtauld Trust, The Courtauld Gallery, London (Collection Antoine Seilern)

Descent from the Cross in the cathedral in Antwerp and for the ceiling paintings of the St. Charles Borromeo Church, also in Antwerp, which were sadly
destroyed by a fire. For these purchases Seilern was steadfastly supported by
none other than his friend Ludwig Burchard, an expert on Rubens. In 1937 Seilern published a catalogue about his collection, which was already extensive by
this time. After World War II he added the intimate portrait of the *Family of Jan
Brueghel the Elder* and a remarkable *Entombment*. When Rubens's paintings
became too expensive even for Seilern, he devoted himself to purchasing the
master's drawings.

Seilern's collection was not initially accessible to everyone. He insisted on privacy and in fact lived as a recluse in a large, bizarre and gloomy house in Prince's Gate, London. After his death in 1978 his collection was donated to the renowned Courtauld Gallery, as Seilern had stipulated in his will. The Courtauld has since moved to the sumptuous, labyrinthine yet intimate, Somerset House on the Strand in London. Rubens permanently takes centre stage there. Seilern wanted to honour the Flemish baroque master in all his genius: as a portrait and landscape painter, a decorator on an epic scale, designer of tapestries and books, and inquisitive student who paid homage to illustrious forebears such as Titian and Tintoretto. He thoroughly succeeded in his aim. ■

FURTHER READING

Claire Baisier and Ulrike Müller, 'Fritz (1858-1901) en Henriëtte Mayer van den Bergh', in: *500 jaar verzamelen in Antwerpen. Een passioneel verhaal* (500 Years of Collecting in Antwerp. A Passionate Tale), Leuven, Davidsfonds, 2013, pp. 147-159.

Helen Braham, *The Princes Gate Collection*, London, Home House Society Trustees / Courtauld Institute Galleries, 1981.

Greta Van Broeckhoven and Jozef Glassée, 'Museum en mecenaat' ('Museum and Patronage'), in: Leen de Jong (e.a.), *Het Koninklijk Museum voor Schone Kunsten Antwerpen. Een geschiedenis 1810-2007* (The Royal Museum of Fine Arts Antwerp. A History 1810-2007), Oostkamp, Stichting Kunstboek, 2008, pp. 187-207.

The Frick Collection, New York, New York - Paris, The Frick Collection - Fondation BNP Paribas - Réunion des Musées Nationaux, 2011.

Jozef Glassée, 'Van collectioneur naar donateur. Florent van Ertborn (1784-1840) en de betekenissen van een schilderijenverzameling' ('From Collector to Donor. Florent van Ertborn (1784-1840) and the Significance of a Collection of Paintings'), in: *500 jaar verzamelen in Antwerpen. Een passioneel verhaal* (500 Years of Collecting in Antwerp. A Passionate Tale), Leuven, Davidsfonds, 2013, pp. 131-145.

Leen Huet, *Pieter Bruegel. De biografie*, Antwerp, Uitgeverij Polis, 2016.

Jan Lampo, 'Florent (Floris) ridder van Ertborn (1784-1840), een van Europa's eerste verzamelaars van 15de-eeuwse schilderkunst' ('Sir Florent (Floris) van Ertborn (1784-1840), One of Europe's First Collectors of 15th-Century Painting') via https://janlampo.com/2012/10/18/florent-floris-ridder-van-ertborn-1784-1840-een-van-europas-eerste-verzamelaars-van-15de-eeuwse-schilderkunst/ (consulted on 24 October 2017).

Le Musée Jacquemart-André. Livre guide, s.l., Culture Espace et DR&A, 1998.

Musée Jacquemart-André. Catalogue itinéraire. Troisième édition, Paris, Editeur J.-E. Bulloz, s.a.

John Russell, 'Gallery View. An Estimable Collection Sees the Light of Day', in *The New York Times*, 13 December 1981.

James Byam Shaw, 'Count Antoine Seilern (1901-1978)', in: *The Burlington Magazine*, November 1978 (vol. 120, no. 908), pp. 760-762.

Lea van der Vinde, *The Frick Collection. Kunstschatten uit New York* (The Frick Collection. Art Collections from New York), The Hague - Zwolle, Mauritshuis - Waanders Uitgevers, 2015.

Translated by Anna Asbury

A Portrait of the Market as a Seismograph

Dutch Masters on the Art Market

[EVERHARD KORTHALS ALTES]

Caravaggio and Vermeer are among today's most popular Old Masters. They enjoy some kind of star status and any exhibition of their work is guaranteed to be a blockbuster. But what is so singular is that their paintings have not always been so well regarded. In fact, for a long time they were little known or little loved.

What do the prices that were paid for artists' work on the art market in the past tell us about changes in the appreciation of their work? How much is paid for a painting depends on a great many factors. It is not only the artist's reputation that counts, but also the authenticity of the work (did the artist create the work of art entirely with his own hands?), the method of execution, the subject, the format, the number of figures depicted, and the condition and provenance of the painting. And in addition there are all manner of economic factors that have an influence on the price of a work of art, such as supply and demand. Whether the work is sold by auction or privately also has an effect. In what follows, I shall take a closer look at this issue on the basis of a case study. I shall be concentrating primarily on seventeenth-century Dutch painting.

Changes in supply and demand

Unlike such painters of the Southern Netherlands as Peter Paul Rubens and Anthony van Dyck, who received numerous commissions from the church, nobility and court, and had impressive international careers, painters in the Republic of the United Netherlands worked mainly for the open domestic market. It's true that there were occasional exports, but they were by no means regular or on a large scale. This all changed around 1700: the demand from abroad started to increase dramatically. Although the Italian art of the High Renaissance continued to be the most well regarded among collectors almost all over Europe until well into the nineteenth century, with the work of Raphael in the undisputed lead, Dutch art increasingly gained ground.

At the end of the Golden Age, the economic position of the Republic deteriorated in relation to that of other countries. Domestic demand for luxury consumer goods stagnated, while a huge supply of Northern-Netherlandish paint-

Raphael, *Sistine Madonna*,
c. 1512/13, oil on canvas,
256 x 196 cm,
Staatliche Kunstsammlungen,
Gemäldegalerie Alte Meister,
Dresden

ings was available on the art market. At the same time, good Italian paintings were relatively scarce and expensive. So foreign collectors were now able to get their hands on most Northern-Netherlandish paintings quite easily and at a relatively favourable price.

The influence of traditional academic art theory

The traditional academic theory of art that developed mainly in Italy and France in the seventeenth and eighteenth centuries has been a decisive factor in the history of taste. In this context, the sixteenth-century Italian painting of the High Renaissance and seventeenth-century French painting were considered to be high points in the history of art. The work of such masters as Raphael

Philips Wouwerman, *Battle Scene*, c. 1655-1660, oil on canvas, 127 x 245 cm, Mauritshuis, The Hague.

This painting was purchased for 4,575 guilders by Prince William of Orange at an auction in The Hague in 1764 making it one of the most expensive Dutch paintings in the eighteenth century.

and Nicolas Poussin set the standard of quality by which all others were to be gauged. These painters had taken their cue from both the formal idiom and the subjects of the art of classical antiquity. They also painted many biblical subjects. Their art was based very much on reason: universal rules for art were formulated and they had to be strictly adhered to. For example, only the most beautiful elements in nature were to be selected. Works of art that were composed using the imagination received greater approval than paintings that were done directly from nature. In addition, the design and the line were considered more important than the use of colour.

Dutch art was accepted only with difficulty

Because most Dutch painting did not fulfil these ideals, it was for a long time subject to criticism. It was only at the start of the eighteenth century, after the triumph of the *Rubénistes* (the followers of Peter Paul Rubens, from the Southern Netherlands) over the *Poussinistes* (the followers of Poussin) in the *Querelle du coloris*, the dispute about whether colour and drawing were of equal importance in painting, that tastes changed and the tide turned in favour of the masters of the Southern Netherlands and then also those of the Northern Netherlands. In France, writing on the artists of the Northern Netherlands gradually became more positive and their work also became more avidly collected. The following quote from an eighteenth-century collector is typical: 'I have distinguished two sub-schools within the school of the Low Countries, and they are the Flemish and the Dutch, and I have even added a number of German painters to them, because they worked in the same genres (...) In some respects, the Dutch school successfully distinguishes itself from other schools. It handles nature with the highest possible degree of faithfulness (...) The paintings are executed in extreme detail. The Dutch have also thoroughly mastered the art of shades and contrasts of colour: in this way they succeed in painting the light itself, if one may so express it.'

Trendsetters

When it came to collecting works at the top end of the art market, certain royal courts and noble families in Germany and France will have played an exemplary role, guided by their agents in the Republic. Arnold Houbraken, an early eighteenth-century biographer of several artists, described how collectors imitated each other in their preferences, taking as his example the paintings of Philips Wouwerman: 'It is true that the products of his brushwork have risen to a much higher price many years after his death than during his life, since the Dolphin [Dauphin] of France, and the Elector of Bavaria (which prompted other courts to do the same) had all his works in Holland purchased for them.'

So you might say that seeing others buy makes you yourself buy: according to Houbraken, virtually every royal collector tried to acquire works by this Haarlem painter, in imitation of such trendsetters as Louis of France (1661-1711), the eldest son of King Louis XIV, and Maximilian II Emanuel, the Elector of Bavaria (1662-1726).

Adriaen van der Werff, *Lot and his Daughters*, 1711, oil on panel, 44.5 x 35 cm, Hermitage Museum, Saint Petersburg

This painting sold for 4,100 guilders at an auction in Rotterdam in 1713
making it one of the most expensive Dutch paintings in the early eighteenth century.

Which Northern Netherlands masters?

The average yield from paintings at Dutch auctions in the early eighteenth century would seem to give a good indication of the popularity of the various artists.
    Among the most expensive paintings were those of Adriaen van der Werff
(an average of 858 guilders), a painter in the classical style at work in the late
Golden Age, who was tremendously popular among European collectors in the
eighteenth century, because to a large extent his work met the demands of
the traditional academic theory of art – whereas in later periods it was hardly
appreciated at all, though for the very same reason. The same applies to the

Rembrandt van Rijn, *Christ and the Woman Taken in Adultery*, 1644, oil on oak, 83.8 x 65.4 cm, The National Gallery, London

This painting sold for 2,510 guilders at an auction in Amsterdam in 1733
making it one of the most expensive paintings by Rembrandt in the early eighteenth century.

work of another classicist painter of the late Golden Age, Gerard de Lairesse, though the average yield from his paintings was not so high (272 guilders). By comparison, the annual income of a Dutch teacher, grocer or pharmacist in 1742 amounted to between 600 and 800 guilders.

Rembrandt

Although it's true that the art of Rembrandt van Rijn was well liked by collectors in the Netherlands, France, Germany and England in the eighteenth century, he was also the subject of much criticism, especially in France. He was said to have drawn outlines incorrectly and not shown any interest in the art of classical antiquity, only wanting to imitate living nature, which he copied exactly as it was and not in an improved, idealised form. His sketchy manner of painting also regularly attracted criticism, though sometimes great praise too. According to the seventeenth-century biographer and art theorist André Félibien, the effect of his painting only really became apparent from a distance: '[Rembrandt] juxtaposed his tints and half-tints so well and rendered his areas of light and shade so effectively that the things he painted so roughly and which often appear like sketches do not come across when one stands too close to the painting. But when one moves further away, the thick and vigorous brush-strokes become less visible and merge into a single whole whereby the desired effect is achieved.'

The diverging estimation of Rembrandt's art seems to have had an effect on the average yield from his paintings at auction in the early eighteenth century. The average price of 140 guilders is considerably lower than for the work of Adriaen van der Werff and Gerard de Lairesse.

Gerrit Dou, *The Night School*, c. 1660-1665, oil on panel, 74 x 64 cm, Rijksmuseum, Amsterdam

This painting sold for 4,000 guilders at an auction in Leiden in 1766 making it one of the most expensive Dutch paintings in the eighteenth century.

Genre works

Throughout the eighteenth century, the Leiden painters Gerrit Dou and Frans van Mieris the Elder were the most highly regarded Northern-Netherlandish genre painters, both in their home country and abroad, and it was their work that yielded the most: Dou an average of 440 guilders and Van Mieris 437 guilders. The great attraction of these small paintings was their extreme precision and convincing illusionism. The work of Gabriel Metsu (179 guilders) and Godfried Schalcken (188 guilders) also did well on the art market and increasingly benefited from international interest. With an average of 107 guilders, Johannes Vermeer did not do badly, but he was relatively unknown, especially outside the Netherlands, because of the small number of works he produced.

Johannes Vermeer, *Allegory of the Catholic Faith*, c. 1670-1674, oil on canvas, 114.3 x 88.9 cm, Metropolitan Museum of Art, New York

This painting sold for 500 guilders at an auction in Amsterdam in 1718, making it one of the most expensive paintings by Vermeer in the early eighteenth century. It's an historical painting and not a genre painting, rather atypical in the oeuvre of Vermeer.

Portraits

One possible explanation for the limited popularity of Northern-Netherlandish portraits among eighteenth-century collectors is to be found in the writings of Johan van Gool, a biographer of artists who in 1750 had observed that portraits were in general not much collected because they had little value outside the subject's family circle, except in the case of such renowned artists as Peter Paul Rubens, Anthony van Dyck, Rembrandt and Frans Hals, who were popular because of their artistic worth. For that matter, in the early eighteenth century Hals, a portraitist *pur sang*, achieved only an exceedingly meagre average of nineteen guilders, compared to 641 guilders for the work of Van Dyck and 292 for that of Rubens (though of course in the two latter cases they included not only portraits but also history pieces).

Italian and Dutch landscapes

It was landscapes, sometimes populated with biblical figures, shepherds, hunters or soldiers, that generally made up the majority of Northern-Netherlandish paintings in eighteenth-century collections. These almost always included a substantial number of paintings by the much-loved *Italianisanten*,

Nicolaes Berchem, *Shepherds beside Roman Ruins*, after 1661, oil on canvas, 63.5 x 76.5 cm, Mauritshuis, The Hague

This painting was purchased for 2,105 guilders by Prince William of Orange at an auction in Amsterdam in 1765 making it one of the most expensive paintings by Berchem in the eighteenth century.

Northern painters who had painted sun-drenched, Italian-looking landscapes, often inspired by travels to Italy. Such artists as Jan van Goyen, who had concentrated exclusively on the Dutch landscape, were significantly less popular. He achieved an average yield of only six guilders at Dutch auctions in the first half of the eighteenth century.

The highest yields were for the work of Nicolaes Berchem (an average of 133 guilders), Adriaen van de Velde (167 guilders), Paulus Potter (204 guilders) and Philips Wouwerman (232 guilders). Wouwerman's landscapes, in which horses almost always played a leading part, were particularly in vogue among royal and aristocratic collectors. The appeal of Paulus Potter's paintings was due to his highly detailed and refined technique and his choice of subject: farmers or hunters with their animals in a landscape. Huge prices were often paid for them. We can easily illustrate the speed at which the price of his work increased in the course of the eighteenth century on the basis of the well-known work *Grote Ossendrift* in the Braamcamp collection, a major work that Catherine the Great purchased in 1771, but which was lost in a storm at sea on its way to Russia. In 1707 it cost 455 guilders, in 1734 it was already at 1,760 guilders, in 1754 no less than 3,110 guilders, in 1761 3,975 guilders and in 1771 finally reached the astronomical price of 9,050 guilders.

Paulus Potter, *Cattle in a Meadow*, 1652, oil on panel, 35.8 x 46.9 cm, Mauritshuis, The Hague

This painting sold for 730 guilders at an auction in Amsterdam in 1738 making it one of the most expensive paintings by Potter in the early eighteenth century.

Jacob van Ruisdael, *The Jewish Cemetery*, c. 1655, oil on canvas, 84 x 95 cm,
Staatliche Kunstsammlungen, Gemäldegalerie Alte Meister, Dresden

This painting is possibly identical with one auctioned in 1739 in Amsterdam for only eleven guilders.
Before 1754 it had been purchased by August III, Elector of Saxony and King of Poland.
Goethe's 'Ruisdael as Poet' from 1816 made it very famous.

Translated by Gregory Ball

To conclude, a brief observation on an artist who is currently one of the best-known landscape painters of the Golden Age: Jacob van Ruisdael. Although his paintings of North European landscapes could be purchased relatively cheaply on the art market in the first half of the eighteenth century (an average of only forty-two guilders), this changed in the second half of that century when the appreciation of his work appeared to increase rapidly. A little later still, during the Romantic period, he became one of the best-loved painters of the Golden Age. ■

Lantern Bearers and Pathfinders

The Journey to Italy in the Sixteenth Century

[LEEN HUET]

Italy: sun, the Mediterranean, beautiful landscapes, delicious food, cities and villages filled with art. This is how we northerners now view this southern land. Our ancestors in the sixteenth century had a somewhat different list: terrifying Alps, sun, art, the pope in Rome (even a Dutch pope at one point), Ottoman pirates on the Mediterranean, fellow subjects of Emperor Charles in Naples and deeper down into the boot, where they would feel at home; Virgil's birthplace, in Mantua; Virgil's grave, in Naples; the Lago di Averno, where Virgil's Aeneas descended into the underworld; good business deals. Anyone who spoke and wrote humanist Latin could, with the right recommendations, go to Italy and find an interesting career as a secretary or a librarian. Those who had mastered the universal language of art could work anywhere in the country, in studios both large and small. Travellers from the north, who were all, for the sake of convenience, known as *fiamminghi* (Flemings), were usually quick to find work in what Italians considered their speciality: painting landscapes. As Michelangelo, the greatest Italian artist of the sixteenth century, declared in 1547, 'To be honest, in Flanders they paint to deceive the outwardly focused gaze, either by depicting scenes that are pleasant to the eye, or by choosing subjects about which nothing bad can be said, such as saints or prophets. In their tableaux, it is all laundry, ruins, green fields, shadows of trees, rivers and bridges, which they call landscapes, and here a whole throng of figures and there a whole throng of figures. And all of this, although some people seem to find it beautiful, is in reality done without reflection or artistic sensitivity, without a sense of symmetry and proportion, without discernment and playfulness, in short, without any substance or power...'.[1]

Fiamminghi

In the sixteenth century, people in Italy were accustomed to travelling artists from the north, who came to study the artistic masterpieces of antiquity and of the Renaissance. This had not always been the case. A hundred years earlier, a Sicilian artist, Antonello da Messina, had travelled to Bruges in an attempt to meet Jan van Eyck and to learn the secret of his oil-painting technique from

him. At least, this is what Giorgio Vasari wrote in his standard work about the lives of the famous Italian painters, sculptors and architects, and it was widely believed.[2] After the blossoming of the art of the Flemish Primitives, the artistic centre of Europe shifted to the south. In the Low Countries, art experts assume that Jan Gossaert van Maubeuge (1478-1532) was the first *fiammingo* to travel to Italy to become acquainted with the works of the Renaissance masters. Gossaert travelled to Rome on a diplomatic mission in the retinue of his patron, Philip of Burgundy. Philip, the illegitimate son of Duke Philip the Good, was there to negotiate with Pope Julius II. The humanist Gerardus Geldenhauer Noviomagus noted in his biography of Philip: 'Nothing gave him greater pleasure in Rome than the holy monuments of her Antiquity, which he commanded his very famous painter, Jan Gossaert, to capture for him.'[3] Gossaert stayed in Rome in 1509 and after his return was the first northerner to paint 'poesie', poetic mythological scenes in the Italian style, for Philip after he became the bishop of Utrecht. One striking work is Gossaert's drawing of the Colosseum, a dilapidated monument of enormous proportions that would develop in the minds of northern artists into a symbol of the Tower of Babel. Jan Gossaert was, incidentally, not the only artist in the service of Philip of Burgundy. The Venetian Jacopo de' Barbari (?-1516) worked for the bishop in Utrecht for some time and subsequently became the court painter for Margaret of Austria, governor of the Habsburg Netherlands, in Mechelen. Gerardus Geldenhauer, who knew both men, called them the Zeuxis and the Apelles of the Netherlands, a flattering comparison to the most famous painters of ancient Greece.[4]

Maarten van Heemskerck,
Self-portrait, with the
Colosseum, Rome, 1553,
oil on panel, 42 x 54 cm,
Fitzwilliam Museum,
Cambridge

Some years later, the only Dutch pope, Adrian VI, born in Utrecht, attracted many Netherlanders to the south, including the outstanding painter Jan van Scorel (1495-1562). Van Scorel had previously spent time in Venice and as a pilgrim in the Holy Land. In 1522, Pope Adrian appointed him as the keeper of the antique sculptures in the Belvedere. Those sculptures included the famous *Laocoön Group*, which was excavated from a Roman vineyard on 14 January 1506. Van Scorel succeeded none other than Raphael in this role. The Dutch dream in Rome did not last long. Adrian VI died suddenly in August 1523, and Van Scorel returned to the north and settled as a canon and artist in Utrecht. His best student, Maarten van Heemskerck (1498-1574), later followed in his footsteps and travelled to Italy. Van Heemskerck left behind an impressive self-portrait with the Colosseum in the background.

Networks

Jan Gossaert and Jan van Scorel are still well known for having paved the way for all Dutch artists who wanted to delve into the stylistic idiom of the Renaissance and Mannerism. They are the most striking figures in what could be called the Utrecht Network, which originated around Bishop Philip of Burgundy. Jan van Scorel enjoyed an even greater reputation with later artists, as he had not travelled to the south in the company of a noble, but on his own initiative: Frans Floris called him 'the lantern bearer and pathfinder' of the Romanists, the painters and sculptors who had visited Rome.[5]

Out of the Utrecht Network, the Liège Network developed, crucial for artists in our region. The Liège painter Lambert Lombard (1505/6-1566) may have had lessons from Jan Gossaert and Jan van Scorel, and he later became a court painter in the city of his birth. Whenever he could, he studied Italian paintings in collections, analysing their composition so well that his contemporaries thought his work was that of a born and bred Italian. This fact is proudly record-ed in Lombard's biography, written by the humanist Lampsonius and published in 1565[6] – which is, incidentally, the only standalone biography of a Dutch artist from the sixteenth century. In 1537, Lombard finally received a commission and funding from the Liège prince bishop Erard de la Marck to travel to Rome, so that he could buy sculptures and become a first-class advisor on artistic mat-ters. Lombard could only stay a year in Rome, but he emerged as one of the most original Romanists of the sixteenth century. His correspondence, for instance, reveals his interest in Romanesque and Gothic painting – the sort of artworks that in the sixteenth century were generally regarded as barbarian, completely outdated and ridiculous. In 1565, he wrote to Giorgio Vasari: 'It is my great wish, through your benevolent intercession, to receive a History [drawn composition] by Margaritone [second half of the thirteenth century], and also by Gaddi and by Giotto; I would like to compare them with the stained-glass windows that are to be found here in old monasteries, and bronze bas-reliefs in which one usually sees the figures standing on the tips of their toes, and yet which have given me more to think about than some works that are only one hundred years old.'[7] This fondness for older art also sparked an academic interest in the archaeological and numismatic history of northern Europe. Lombard made studies of the Igel Column, a late classical burial moment in Trier. He designed prints based on classical themes for the publisher Hieronymus Cock in Antwerp, designs that were both aesthetically pleasing and academically sound, in their reproduction of clothing, objects and events from classical antiquity. His *Sacrifice to Priapus* is an attractive example of this thorough approach.

Lambert Lombard, *Sacrifice to Priapus*, 1540, Ashmolean Museum, Oxford

An artist with the intellectual vigour of Lambert Lombard attracted ambitious students, all the more so because he also truly dedicated himself to teaching, developing a curriculum in his home to give young artists a broad intellectual education: the first academy in the Low Countries. His most famous students were Frans Floris, Willem Key, his later biographer Lampsonius and the Bruges humanist Hubert Goltzius. Goltzius produced such ground-breaking work with his illustrated publications in the field of numismatics that, in 1567, he was offered the citizenship of Rome, a great accomplishment for a humanist from the north. By way of comparison, this honour was never granted to our most renowned humanist, Desiderius Erasmus. Frans Floris became the tutor of the painter-poet Lucas d'Heere in Ghent, who in turn taught Karel van Mander. In 1604, Van Mander published the *Schilder-Boeck*, or 'Book of Painters', the first major study of art in the Low Countries, still an essential source for art historians, and a late fruit, it might be said, of Lombard's intellectual approach to art. Dominicus Lampsonius became the teacher of Otto van Veen, who later tutored Peter Paul Rubens, just about the apotheosis of the humanist artist in our region.

Pieter Bruegel the Elder

In the second half of the sixteenth century, the artistic traffic on the roads to the south increased. Study trips to Italy remained expensive and risky undertakings though, and only for the most highly motivated of artists. Travellers could earn a living on the way by taking on commissions, but they would certainly have required a lot of savings before setting off, not to mention the social capital of self-confidence, letters of recommendation, and connections. The

Pieter Bruegel the Elder, *View of the Ripa Grande, Rome*, c. 1553, pen and brown ink, 20.7 x 28.3 cm, The Devonshire Collection, Chatsworth House

most remarkable Romanist was undoubtedly Pieter Bruegel the Elder (1525?-1569). At first glance, his oeuvre contains few traces of Italian influence. Yet he spent two intense and educational years in Italy. We can follow his trail from Mantua to Venice and Milan, Bologna, Rome, Naples and Sicily. In Venice, he studied Titian's woodcuts, and in Rome he became friends with the miniaturist Giulio Clovio, 'Michelangelo in a small format'.[8] He painted a Tower of Babylon on ivory for Clovio, probably a precursor to his famous and magnificent Towers of Babel, inspired by the Colosseum and preserved in the Museum Boijmans Van Beuningen in Rotterdam and the Kunsthistorisches Museum in Vienna. Like Lambert Lombard, Bruegel had an eye for older forms of art: manuscript illuminations, medieval frescos depicting the Triumph of Death, paintings by Hieronymus Bosch and Jan van Eyck in Italian collections. And the Alps, too, made a great impression on him: after his return to Antwerp, he came to fame with a series of designs for prints of stunning mountain landscapes, published by Hieronymus Cock.

Giambologna, *The Rape of the Sabine Women* (details), 1582, marble, Loggia dei Lanzi, Florence

We can consider ourselves fortunate that Pieter Bruegel returned to the flat north. Not all *fiamminghi* did so. Some of them built up fine careers in Italy. Jean de Boulogne (1529-1608) from Douai became a first-class sculptor in Florence under the name of Giambologna, and every tourist there nowadays sees his unrivalled *Rape of the Sabine Women* in the Loggia dei Lanzi. Jan van der Straet (1523-1605) from Bruges set up shop in the same Italian city in around 1550, where he worked for the court painter Giorgio Vasari. Van der Straet was from then on known as Giovanni da Strada or Giovanni Stradano. 'Like a cunning Circe, the greedy, flower-filled Florence keeps this Bruges artist away from his homeland and makes him grey and white there with her', Van Mander wrote on the subject.[9] Stradano contributed to frescos in the Palazzo Vecchio, created designs for tapestries that complemented the wall paintings, and designed many series of tapestries and prints of hunting scenes, which appealed to an international audience with their elegance and wealth of details. He also illustrated Dante's *Inferno*. Stradano did not break all ties with his homeland; most of his prints were engraved in Antwerp, including some by Bruegel's publisher, Cock. So he was well placed to provide Giorgio Vasari with information about his northern colleagues for the second edition of his *Lives of the Artists* (1568), still our most important source of knowledge about Renaissance art.

Venice as a hub

Rome is often seen as the natural final destination of a journey to Italy, but as this essay has shown above, other Italian cities exerted an equally great attraction. The artists' personal preferences also played a role. Van Mander noted approvingly that the young Brussels painter Adriaan De Weert (1536?-1590) went specially to Parma to study the work of his favourite master, Parmigianino.[10] The powerful trading state of Venice functioned in all respects as a hub for the contact between Italy and the Low Countries. Titian worked there as a portrait painter in the service of Emperor Charles V, and his interest in prints as a means of making his work more widely known led to fruitful collaboration with artists from the north. In 1565, he hired the engraver Cornelis Cort (1533-1578), who until then had worked for Hieronymus Cock. In Venice, Cort soon revealed himself to be among the very finest of engravers, achieving astounding results with large prints full of lively chiaroscuro based on Titian's compositions. Later Cort briefly worked with Stradano in Florence; he subsequently established himself in Rome as a freelance large-format engraver, the most widely imitated of his day.

Rubens

Family role models are an important form of social capital. In 1589, Pieter Bruegel's youngest son, Jan (1568-1628), travelled to Naples and possibly Sicily. He had undoubtedly heard stories as a child about the things his father had seen and experienced there. In Naples he received a payment for painting a clock that belonged to the abbot Francesco Caracciolo.[11] This is an early indication of his fondness for working on a small scale. In 1591, he went to Rome, where after some years he took up residence with an excellent patron, Cardinal Federico Borromeo. The cardinal, as we can gather from Jan's letters, had liberated the young artist from a Roman prison at some point. Borromeo purchased a large number of works by Jan Bruegel and later described them with great insight in a small guide to his collection, with the title of *Musaeum*. 'The painter Brueghel himself indicated the price of this flower painting in a particularly witty manner. He painted a diamond brooch at the foot of the vase. Anyone who saw it understood that the price of this painting was equal to the value of the jewel (even though this was already clear), and so that is the amount I paid the artist.'[12] When Borromeo was made archbishop of Milan in 1595, Jan travelled there with the rest of the household. He did not return to Antwerp until 1596. Throughout his life, he continued to correspond with Borromeo's agents and with the cardinal himself. A number of these letters were, incidentally, written by Peter Paul Rubens (1577-1640), a good friend of Jan's and more comfortable with Italian. Family role models were also important for Rubens: his father had studied law in Padua, and his brother Philip stayed in Rome as the protégé of the humanist Justus Lipsius. Rubens's time in Italy in 1600-1608 is one of the best-documented journeys to the south, as we still have a good number of the letters that he wrote while there. Those letters show that the north only narrowly succeeded in getting back Rubens, the most important master of the seventeenth century. He was making a fine career for himself

Peter Paul Rubens, *Self-Portrait in a Circle of Friends from Mantua*,
c. 1602-1604, oil on canvas, 77.5 x 161 cm,
Wallraf-Richartz-Museum, Cologne

with major commissions in Rome, when his mother died in 1608. Rubens came back to Antwerp for the funeral, with the firm intention of returning to Rome. 'Even to this day I do not know which decision I should best take, to stay here in my fatherland or to return forever to Rome, whence I receive offers under the best of conditions.'[13] Thanks to orders placed by the citizens of Antwerp, flattering commissions from Archduke Albert and Archduchess Isabella, and to the beautiful Isabella Brant, things turned out differently. ▪

NOTES

1   F. de Holanda, p. 25.

2   Vasari, vol. 2, pp. 568-569. The first edition of Vasari's *Vite* was published in 1565, the second, greatly expanded, in 1568.

3   Geldenhauer, p. 233.

4   Geldenhauer, p. 235.

5   Recorded by Karel van Mander in his biography of Scorel. Quoted in Dacos, p. 237, note 2.

6   Hubaux and Puraye, p. 65.

7   Denhaene, p. 319.

8   L. Huet, pp. 105-146.

9   Van Mander, p. 164.

10 Van Mander, p. 90.

11 Bedoni, pp. 20-21.

12 Borromeo, pp. 182-183.

13 Rubens, p. 44. Letter from Antwerp to a friend in Rome, 10 April 1609.

FURTHER READING

Hieronymus Cock. De renaissance in prent, exh. cat. Leuven, 2013.

S. Bedoni, *Jan Brueghel in Italia e il collezionismo del Seicento*, Florence, 1983.

F. Borromeo, *Sacred Painting. Museum*, edited and translated by K.S. Rothwell, Jr., with an introduction and notes by P.M. Jones (*The I Tatti Renaissance Library*), Cambridge, Mass. – London, 2010.

N. Dacos, *Voyage à Rome. Les artistes européens au XVIe siècle*, Brussels, 2012.

F. de Holanda, *Romeinse dialogen. Gesprekken met Michelangelo en Vittoria Colonna*, translated from Portuguese by A. Boon, Amsterdam, 1993.

G. Denhaene, *Lambert Lombard. Renaissance en humanisme te Luik*, translated from French by B. Van Imschoot-Hoing, Antwerp, 1990.

G. Geldenhauer, *Collectanea van Gerardus Geldenhauer Noviomagus, gevolgd door een herdruk van eenige zijner werken*, edited and elucidated by Dr. J. Prinsen J. Lz., Amsterdam, 1901.

J. Hubaux and J. Puraye, *Dominique Lampson. Lamberti Lombardi ... Vita*, in *Belgisch Tijdschrift voor oudheidkunde en kunstgeschiedenis*, 1949, XVIII, pp. 53-77.

L. Huet, *Pieter Bruegel. De biografie*, Antwerp, 2016.

P.P. Rubens, *Brieven* (Letters), selected and translated by L. Huet, Antwerp, 2014.

M. Sellink, *Cornelis Cort*, 3 vols. (*The New Hollstein Dutch and Flemish Etchings, Engravings and Woodcuts 1400-1700*), Rotterdam, 2000.

K. van Mander, *Het schilder boek. Het leven der doorluchtige Nederlandsche en Hoogduitsche schilders*, reworked by A. F. Mirande and G.S. Overdiep, third edition, Amsterdam, 1946.

G. Vasari, *Le Opere di Giorgio Vasari con nuove annotazioni e commenti di Gaetano Milanesi*, 9 vols., Florence 1906 (anastatic reprint, Florence, 1981).

Translated by Laura Watkinson

Rubens in Holland, Rembrandt in Flanders

Peter Paul Rubens was not what you would call a man of one piece. In point of fact, and it hurts me to say so, he could be downright devious. Take his visits to the Republic of the Seven United Netherlands in July 1627 and December 1631. When Rubens showed up in Utrecht on the earlier visit, he was feted by Gerrit van Honthorst with a dinner in his honour to which all the prominent artists of the city were invited. He praised the paintings of his host, especially the night scenes (he surely knew that in Italy Honthorst was known as Gherardo delle Notti), and on subsequent days visited the main masters in their studios, buying a number of pictures by Cornelis van Poelenburgh. This part of the story was published sixty years later by someone who was at the events – Joachim von Sandrart, who in summer 1627 was a young German apprentice to Honthorst and went on to become a major figure as a painter and writer on art. Because Honthorst was indisposed, Sandrart got to accompany Rubens on his studio visits in Utrecht and Amsterdam, which understandably he wrote up as the highpoint of events.

There is a story behind the story, however, which we know about from the correspondence of key insiders. First of all, Rubens had no desire whatsoever to come to the Republic, with which his country, the Habsburg Netherlands, was at war. He and his friend Balthasar Gerbier were engaged in the sale to the duke of Buckingham, for a hefty 200,000 francs, of a collection of ancient marbles. Rubens was anxious to conduct the business in neutral territory between the northern and southern Netherlands, in the town of Zevenbergen. It was Gerbier who insisted on combining their talks with studio visits in Delft, Utrecht and Amsterdam.

That is not even the innermost of these circles within circles. The entire enterprise, Dutch painters and Gerbier's statues both, was nothing other than a pretext to cover a spying mission Rubens was carrying out, on the order of Infanta Isabella Clara Eugenia of Spain, regentess of the Habsburg Netherlands, to throw a wrench into renewed negotiations on a peace treaty between the Republic and Spain.

Rubens's position on the secret council of the Spanish king and confidant of the Infanta also lay behind his disastrous trip to The Hague four years later. On his Lady's orders, Rubens transgressed diplomatic protocol and showed

Rembrandt, *Self-portrait*, 1631
etching, touched up in black chalk, 14.8 x 13 cm,
British Museum, London

Paulus Pontius, after Peter Paul Rubens,
Self-portrait by Peter Paul Rubens, 1630,
engraving on paper, 36.5 x 27.2 cm
Teylers Museum, Haarlem

up unannounced at the court of the stadholder, Frederik Hendrik. Despite his proud ownership of six paintings by the famous master and his desire for more, the stadholder had no choice but to send him packing. Two days after his arrival, Rubens left the Republic with his tail between his legs, going back to face the extreme annoyance of Flemish aristocrats at home, who saw their own diplomacy being undermined by the Infanta and her favourite.

To be generous, it must be said that Rubens's shifty behaviour was occasioned at least as much by the circumstances attending the Eighty Years War (1568-1648) as by his character. Having said which, it must be noted that the events of his life and the civil war between north and south were closely intertwined. The war began nine years before Rubens was born in 1577 and did not end until eight years after he died, in 1640. He was born in Germany because in 1568 his Protestant father Jan had fled Antwerp for safety from the Spanish oppression of Protestants in the city of which he was town secretary. Jan drew even closer to the Revolt when he became the lover of Anna van Saksen, the wife of Prince William of Orange. He was rescued from the death sentence pronounced on him only through the impassioned appeal of his wife, the more than admirable Maria Pijpelinckx. After Jan's death in 1587, Maria took her two sons back to Antwerp and re-entered the Catholic church.

Like the other inhabitants of the Netherlands, Rubens enjoyed a reprieve from hostilities during the twelve years of the truce between north and south, from 1609 to 1621. (In the north, this was a relative blessing. The Republic seized the occasion to hold a mini-civil war of its own, between Calvinists and Remonstrants.) The truce went into effect on 9 April 1609, half a year after Rubens's return to Antwerp from Italy. Setting himself up in a studio that was soon internationally famous, it came to his attention that printmakers from The Hague, Haarlem and Leiden had begun to copy paintings of his engravings of the highest standard. Rubens paintings that happened to be in the north were engraved by Willem van Swanenburg in 1612 and Andreas Stock in 1614, while in 1613 Willem Buytewech produced etchings after designs by Rubens and Jacob Matham brought out a print after his *Samson and Delilah*, a proud possession of Burgomaster Nicolas Rockox of Antwerp. Rubens was so impressed that he came north to stimulate more of the same. After the death in 1617 of the great Hendrik Goltzius, the foremost engraver of his time, Balthasar Gerbier wrote a forty-eight-page eulogy including the following slightly weird annotation, in literal translation: 'Rubens, [Jan] Breughel, [Hendrik] van Balen and some more [Flemish artists] being in Holland, Goltzius and other Haarlemers traveled from that city to encounter them in a village where – having played the joke of not identifying themselves – they arrested them in order to pay honor to the noble spirits, which they did by raising an undisguisedly joking wineglass [why joking?] in order to drink to mutual friendship and trust.'

Rubens was so impressed by the quality of Dutch printmakers that he took two of them consecutively in service, Pieter Soutman and Lucas Vorsterman. In 1619 Rubens applied through a befriended Dutch officeholder for copyright in the Republic of Vorsterman's prints after his paintings.

If anyone in Holland knew all about this, it was the omnivorous adapter and collector of other artists' creations Rembrandt van Rijn. In 1627, when Rubens visited the Republic, Rembrandt was poised to hit his stride in The Hague as a well-paid painter for the Rubens-loving court of Frederik Hendrik. Rubens was the man to beat in Netherlandish art, and Rembrandt set out to emulate if not to surpass him. As Simon Schama wrote in his brilliant disquisition on the two masters: 'Rembrandt ... could not quite leave off wanting to be Rubens.' That desire expressed itself astonishingly literally in a self-portrait etching of 1631, a year after the model provided by Rubens through an engraving by Paulus Pontius.

A more subtle cross-border connection became apparent a few years later. In 1633 Rembrandt took on the guise of the most famous Leiden artist before him, Lucas van Leyden. He borrowed Lucas's appearance from a print by Andries Stock after a painted self-portrait, which was provided with a caption telling that Lucas died in 1533. Rembrandt's print was a centennial tribute to Lucas as well as a self-glorifying claim to be his successor. Around the same time Rubens copied the same image, probably from the print rather than the painting, with allegorical attributes that pay hommage to Lucas as the very embodiment of artistic fame. The legend below attributes mystical qualities to the artist, calling Lucas the light, moon and sun of the paintbrush. Rubens, Rembrandt and Lucas van Leyden were participants in a Low Countries artistic culture that covered all seventeen provinces of north and south.

Andries Jacobsz Stock after Lucas van Leyden, *Self-portrait*, c. 1620, engraving, 21.8 x 16.7 cm, Rijksmuseum, Amsterdam

Peter Paul Rubens after Andries Stock after Lucas van Leyden, *Self-portrait*, c. 1633, brush and ink, white and yellow body colour over a sketch in black chalk, 27.9 x 20 cm, Fondation Custodia, Collection Frits Lugt, Paris

Rembrandt, *Self-portrait*, 1633, etching, 13.2 x 10.3 cm, Rijksmuseum, Amsterdam

1631 was the year that saw Rembrandt turn seriously to Rubens as a source and model. The self-portrait print has a funny equivalent in his *Self-Portrait in Oriental Costume with Poodle*, in which Rembrandt dresses himself in Oriental garb like a figure in Rubens's *Adoration of the Magi* and like his wealthy Antwerp sitter Nicolas de Respaigne. Rembrandt's *Crucifixion* of 1631 is based on a print after a Rubens design, as are his *Raising of* and *Descent from the Cross* of about 1633. The latter were painted for Frederik Hendrik in a series of the Passion of Christ, commissioned following Rubens's ill-fated two days in The Hague. I must confess that I have been unable, for long years now, to suppress the thought that Rembrandt visited Antwerp not long before making those Rubens-esque self-portraits of 1631. The Rembrandt documents show a gap between 15 November 1630, when he signed an apprenticeship agreement in Leiden, and 1 March 1631, when he bought a piece of land outside Leiden. In those four months Rubens was in Antwerp and could have received his younger colleague before or after his marriage to Helena Fourment on 6 December 1630.

This hypothesis, which I fear is unprovable, would help to explain why Rembrandt, more than any other artist of his time, associated himself so emphatically with Rubens. His dedication to the Flemish master extended to the purchase of an early Rubens painting, *Hero and Leander*. He also owned seven paintings by another Antwerp artist whom Rubens admired and envied for his truth to (low) life, Adriaen Brouwer. My favourite example of Rembrandt's appropriation of motifs from Flemish painting concerns his first Amsterdam masterpiece, the *Anatomy Lesson of Dr. Nicolaes Tulp*, painted in early 1632.

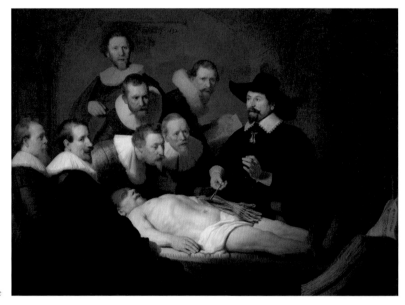

Rembrandt, *The Anatomy Lesson of Dr. Nicolaes Tulp*, 1632, oil on canvas, 169.5 x 216.5 cm, Mauritshuis website, The Hague

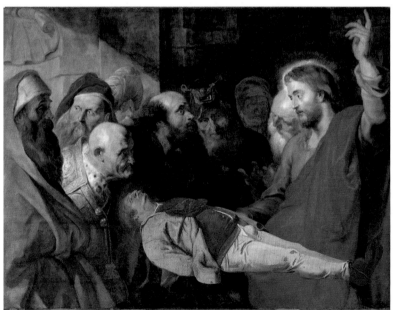

Montage of detail from Adriaen Brouwer, *Drunken Peasant Passed out in a Tavern*, c. 1630, Museum Boijmans Van Beuningen, Rotterdam onto Peter Paul Rubens, *The Tribute Money*, c. 1612, Legion of Honor Museum, San Francisco (also copied in an engraving by Claes Jansz Visscher)

Insofar as the painting owes its success to its introduction into the usually static formula of the group portrait elements from narrative and genre painting, the sources for that tactic lay in Antwerp, in Rubens's *Tribute money* (1612) and Brouwer's *Drunken Peasant Passed out in a Tavern* (c. 1630). History does not tell what the Brabant masters thought of this tribute to their art.

Because the difference between Rubens and Rembrandt, like that between their countries, is often reduced to Catholicism versus Calvinism, it is worthwhile looking at this issue more closely. When the Antwerp art historian Frans Baudouin, director in life of the Rubens House and founding father of the Rubenianum Study Centre, delved into the religious history of the Rubens's family, he came to a surprising conclusion. That is, that the return of Maria Pijpelinckx to Catholicism when she moved to Antwerp with her sons was inspired more by opportunism than by conviction. Even more than Jan Rubens, Maria was attached to Lutheranism, the religion of her mother. Rubens was therefore brought up as a kind of Lutheran marrano, a Protestant Catholic. As for Rembrandt, the Amsterdam archivist Bas Dudok van Heel places him unreservedly in the ranks of the Dutch Remonstrants, a Reformed movement that its detractors call Catholic Protestants. Both artists had an uneasy relationship with the dominant creed in their countries.

This nuance has long been lost. It was especially absent in the mid-nineteenth century, when Rubens and Rembrandt became symbols of their respective nations. In 1843 the new Monarchy of Belgium placed a statue of Rubens in the square adjoining Antwerp Cathedral. The square, the Groenplaats, had been a cemetery, and the statue of Rubens was placed on the sacred spot where the churchyard cross had stood. The response from the north was more defensive. As a nationalist hero, Rembrandt could not compete with the humanist diplomat giant of European culture that Rubens had been. On the eve of the inauguration of the Rembrandt statue, on a commercial Amsterdam market square, the Amsterdam archivist Pieter Scheltema felt called upon to hold an hours-long lecture defending Rembrandt from charges of boorishness, moneygrubbing and bad behaviour. Because these accusations were mainly true, scholarly study of Rembrandt got off to a false start from which it has never entirely recovered. Rembrandt's own ambition to vie with Rubens was revived and taken on by his admirers 200 years later. Admirers who were moved more by patriotism than love of art, let alone of historical truth.

Coming at the dawn of the age of nationalist museology, this strained posthumous competition led to predictably unhappy results. No collection of Rubens paintings became a lasting part of Dutch cultural heritage until the mid-twentieth century, nor were paintings by Rembrandt acquired in Belgium. There are only two paintings by Rembrandt in public collections in Belgium, and a mere handful by Rubens in Holland, not counting the mid-twentieth century donation to Museum Boijmans Van Beuningen of twenty oil sketches. These are pitiful figures for major collecting nations. It took positive distaste to attain a record like this.

To this unfortunate rule there is one historical exception. That was the painting collection built by King William II of the Netherlands (1792-1849; r. 1840-49). The catalogue of the auction sale held of his collection in 1850 lists eight paintings by Rembrandt and eight by Rubens; the rest of the collection attests to a deliberate attempt to balance the art of the northern and southern

Netherlands, with twenty-seven seventeenth-century paintings from Flanders and twenty-six from Holland. This approach to the art of his fatherland, I am convinced, was due to William's personal ambitions. Fatherland is indeed the word; when William began to collect, his father was king of a shortlived monarchy joining the southern provinces of the Netherlands to the northern ones. That arrangement, so attractive to the House of Orange, did not last long, but son William never gave up the unrealistic hope that he would some day rule over all of the Seventeen Provinces. His art collection may have reflected William's personal taste as well, but it surely corresponded to his dynastic dream. He promoted the status of his own art collection by opposing any and all public spending on acquisitions for the national museums.

In 2006, the year when Rembrandt's 400th birthday was celebrated all over the world, I lectured on this subject to the Royal Flemish Academy of Belgium for Science and the Arts in Brussels. It was a thrilling experience for me, since the Academy is housed in the very building, erected in 1824 by William I as a Brussels palace, where William II and his wife Anna Pavlovna lived before the Belgian breakaway of 1839 drove them to The Hague. The collection went with them, to be reinstalled in the Gothic Hall behind a town palace on the Kneuterdijk, where it was open to the public when the royal pair was not in residence. When William died unexpectedly in 1849, it turned out that six months earlier he had secretly borrowed one million guilders from his brother-in-law Tsar Nicholas I, putting up his art collection as collateral. His heirs refused to honour the debt, and a proposal in Parliament to form a fund of private money and a loan from the state to buy the collection for that paltry million was voted down by fifty votes to eight. At auction, the finest private art collection ever assembled in the Netherlands, including masterpieces not only by Rubens and Rembrandt but also Jan van Eyck and Rogier van der Weyden, Dieric Bouts and Hans Memling, Perugino and Sebastiano del Piombo, Lucas Cranach and Hans Holbein, Raphael and Titian (well, almost Raphael and Titian), Claude Lorrain and Gaspar Dughet, Murillo and Ribera, went blowing in the wind.

After the lecture I was approached by a friendly man who had kept silent in the question period. 'Mr. Schwartz,' he said, 'I have something to show you that is not known to many people. The room next door where the Academy is now serving drinks was the gallery where those paintings you were talking about once hung. There are still traces of that function on the walls. The hooks from which the paintings were hung are still in place. Because the Palace of the Academy was recently placed on the list of protected monuments, fixtures like those cannot be removed.' We moved next door, and indeed there they were.

The picture I made with my telephone camera shows more than the glow on the wall. I too was gleaming. ■

FURTHER READING

Frans Baudouin, 'Rubens' kinderjaren in Keulen en in Antwerpen,' in *Rubens in Context: Selected Studies. Liber Memorialis*, Centrum voor de Vlaamse Kunst van de 16e en de 17e eeuw.

S.A.C. Dudok van Heel, *De jonge Rembrandt onder tijdgenoten: godsdienst en schilderkunst in Leiden en Amsterdam* (The Young Rembrandt Among his Contemporaries: Religion and Painting in Leiden and Amsterdam), Rotterdam, 2006.

J.G. van Gelder, 'Rubens in Holland', *Nederlandsch Kunsthistorisch Jaarboek* 3 (1950-51), pp. 103-150.

Carlos van Hasselt, exhib. cat. *Flemish Drawings of the Seventeenth Century from the Collection of Frits Lugt*, Victoria and Albert Museum, London, 1972.

Erik Hinterding and Femy Horsch, 'A Small but Choice Collection: the Art Gallery of King Willem II of the Netherlands (1792-1849)', *Simiolus: Netherlands Quarterly for the History of Art* 19 (1989), pp. 5-122.

Max Rooses and Charles-Louis Ruelens, *Correspondance de Rubens et documents épistolaires concernant sa vie et ses œuvres*, 6 vols., Antwerp, 1887-1909 (available online at Google Books).

Gary Schwartz, *Rembrandt's Universe*, London, 2006.

Bruegel Revisited

A Look at the Master in Anticipation of Bruegel Year 2019

[MANFRED SELLINK]

It is somewhat dull and predictable to always begin texts about Pieter Bruegel the Elder with the observation that art historians know so incredibly little about this great master. The number of studies and dissertations on his work are in sharp contrast to the few factual details that are known about the person and his life. What do we know with certainty? Bruegel was born somewhere between 1525 and 1530. Some think this was in the (Netherlands) Brabant village of Breugel, others think it must have been in Breda, local historians in Belgian Limburg opt for Bree or Brogel and yet others – including the undersigned – think that it was most likely Antwerp. Although there is no archival proof, it is generally accepted that he received his artistic training in the Scheldt city in the 1540s, at Pieter Coecke van Aelst's workshop. What is certain is that Bruegel was enrolled as a master – and therefore as a fully qualified artist – in the Guild of St. Luke in Antwerp in 1551. In 1551/52 he worked with the painter Pieter Balten on the side panels of a lost altarpiece for the St Rombout's Cathedral in Mechelen. Shortly after that, in the years 1552-54, he must have set off on a journey to Italy. Presumably he went via Lyon. In Italy he certainly spent quite a long time in Rome and travelled further south as far as Reggio di Calabria. He probably returned via Venice and then northwards through the Alps back to Antwerp. There he worked primarily as a landscape draughtsman and print designer for In de Vier Winden/Aux quatres vents (At the Sign of the Four Winds), Hieronymus Cock's internationally renowned print publishing house. Paintings dated from 1557 have survived and, as of 1561/62, it is clear that Bruegel concentrated increasingly on painting. In the autumn of 1562 he married Mayken Coecke, the daughter of his teacher, Pieter Coecke van Aelst, and moved to Brussels – where he was to devote himself completely to his career as a painter. The artist died in the autumn of 1569 and was buried in (or near) the Chapel Church in Brussels. There are dated works until 1568. The oeuvre from his own hand that has been passed down is small, approximately forty-five paintings and sixty-five drawings. The precise number depends on a small handful of problematic attributions. Pieter Bruegel left two sons, both of whom made their careers as painters. Pieter Brueghel the Younger (1564-1638) was to devote himself completely to producing copies and paintings in the style of his father. The more versatile and considerably more talented Jan Brueghel

The Artist and the Connaisseur, c. 1565, drawing, 25.5 x 21.5 cm,
Graphische Sammlung Albertina, Vienna

the Elder (1568-1625) became one of the most important and most successful painters in Antwerp in the first decade of the seventeenth century. The presumably already small oeuvre of the older Bruegel – relatively few paintings seem to have been lost – was as rare after his death as it was in demand and was quickly dispersed among prominent European (royal and aristocratic) collections.

A once-in-a-lifetime opportunity

As the conditional wording of this biographical sketch shows, contemporary sources and documents offer little real knowledge about Pieter Bruegel – most is based on indirect sources, the study of his works and circumstantial evidence. One of the few biographical certainties that we have is that he died in

Brussels in the autumn of 1569. That is why 2019 is considered internationally to be Bruegel Year, as it marks 450 years since the artist died. As already mentioned, his exact year of birth is not known. Years commemorating writers, composers and artists are not uncontroversial in the world of art and culture and are often dismissed as primarily economically driven initiatives for the benefit of (cultural) tourism and city marketing. That is always a risk and it is easy to think of examples of activities in this type of commemorative year where the content totally fails to make the grade. On the other hand, there are many examples of the opposite. Bosch Year 2016 is, in my opinion, one of these.[1]

Obviously, one can always criticise overwhelming public interest as a measure of success, but the Hieronymus Bosch exhibitions in Den Bosch and Madrid were of the very highest quality and a once-in-a-lifetime opportunity for any art enthusiast in the Low Countries. The years of research into the master's oeuvre and his workshop were only possible thanks to financing from the jubilee year. Besides the public appreciation, it is already clear that this fundamental art historic and material technological research has provided not only many new insights in terms of both content and the discipline itself, but has also raised many questions, setting the agenda for research into Bosch and his workshop practices for the coming years. Presumably it will be no different with Bruegel. It is an incredible opportunity – both for the general public

The Land of Cockaigne (detail), 1567, oil on wood, 52 x 78 cm, Alte Pinakothek, Munich

and for the discipline – that precisely these two artists should be the subject of thematic years so soon one after the other. Indeed, in the Low Countries the sixteenth century – a period that is certainly THE Golden Age in the Southern Netherlands – is dominated by these two unique grand masters. It is not without reason that this period is often summarised as the century 'from Bosch to Bruegel' – not only because of their chronological succession but, in particular, because of the influence of their work and imagery.

Vienna rules

Bruegel Year will start already in the autumn and winter of 2018/19, in the Kunsthistorisches Museum in Vienna. For the first time ever, a large monographic review of the master's paintings will go on show there, together with a wide selection of his drawings and graphics of his design. While the drawings (and graphics) have almost all been brought together before (Rotterdam and New York 2001), it has never been possible to bring together more than a handful of paintings from his hand, as part of a more broadly based exhibition. The fact that the Kunsthistorisches Museum will probably manage to assemble thirty, perhaps even more, panels in Vienna – out of a total of forty-five, as mentioned above – is only possible thanks to the fact that the museum itself possesses twelve absolute masterpieces by Bruegel and, equally, the dynamic and resources generated by the symbolic jubilee year 2019. Bruegel's works are, almost without exception, fragile panels that belong to the core collec-

View on the Scheldt near Baasrode, c. 1555, drawing, 24.9 x 42.1 cm,
Kupferstichkabinett, Staatliche Museen, Berlin

tions of the museums where they hang. That, plus the fact that the oeuvre is so small, makes obtaining the loan of a panel by Pieter Bruegel the Elder one of the most difficult tasks in the museum world – as is the case with Bosch. That at least thirty panels, around thirty drawings and thirty-five prints of his design will be on show together soon is more than a once-in-a-lifetime opportunity – an expression that is all too easily used by museum directors and marketers. The chance of seeing this particular collection again can be ruled out for many decades. Here the Bruegel Year clearly works as leverage. Everyone realises that this is a unique event, both for the public and for further research and insight into the artist. Furthermore, there will be no second venue – however much museums in Paris, London, Madrid and Flanders would like it.

The fascination of the original

The exhibition in Vienna – of which I have the incredible privilege to be one of the curators – has a specific focus: the creative process, or the way in which the master created his works in terms of concept, techniques, form and style. That is a research question that seems to have appealed quite frequently in recent years to both the general public and specialists. It is useful to understand why. In an age when an abundance of images and information is immediately available (virtually) with the click of a mouse or the swipe of a finger, museums are increasingly aware that their great advantage lies in the fact that they have the original works within their walls – either as part of the permanent collection or brought together temporarily in an exhibition. Being eye to eye with the originals creates an enormous fascination, a desire to get into the mind of the master and learn more about how Bruegel's astonishing masterworks came into being, from conception to execution; to understand how the rare combination of minute details and suggestive lack of clarity blend into one coherent composition; to know whether and how he changed his mind while he was painting; to know how he managed with an extraordinary economy of means to conjure up such a broad and kaleidoscopic and, in particular, such a layered image; to understand how Bruegel used rhetorical and – without being aware of the concept – psychological tricks to 'play' the viewer and draw him into his composition.

A search for the essence

There is something else, too. In the second half of the twentieth century, connoisseurship and a stylistic approach towards older art has to some degree fallen into discredit, for being too intuitive, too subjective and not scientific enough, a criticism that is in many ways understandable and not entirely wrong. But in the past decade a lot has changed, particularly because of the exhaustive scientific approach to restoration and conservation, on the one hand, and the rise of material technical research as a skilled and highly specialised discipline within art history on the other. This latter type of research – known within our field as conservation science – combines state-of-the-art research and technology in the field of natural sciences, chemistry and imagery with the insights of art historians, archival researchers and restorers. This team-oriented and multidisciplinary analysis of artworks seems increasingly to be producing results. This is partly because of incredibly fast technological developments and ever more specific applications, such as chemical analysis of the pigments and materials used, dendrochronology (the dating of panels by statistical analyses of tree rings) and analysis of images based on techniques such as infrared, ultraviolet

The Harvesters (detail),
1565, oil on wood, 119 x 162 cm,
Metropolitan Museum of Art,
New York

and X-ray. All this is supported by equally fast developments in the field of ICT and data storage, whereby it is possible, for example, to take and use detail shots – so-called macro photography – which zoom in on a square millimetre of the structure and paint surface of Bruegel the Elder's panels. This might all sound abstract and not very exciting, but these developments have all made it possible to acquire much better insight into how an artist like Bruegel produced his works. The exhibition Vienna aspires to is – rather like the Bosch exhibitions in Den Bosch and Madrid – much more than an analysis of Bruegel's technical craftsmanship and skills, it is a search for the essence of his artistry.

New insights

Moreover, there is a striking and important side-effect of a thematic year and a large retrospective exhibition – one that gives the quest for knowledge about the creation of Bruegel's paintings an extra stimulus. In the years-long run up to 2019, new (material technological) research has been done in many muse-

The Triumph of Death (detail), c. 1562, oil on wood, 117 x 162 cm, Museo del Prado, Madrid

Skaters at the Sint Joris Gate, Antwerp, 1559, drawing, 20.8 x 29.3 cm, Private Collection

ums where his works hangs, and some damaged panels have been cleaned or even thoroughly restored. That is the case, for example, with the *Dulle Griet* (aka *Dull Gret* or *Mad Meg*) in the Mayer van den Bergh Museum in Antwerp and *The Triumph of Death* (*De Triomf van de Dood*) in the Prado. Both panels – which are often considered to have been painted at more or less the same time in Bruegel's workshop and which will be on show together for the first time in Vienna – were studied and restored in 2017-2018. Even works that, due to their fragility, cannot travel – such as the *Peasant Wedding* in Detroit – are being studied in detail during this preparatory phase. All this research and the intensive exchange of information is providing many new insights, which will throw new light on Bruegel as a painter, not only in the exhibition in Vienna but in other publications too. Moreover, insight is increasing into the creative process in more than just his paintings. For example, the Royal Library of Belgium and the University of Leuven (KUL) have collaborated on a high-tech research project and an exhibition, which will open in the spring of 2019, in which the creation of his prints and drawings will be reconstructed in detail – including an analysis of the use of various inks and pens. This will apparently make it possible to reconstruct the order and phase in which Bruegel produced his drawings.

Perceptions and clichés

However much politicians and the public in Flanders hoped that it would be possible to organise a monographic retrospective exhibition in Antwerp or Brussels, with as many works from the hand of Pieter Bruegel as possible, it was clear from the beginning to all museum insiders that the Bruegel year

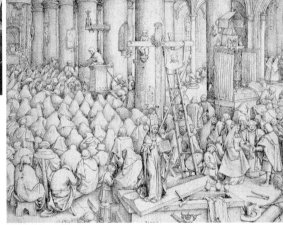

The Faith,
1559, drawing, 22.5 x 29.5 cm,
Rijksprentenkabinet,
Rijksmuseum, Amsterdam

The Fall of the Rebel Angels (detail), 1562, oil on wood, 117 x 162 cm,
Royal Museum of Fine Arts, Brussels

would have to find a different expression here. On the one hand the year will be interpreted in a much broader sense and will contextualise the artist, while on the other his influence, significance and imagery will be explored in a range of exhibitions, publications and workshops. What is striking is that a number of workshops and a couple of museums that the general public do not immediately associate with Bruegel will focus on the perception of the artist in Belgium and Flanders in the twentieth century. As part of a reappraisal of the Flemish Primitives and early Netherlandish art – the period of Van Eyck to Bruegel has long been seen as one long and continuous art historical development – Pieter Bruegel rapidly grew in popularity, from the end of the nineteenth century and through the twentieth century, to become one of the most popular Flemish artists. Furthermore – partly under the influence of authors such as Pieter Timmermans, but also through themes that were picked up by visual artists from the early twentieth century onwards – 'Peasant Bruegel' almost became the (self) image of the typical Fleming: deeply rooted in the traditions of the Flemish countryside, distinctly 'Burgundian', and with a strong, rather popular sense of humour that has little time for central government and the powers-that-be. It is a completely one-sided and totally untenable interpretation of the artist and his work, but nonetheless a stubborn cliché that still lives on. Both in Gaasbeek Castle (artistic treatment of the oeuvre in the twentieth century) as in the open-air museum in Bokrijk (the artist who portrays the prototypical Flanders) Bruegel's imagery is associated with this sort of cliché about his life and work. It will be no surprise that, at a time when there is great confusion and heated debate about what exactly the (historic) identity of this region and its inhabitants is, this approach is as topical as it is fascinating.

A look at our own period

The second half of the sixteenth century in the Southern Netherlands generally lends itself extremely well to focussing attention on issues that affect us today: fast-growing towns and cities with huge social inequalities, the manageability of health, care and security in urban areas, increasingly heated discussion and irreconcilability between religions, ever-increasing economic, social and po-litical uncertainty, at the same time as being a period of economic innovation, discovery and an unprecedented flourishing of the arts and sciences. And it is precisely in the work of Bruegel and his contemporaries that the character-istics of this both fascinating and complex era are implicitly and sometimes explicitly portrayed. The various exhibitions being organised in Brussels and Antwerp on Bruegel and his period contextualise Bruegel and his imagery. They map out the booming cities that were so characteristic of the Low Coun-tries, they highlight the blurring of the borders between towns and the country-side surrounding them, and they zoom in on Bruegel's intensive involvement in 'new' media such as printing.

Without falling into the trap of suggesting a direct link between that era and our own, the various exhibitions each offer an insight into or a view of the work of Bruegel and his time, and they encourage us to look from (and with) Bruegel at our own time. It is only the greatest and most timeless artists whose work makes this possible and who can be discovered and rediscovered again and again by new generations. Pieter Bruegel is certainly one of them. Bruegel Year 2019 is THE opportunity to get to know and value his work and significance. ▨

For the Bruegel exhibition in Vienna, see:
www.khm.at/en/visit/exhibitions/bruegel

For the programme of Bruegel Year 2019, see:
www.visitflanders.com/en/themes/arts.../flemish-masters/index.jsp

Translated by Lindsay Edwards

NOTES

1   See: Manfred Sellink, 'Hieronymus Bosch – Both Trendsetter and Representative of His Time. Reflections on the Significance of His Oeuvre': in *The Low Countries. Arts and Society in Flanders and the Netherlands* 24 (2016), pp. 124-133.

These Things Are Immortal

The Wanderings of Rembrandt's *Polish Rider*

Gowns like quilts. Moist oysters.
These things are immortal, but don't serve us.
Adam Zagajewski, 'Dutch Painters', translated by Clare Cavanagh

You might wonder as you stand in the richly filled galleries of the Frick Collection and look at Rembrandt's *The Polish Rider*: that lady in the sunglasses, that tourist with the camera on his stomach, that whining child – are they all looking at the same painting? Are they seeing the same rider, the same horse, the same red of the breeches? Do they see the same bit in the animal's mouth, the same hand clasping the war hammer? Do they see that same hammer and the same landscape, half washed away? Do they see the same exotic hat, the same buttons on the cream-coloured *żupan*, the same heel of the boot? And what of the Dutch connoisseur, the Polish king, the American industrialist? Did they too see, in places that no longer exist, these same immortal things?

The connoisseur and the count

Since that time, it has not changed, and yet everything there has changed: the landscape that Abraham Bredius looked out at in 1897 from his train compartment. The *k.k. Galizische Carl Ludwig-Bahn*, named after the brother of Emperor Franz Joseph I of Austria, was taking him from Krakow to Tarnobrzeg and far beyond: deep, deep into Galicia.

'It was a long way,' Bredius, the director of the Mauritshuis and a Rembrandt connoisseur, reported much later from Moscow. 'And those little branch lines of the Galician railways – it goes so slowly that you could walk alongside at a trot.' Sunk deeply into the burgundy velvet cushions of his first-class carriage – that is how I picture him – he saw the rolling cornfields and the birch forests, the rivers and the watermills, the stud farms and the skies, which stretch much lower above the land in this European border country than in the paintings of the Dutch masters that he knew so well. The onion-shaped cupolas of

the Ruthenian Orthodox churches must have seemed exotic to him as well. In that distant Galicia, then a crown land of the Habsburg Empire, Bredius was to make the greatest discovery of his career as a Rembrandt scholar.

This scholar was on a special mission in 1897. He was travelling to Saint Petersburg, Moscow and Kiev to study Rembrandt's paintings in those places, not only in renowned museums but also on the country estates and in the city palaces of wealthy aristocrats. Names such as Zamoyski, Czartoryski and Semenov, families who owned impressive art collections, made his mouth water. He knew of the existence of the Rembrandts in these collections only from reproductions and archive material. Now he had finally undertaken this long journey to inspect the paintings with his own eyes and to determine if they could be regarded as genuine Rembrandts. He was also searching for special works by the Dutch master for the major Rembrandt exhibition that was to be held at Amsterdam's Stedelijk Museum in 1898 to mark the inauguration of Queen Wilhelmina.

Rembrandt, *The Polish Rider* (details)

On his way to Russia, Bredius made a stop in Berlin, where he met another famous art expert: Wilhelm Bode. 'Ah,' Bode had said to him, 'now that you're going to Krakow anyway, try to see if you can view the Rembrandt at Count Tarnowski's castle, about which there have been such varying opinions; I would like to know if it is genuine.'

And so he did. Bredius took a room at a hotel in Krakow, where he went to see Rembrandt's 'remarkable landscape' in the Czartoryski Museum and attempted to make contact with the Tarnowskis. Fate lent him a hand. 'When I saw a fine carriage driving past my hotel and heard from the porter that it was Count Tarnowski, who had become engaged to the beautiful Countess Potocka some days ago, who would bring him a most substantial fortune, I little imagined that the man was also the fortunate owner of one of the most magnificent works by our great Master. This, however, proved to be the case.' Our connoisseur wasted no time: 'I naturally requested permission to see the paintings at Dzików Castle. Yes, but it would not be easy – it was a long way – so I would just have to stay a night, and everything there would be taken care of for me. In addition, Count Mycielski, the cousin of Count Tarnowski, declared himself willing to come with me and to show me around.' And that was how the museum director from The Hague came to be on the train that took him at walking pace through the fields and past the churches of Galicia.

The residence of the Tarnowskis, with its central section crowned with a tower, its neo-Gothic ornamentation, the majestic square in front: at first sight it must have made quite an impression on Bredius. The whole castle was in a state of commotion because of the arrival of Tarnowski's brand-new bride. Bredius entered the palace to see 'a great deal of trash in this curious building' alongside a few fine pictures by the Dutch masters that hung on its ancient walls: a Teniers, a Lucas van Leyden, a Cuyp, and a 'spirited' portrait of a woman. But the painting that instantly made a huge impression on him was *The Polish Rider* by Rembrandt.

'I had heard talk of it, yes, that Rembrandt – it is not marked, and various people said it could well be by an apprentice, for example, Aert de Gelder etc. So my expectations were not high. And there it was! Just one glance, and a few seconds' study of its technique were necessary to convince me entirely that, here in this remote outpost, one of Rembrandt's greatest masterpieces has been hanging for almost 100 years!'

There follows a lyrical description of the painting, certain parts of which Bredius finds 'delightfully painted.' 'And for how much longer should such a delicious piece remain hanging miles away from anywhere in an almost inaccessible castle in Galicia? All of my attempts to win it for Holland came to grief. They are doubly attached to this work as it was part of the collection of the last ruler of Poland, Stanisław Poniatowski.'

Because it was not only Abraham Bredius, Count Tarnowski and Countess Potocka who had stood face to face with *The Polish Rider*. For years it had belonged to Stanisław August Poniatowski, the last Polish king.

Hendrik Haverman,
Portrait of Abraham Bredius,
1899, black chalk and pencil
on paper, 23.8 x 20.7 cm,
RKD, The Hague

The king and the diplomat

In the extensive grounds of Łazienki Park, far from the busy centre of War-saw, is the private palace of Stanisław August Rex. The high windows gaze at themselves in the large pond where the white stone building with its steps and columns appears to float. Here, in 1793, behind the windows of this Palace on the Isle, the king established his *galerie en bas* to display the gems of his paint-ing collection. Within his artistic concept, this gallery formed a highly personal counterpoint to the Royal Palace in the heart of the Polish capital. That was the representative centre of power and therefore the right place for state portraits of the king, gifts and likenesses of friendly heads of state. It was where he had his court and where he was surrounded by his advisors and court painters, his footmen and cooks, his dwarfs and his mistresses.

But at the Palace on the Isle, His Majesty created a very different atmos-phere. He invited his friends, who were allowed to call him by his first name there, and he filled the galleries with the works of art that he loved best. There were 145 works to see on the upper floor, with 180 paintings downstairs. The king selected 65 pieces for the *galerie en bas* – his showpiece.

Juliusz Kossak, *The Polish Rider*,
after Rembrandt, c. 1860-1865,
oil on canvas, 55 x 45.5 cm,
National Museum, Warsaw

The linden green walls were adorned with his favourite works by Titian, Rubens and Giordano, in identical gilded frames, decorated with the royal monogram, arranged according to a principle that was popular at the time: the walls covered with paintings from top to bottom, with the smaller works below and the larger ones above. An inventory tells us that the king was very fond of Rembrandt, particularly appreciating his *grand effet de lumière et un coloris vigoureux* – great light effect and powerful colours. In his *galerie en bas*, he displayed six of the twelve Rembrandt paintings in his collection that, according to the royal catalogue, were considered to be genuine. One of those paintings was *The Polish Rider*, which at some point was moved from the *antichambre en haut* to the *galerie en bas*. That work had found its way into his collection via an interesting route.

Like many collectors at the time, Poniatowski made use of a network of advisors, agents, bankers and diplomats who facilitated international art acquisitions. In Italy, the king often purchased works through his court painter and curator Marcello Bacciarelli and his agents, while in Paris the celebrated salonnière Madame Geoffrin was one of his trusted intermediaries. Poniatowski also had his advisors in the Low Countries, of course. But the king did not only expand his collection with purchases. The exchange of gifts was one of the most important rituals of courtly culture. As the king was widely known to be a great art lover, he often received gifts of paintings, sculptures and prints, rather than horses, dogs or jewellery. *The Polish Rider* was one such work that the king received in return for a number of orange trees he had given to Michał Kazimierz Ogiński – *hetman* (military commander) and confidant of the king. Ogiński sent him *The Polish Rider* from The Hague in the spring or summer of 1791. In a letter that was added to the royal archive in 'mediis Augusti' 1791, Ogiński wrote: 'Sire, I send Your Majesty a Cossack, placed upon his horse by Rembrandt. During his stay, the horse ate 420 German guilders' worth at my expense. Your righteousness and generosity allow me to expect that the orange trees will blossom to the same extent. Bowing at Your feet, Your Majesty's most humble servant, Michal Ogiński, G[reat] H[etman] of L[ithuania]].' The painting became part of Poniatowski's art collection and was included in the royal paintings catalogue in 1793 as *Cosaque à cheval*, with a value of 180 ducats. The painting soon became known in Poland as the *Lisowczyk*, as the king had recognised the rider's clothing as the uniform of Aleksander Lisowski's cavalry.

Three months before Poniatowski archived Ogiński's letter, Poland had adopted a new constitution, the most progressive in Europe. Russia and Prussia feared a sort of French Revolution in their neighbouring country and so invaded Poland. This led to the Second and Third Partitions of Poland, and the king was forced to move to Russia. A few years later, in 1797, the last king of a great empire that had ceased to exist died in exile in Saint Petersburg. The childless royal had had to leave most of his collection behind in Warsaw. After the death of his heirs, many items from his estate, including *The Polish Rider*, came onto the market. Via dowries and inheritance, *The Polish Rider* eventually found its way to Dzików Castle, where Bredius went to admire the painting precisely 100 years after the king's death and, with his expert eye, ascertained with 'one look at the whole' that it was indeed a genuine Rembrandt.

Given the remarkable history of the painting, it was no wonder that the Tarnowskis did not want to say farewell to *The Polish Rider*. But Bredius's powers of persuasion must have been strong and the royal context irresistible: they finally gave permission for the painting to travel to the Netherlands, where it was displayed at the exhibition *Rembrandt. Schilderijen bijeengebracht ter gelegenheid van de inhuldiging van Hare Majesteit Koningin Wilhelmina* (Rembrandt. Paintings Brought Together on the Occasion of the Inauguration of Her Majesty Queen Wilhelmina), which took place from 8 September to 31 October 1898 at the Stedelijk Museum in Amsterdam.

It was an international debut for *The Polish Rider*, which was to determine the painting's future. The story of this unusual Rembrandt – the rider, the horse, the landscape in the background – quickly spread amongst collectors. In the early twentieth century, when Count Tarnowski found himself in urgent need of money because he wanted to purchase a large tract of land adjacent to the Dzików estate to prevent it from falling into foreign hands, he sold the work in 1910 to the American coal magnate Henry Clay Frick for 60,000 pounds – much to the consternation of many Polish art historians. To ease his pain a little, Tarnowski had a copy of the painting made for the castle in Dzików before letting the *Rider* go. And so *The Polish Rider* crossed the ocean, where it finally received a place of honour in the famous Frick Collection on Fifth Avenue in New York after it had previously hung in the palace-like residence of Henry Frick.

Jan Lebenstein, *The Polish Rider*,
ink on paper, Private Collection

The Frick Collection, New York

The trenches of the First World War, the Russian Revolution making its way across country estates, the Second World War wreaking havoc on the 'bloodlands', and then Soviet Communism put a permanent end to the fairy-tale existence of the Polish aristocracy on their estates in Galicia. Their art collections were stolen, 'nationalised', or went up in flames. Many of the Tarnowskis' belongings met such fates. The copy of *The Polish Rider*, so meticulously made by the English portraitist Ambrose McEvoy (1878-1927), was destroyed in 1927, when Tarnowski's castle burned to the ground. To this day, the Tarnowskis are still fighting for the return of their nationalised possessions. Perhaps it is in fact thanks to that scandalous sale in 1910 that one can stand before *The Polish Rider* in the year 2018, with those lines of verse by Adam Zagajewski in mind.

Us

When things are immortal, they can move not only physically and within time, but also in our memories and in our imaginations. Bredius remembered his journey to see *The Polish Rider* and those few seconds in which he recognised the work as an authentic Rembrandt. In Stanisław August's memory, the painting was undoubtedly linked to the linden green walls of his *galerie en bas*, Aleksander Lisowski's cavalry and a shipment of orange trees. When they looked at *The Polish Rider*, they saw not only their own wanderings but also the painting's journey.

Sometimes things, including certain works of art, are stubbornly immortal. Then they receive a place not only inside the mind of an individual, but also become part of a shared memory. And this is what happened to *The Polish Rider*: it has gained many new lives.

Jacek Sroka, *The Polish Rider*, c. 2011-2013, ink on paper,
Private Collection

The Polish equine artist Juliusz Kossak made a copy based on the painting in around 1865, although rather than Rembrandt's somewhat unwieldy horse, he painted a noble Arab. Jan Lebenstein used *The Polish Rider* for an apocalyptic work depicting the rider as the messenger of Death. Jacek Sroka took the Rembrandt as the starting point for an ironic object, by pasting, over the top of a wild watercolour in which we recognise our rider, a sketch of a completely different Polish horse rider: the *Lajkonik*, a Tatar warrior who prances through the streets of Krakow on his hobbyhorse on the first Thursday after Corpus Christi. And finally, Simon Vestdijk also took on *The Polish Rider*. In his essay of the same name, he asks despairingly what exactly Rembrandt wanted to say to us with this painting. 'The Polish rider's horse staggers, falling forward, knees knocking, swaying as if walking under water, longing for the knacker's yard, from left to right across the painting, like an intimate riddle.'

And how about me? What does *The Polish Rider* bring to mind for me? I try to look with the eyes of all those who have looked before me – and through their eyes I see the journey the painting has made. If I could step through the frame, I would find myself standing in the *galerie en bas*, listening to the cries of the peacocks and the king's voice telling me in lilting French about this beautiful gift and the path it has taken. Or maybe, on the other side of the frame, Abraham Bredius will take me by the hand and pull me into some aristocratic residence in Galicia. 'We would not have dared to dream,' he says, whispering in the dimly lit interior packed with paintings and tapestries, 'that we would see so many beautiful things, so many unknown things along our way.' ▪

Translated by Laura Watkinson

FURTHER READING

Abraham Bredius, 'Onbekende Rembrandts in Polen, Galicië en Rusland', in: *De Nederlandsche Spectator*, 1897.

Cat. *Bredius, Rembrandt en het Mauritshuis!!!*, The Hague, Mauritshuis, 1991.

Corpus of Rembrandt Paintings (1982-2015) Vol. 5 (2011), no. V20 and Vol. 6 (2015), no. 236.

Ewa Manikowska, *Sztuka. Ceremoniał. Informacja. Studium wokół królewskich kolekcji Stanisława Augusta*, Warsaw, 2007.

Tadeusz Mańkowski, *Galeria Stanisława Augusta*, Lwów, 1932.

Rembrandt and His School: Masterworks from the Frick and Lugt Collections, 2011, from this: Colin Bailey, 'Rembrandt van Rijn. *The Polish Rider*', pp. 39-45, and Esmée Quodbach, 'Henry Clay Frick Collects Rembrandt, 1899-1919', pp. 11-28.

Simon Vestdijk, 'De Poolse ruiter', in: *De Poolse ruiter*, The Hague, 1963, pp. 255-259.

Zdzisław Żygulski, jr., 'Further Battles for the *Lisowczyk* (Polish Rider) by Rembrandt', in: *Artibus et Historiae* Vol. 21, No. 41 (2000), pp. 197-205.

www.rodtarnowski.com

www.rkd.nl

The Ambiguous Art of Hyperrestoration

The Case of Jef Van der Veken

[TILL-HOLGER BORCHERT]

A respected figure in the Belgium art world during the last decades of his life-time, the Flemish restorer Jef Van der Veken (1872-1964) was for a long time mostly known to the greater public for his meticulous copy of the *Ghent Altar-piece's* stolen panel of the *Just Judges*. In recent years, however, Van der Veken has become a controversial figure. Since the 'full' extent of his past conserva-tion treatments of a significant number of panels by fifteenth- and early six-teenth-century Masters from the Low Countries was revealed to the scholarly community, and presented to larger audiences in exhibitions and publications a few years ago, more critical attention has been paid to his legacy.[1]

A draughtsman gifted with extraordinary mimetic skills, with long years of experience as a copyist of Old Master paintings, with a fervent passion about the Old Masters, and with a systematic interest in exploring historical painting techniques, Van der Veken rose to be one of the leading painting conserva-tors in Belgium from the Interbellum period onwards. Countless prominent masterpieces from public and private collections were entrusted to his care.[2] However, his treatments of Early Netherlandish panels were sometimes far-reaching and, especially in his work for private clients, bordered on the edge of being outright deceitful. He would spend long hours with a magnifying glass in his workshop in order to create detailed and convincing imitations of crack-patterns that he applied with a thin brush on top of his own retouching. In doing so, he not only concealed his own contribution from the eyes of the beholder but also actively created the illusion that the painting he had been working on had an even surface and was in mint condition.[3]

These meticulous imitations of crack-patterns were harmless, however, compared to the more radical, invasive and irreversible treatments of precious panels that Van der Veken applied during some of his restorations. For exam-ple, his methods included scraping off damaged paint layers and the prepara-tory ground below from the wooden boards with scalpels and other tools in or-der to afterwards carefully reconstruct – rather than to restore – the paintings to his own taste. Treatments such as these that altered paintings in a substan-tial manner have somewhat euphemistically been termed 'hyper-restorations' as it is not entirely clear from the available documents if Van der Veken always acted with bad intentions: he 'improved' them.[4]

Contemporaries, however, were less reluctant to judge; Van der Veken's name was discretely connected with forgeries as early as 1911. But at a time where the borders between the trade, museums and restorers were not as thoroughly transparent as they are today, the experts were unaware, or negligent, of the scale of his activities.

An almost scientific approach

'Accomplished forgers make successful use of old pictures', wrote Max J. Friedländer in 1942, revising a text from 1919, 'which they clean radically – often down to the gesso preparation – in order to subsequently superpose their forgery, glazing carefully and treating with utmost delicacy the *craquelure*, which they leave exposed'.[5] Whether Friedländer had met Jef Van der Veken, who was also involved in the European art market, during his time either in

Berlin or afterwards in his exile in Amsterdam, is not known and it remains un-
clear if the scholar had Van der Veken in mind when he wrote the lines above.
But he certainly referred to his activities when he concluded his thoughts on
forgeries in *Art and Connaisseurship*: 'As the forgers, in conformity to their view
of their activities, are manufacturers, they often produce several versions of a
fake: and it may be particularly noted that duplicates have emerged from the
Belgian workshops which, during the last few decades, have abundantly seen
to the supply of early Netherlandish panels'.[6]

Today, Van der Veken most of all emerges as an ambivalent figure. Leaving
aside the controversial question whether he produced fakes and deceived his
clients intentionally or not: it is clear on one hand that his restoration methods don't comply with today's standards of conservation such as, for example,
reversibility of any treatment. But, on the other hand, his experiments and systematic investigations into historical painting techniques, as well as the photographic documentation of some of his treatments, reveal an almost scientific
approach that makes him one of the ancestors of modern conservation, alongside legendary restorers from the Anglo-German world such as Helmut Ruhemann and William Suhr who were both younger by more than twenty years.[7]

Enhancing art

Joseph-Marie – in short: Jef – Van der Veken, born to small shop-owners in
Antwerp in 1872, was very much a child of his own time. Placing his accom-
plishments into a historical perspective, one has to be reminded that restoration and conservation of Old Master paintings in even the most accomplished
museums was still entrusted to academic painters during most of the nineteenth and early twentieth century, who also more widely acted as curators
and directors of their institutions. Wilhelm von Bode in the 1870s witnessed the
restorer-director Philipp Foltz (1805-1877) of Munich's Alte Pinakothek changing the colour of the curtain in Rubens's monumental *Portrait of Aletheia Talbot,
Countess of Arundel* (1620) from red to green and blue because he believed that
these colours would enhance Rubens's intentions. It was left to his successor
as restorer, Alois Hauser the Elder (1837-1909), to remove the earlier treatments.[8]

After the premature death of his father in 1879, Jef was sent for a few years
to live at an orphanage in Sint Niklaas, since his mother had no means to support the family. Presumably with a clear sense for material wealth, he returned
to Antwerp where he was apprenticed in 1884 by a decorator. In 1890 he started
to attend evening classes and specialised in painting imitations of wood and
marble decorations. When on his twentieth birthday he became eligible for
two years' military service, he enlisted with the University Company so that
he could follow free lessons at the Antwerp Academy of Arts. There he took a
drawing course in 1893/94 in which he was best of his class. During this period, Van der Veken, void of any artistic ambitions or creativity, started to paint
portraits after photographs and to draw and paint meticulous copies after Old
Master paintings that he made from the originals or reproductions.[9]

In order to make a living, Van der Veken started to produce Old Master copies on demand, mostly for dealers who sold antique or old-looking furniture

and used his paintings for decoration purposes. He soon understood, according to his own testimony, that some of his copies passed as originals in the trade and changed his line of business, starting his own gallery in the elegant Regentschapsstraat in the heart of Brussels, *The Early Art Gallery, Van Snick & Van der Veken & Co*, later *The Early Art Gallery, Van der Veken*. Along with his unknown business partners, he sold Old Master copies and old objects, provided expertise, executed restorations and offered to draw up inventories of estates. Judging from the fact that the enterprise had its own telephone line and kept in close contact with leading auction houses in Germany, France and England, business must have been good. With the beginnings of the Great War in 1914, however, Van der Veken's international business collapsed. He transferred part of his inventory to his brother Gustave who fled to London and tried to involve his sister-in-law, who lived in the peaceful Netherlands, in the sale of paintings.

During the war, Van der Veken gradually switched from mere copies and pasticcios of Early Netherlandish masters to partial fakes of degraded or ruined panels that he had purchased cheaply and planned to sell at great profit. In these 'hyperrestorations', he left minor parts of the original paintings intact and painted the greater part of the composition himself, making use of his extensive repertoire of drawn models, tracings and, increasingly, of photographs. He also 'enhanced' anonymous works by giving them the look and feel of a specific master, like Quentin Matsys, Jan Gossaert or Barend van Orley.

Peter Paul Rubens,
*Portrait of Aletheia Talbot,
Countess of Arundel*, 1620,
© Alte Pinakothek, Munich

Soon after the war, he started a close collaboration with the Bruges collector and banker Emile Renders, who had gained notoriety by publishing highly polemic and controversial books about the Van Eycks and the Master of Flémalle.[10] Renders supplied Van der Veken with money, which bought the damaged or mediocre paintings that the latter turned into masterpieces in mint condition in his Brussels workshop. It is thus likely that Renders was aware of the manipulations and at least endorsed, if not requested them. During the Second World War, Renders sold his collection to Hermann Göring, though most of the works were restituted to Belgium after 1945; today, the authenticity of many of them is now considered problematic or doubtful.[11]

Among the most famous works in the Renders collection that Van der Veken treated is Rogier van der Weyden's *Virgin and Child*, now at the Musée des Beaux-Arts in Tournai. Originally the left wing of a diptych for Jean Gros, Van der Veken scraped off the damaged parts and built up the painting from scratch, adding painted cracks on the surface. He then copied the motto and emblem from the reverse of der Weyden's portrait of the Burgundian counsellor Jean Gros, now in Chicago, on the reverse of Renders's painting.[12] Another panel, an *Annunciation* attributed to the Master of the Baroncelli Portraits, is equally a thorough re-invention by Van der Veken, who even made an extensive

Edmond Van Hove, *Portrait of Galilei*,
1885, oil on canvas, 143 x 118 cm
© Groeningemuseum Brugge –
Lukas-Art in Flanders vzw.
Photo Stad Brugge

underdrawing on the preparatory ground. Since the *Annunciation* is depicted in a fictional portrait of Galilei by the Bruges fin-de-siècle painter Edmond Van Hove, Van der Veken must have worked from an existing original that he much enhanced. He then made – as he often did – a copy of his 'hyperrestoration' that entered the art market a few decades ago.[13]

The collector and his restorer collaborated closely until 1927, when Van der Veken revealed to eminent art historians – much to their disbelief – that a panel by the Master of the Baroncelli Portraits shown in an exhibition on Early Flemish Painting in London alongside the 'masterpieces' of the Renders collection, had actually been painted by him. At this point, Renders probably became afraid of the publicity of the scandal that made Van der Veken's name wider known.

His acquaintance with Renders and his growing reputation as restorer of Early Netherlandish masterpieces, though, introduced him to various museums in Belgium that now enlisted his services. He restored several works for the Royal Museum of Fine Arts in Brussels, among them paintings attributed to Van der Goes, Matsys and Van Dyck. He was even entrusted the conservation treatment of Jan van Eyck's masterly *Madonna of Joris van der Paele* from the Groeningemuseum by the municipal authorities in Bruges in the early 1930s, the results of which were received very positively in the international press and provided Van der Veken with lots of publicity. At this time, he was assisted by his son-in-law, the painter Albert Philippot, who after being trained as a restorer by Van der Veken later became chief conservator of the Institut royal du Patrimoine artistique (IRPA) in Brussels after the Second World War.[14]

Humiliation

The treatment of the Bruges panel by Van Eyck had convinced Van der Veken that Van Eyck had used egg-tempera for some of his colours. When he finally received permission to make a copy of the panel of the *Just Judges* from the *Ghent Altarpiece* that had been stolen in 1934 from the Cathedral of Ghent, he therefore used tempera to successfully recreate the image. The personal triumph of the copy that he had produced during the Second World War was followed, however, by what he must have considered deep humiliation. When the panels of the Ghent Altarpiece returned from Altaussee and were examined by the chemists of the Institut royal du Patrimoine artistique, their results proved his empirical insights wrong and scientifically established Van Eyck's use of oils as binding media.[15] The conservation treatment of the panels was entrusted to his son-in-law Albert Philippot.

In 1962, Jef van der Veken, having been almost entirely blind for five years and unable to work as a restorer, died at the age of ninety in the Brussels quarter of Elsene, estranged from his children after a second marriage, years after the death of his first wife. Keeping a studio with his second wife, he had remained active in the field into his eighties. Among the last of his restorations were *The Three Maries at the Tomb*, usually believed to be by a follower of Van Eyck, that he carried out for D.G. van Beuningen from Rotterdam. Recently his treatment has been superseded by a new conservation campaign.[16] ∎

NOTES

1   The Groeningemuseum in Bruges was the first to present the controversy on Van der Veken to a wider audience and, together with the Université Catholique de Louvain, organised the exhibition *Fake/Not Fake: het verhaal van de restauratie van de Vlaamse Primitieven* from 26/11/2004 to 28/2/2005. In 2005, the Institut royal du Patrimoine artistique received a panel that turned out to be a fake and tried to profit from the success of the Bruges show by mounting an exhibition *Autour de la Madeleine Renders* at the Royal Museum of Fine Arts in Brussels (see Hélène Verougstraete, Roger Van Schoute, Till-Holger Borchert with contributions by Elisabeth Bruyns, Jacqueline Couvert, Rudy Pieters and Jean-Luc Pypaert, *Fake or Not Fake? Het Verhaal van de Restauratie van de Vlaamse Primitieven*, Ghent 2004); and Dominique Vanwijnsberghe (ed.), *Autour de la Madeleine Renders: Un aspect de l'histoire des collections, de la restauration et de la contrefaçon en Belgique dans la première moitié du XXe siècle*, Brussels, 2008.

2   *Fake or Not Fake*, pp. 24-34, 110-131.

3   See Didier Martens, 'Joseph Van der Veken faussaire des Primitifs Flamands: découverte ou redécouverte?', in: *Autour de la Madeleine Renders*, pp. 177-188.

4   The term has been coined by Jean-Luc Pypaert in *Fake or Not Fake*, pp.111-112.

5   Max J. Friedländer, *On Art and Connaisseurship*, repr. Boston, 1960, p. 264.

6   ibid. p. 266; see also Suzanne Laemers, 'A matter of character: Max J. Friedländer et ses relations avec Émile Renders et Jef van der Veken', in *Autour de la Madeleine Renders*, pp. 147-176.

7   On Ruhemann, see Morwenna Blewett, 'The Art of Conservation VI: Helmut Ruhemann, Paintings Restorer in Berlin and London', in: *Burlington Magazine* 158 (2016), pp. 638-646. On William Suhr, see: http://archives2.getty.edu:8082/xtf/view?docId=ead/870697/870697.xml (June 2017).

8   Wilhelm von Bode, *Mein Leben*, Berlin, 1930, vol. 1, p. 101.

9   On the following, see the biographical sketch by Jean-Luc Pypaert, Hélène Verougstraete and Roger Van Schoute in *Fake or Not Fake*, pp. 110-121.

10 See Jacques Lust, 'Grandeur et décadence d'Émile Renders. Chronique mouvementée d'une collection d'art Belge', in *Autour de la Madeleine Renders*, pp. 77-146, esp. 79-84.

11 ibid. pp. 84-138.

12 *Fake/Not Fake*, pp. 62-74.

13 *Fake/Not Fake*, pp. 36-49; Andreas Burmester, 'Wechselhafte Geschicke. Von falschen und echten Gemälden', in: *Mercedes in aller Welt* 32 (4) (1987), nr. 208.

14 Paul Philippot, 'De l'histoire de la restauration comme affaire de famille', in: *Autour de la Madeleine Renders*, pp. 189-196.

15 Pim Brinkman, *Het Geheim van Van Eyck*, Zwolle, 1993, pp. 196-205, 214-219.

16 See Stephan Kemperdick and Friso Lammertse (ed.), *The Road to Van Eyck*, Rotterdam, 2012, pp. 293-295.

Portrait of the Museum as a Rendez-Vous

Posthumous Conversations Between Artists

[ANN DEMEESTER]

'Nobody comes from the moon as they say. Everybody comes out of a tradition.'
Johannes Cladders[1]

New or different types of developments often begin with a feeling of powerless-
ness and impotence. Not to mention fear and confusion. A feeling of 'bound-
lessness' that can be channelled by reproducing what already exists. That is
undeniably the case in the English writer A.S. Byatt's meandering essay *Peacock and Vine* (2016), in which she links the work of all-round artists William
Morris and Mariano Fortuny in a positively inimitable fashion. Byatt declares
that – paradoxically enough – the unique strength of the multi-talented Fortuny is the way he borrows and mixes existing motifs from different sources.
He recycles elements from various parts of the world and different periods
and 'restores them to new life'. With these combinations, Fortuny continually
resurrects the art of the past, yet it feels brand new. In Byatt's musings Fortuny becomes synonymous with the peacock, a symbol of the constant cycle
of death and resurrection in art. Byatt seems to suggest that it is essential,
fundamental to keep reproducing, portraying and rewriting, rethinking and re-
formulating existing texts and artworks, and that this does not get in the way of
originality and authenticity. A great work can withstand remakes. Moreover, it
benefits from re-makes and re-enactments, constant rewording and rework-
ing. Western art history, as we know it, is living proof of that. Since antiquity,
making copies of existing works or masterpieces – whether they are faithful
or not – has not only been a way for artists to pay tribute to what is good and
worth imitation, but is also a pragmatic method for honing their own knowhow
and skills, training the eye and improving their own technique. The fact that
copying iconic masterpieces normally no longer features on the curriculum of
most European art schools and that you seldom see (aspiring) artists sketch-
ing in galleries in Belgium or the Netherlands (in contrast to, for example, the
Kunsthistorisches Museum in Vienna or the Musée d'Orsay in Paris) is in that
sense irrelevant. The 'peacock' is still present and parading, in all its glory,
around the arts scene.

Jan de Baen (attributed to),
*The Corpses of the De Witt
Brothers*, c. 1672-1675,
oil on canvas, 69.5 x 56 cm,
Rijksmuseum, Amsterdam

Anonymous artist,
Brigitinnenstraat / Rue des
Brigittines, Brussels

Artists are not lone wolves, nor have they been brought up in total isolation, as Contemporary incarnations of Kaspar Hauser! Quite apart from training or personal interests, every creator is affected or stamped by his or her own time, as well as by the (cultural) history preceding his or her practice. Even CoBrA artists realised that it was impossible to return to a purely instinctive creative point zero. In that respect it does not matter whether artists do or do not use conscious allusions to the art of bygone eras in their work. Since the postmodern age, linear (Western) art history is only one of the many paths to the truth. Artists do not slavishly copy, they reference and collage, developing their own signature by mixing, freely and sometimes wildly, visual references and indirect allusions to artworks from various periods of the history of art and style. Even now, in 2017, eclecticism is still *de rigueur*. For contemporary creators, the gigantic art history sometimes seems to be archive of a grab bag from which elements are greedily fished and plucked. The peacock dies and is resurrected at an extraordinarily pace.

This interest in historic styles and artworks sometimes degenerates into aimless and uncontrolled referencing. At times sentimental, sterile and just plain impotent. In the recently published retrospective architectural manifesto *Solid Objectives: Order, Edge, Aura*, Dutch architect Florian Idenburg from the American-Dutch-Chinese-Greek firm SO-IL wonders:

'Does our inability to find a coherent attitude for tackling the past relate to our blank attitude regarding the future?... [...] Tabula rasa is for cowards, but there are no coherent rules for playing the game on a board filled with pieces. With this in mind we propose a dignified pragmatism: challenge what there is, reactivate it, make it part of the current but allow it to cause friction, to resist. The moment we let go of sentimental values but holistically assess the given and have it fight for its place in the here and now, we might reendow the old with new architectural agency.'

Anonymous artist,
Barthélémylaan /
Boulevard Barthélémy,
Brussels

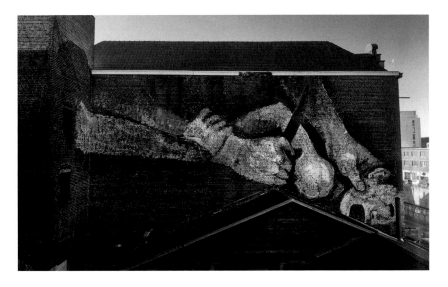

Caravaggio,
The Sacrifice of Isaac, 1603,
oil on canvas, 104 x 135 cm,
Uffizi Gallery, Florence

Assuming that architecture and the visual arts are still two sides of the same coin, this reads like a plea for transhistorical thinking in art that stands not for rational sums but for the sort of free addition and subtraction, division and multiplication that leads to an incalculable result. The list of artists in the Euro-American spectrum that is capable of this seems well-nigh endless. From Jeff Koons, Marlene Dumas and Kelley James Walker through Cindy Sherman, Bill Viola, Peter Greenaway, John Baldessari and Werner Herzog to Anton Henning, Kati Heck, Mark Leckey, Falke Pisano and Shezad Dawood. The nature and manner of the additions and subtractions to which the work of the Great Male Masters of the antique or modern periods is subjected are myriad. Roughly speaking we can distinguish three different methods. Firstly, working in the spirit of – (too) literally or otherwise – in terms of style or content (see, for example, Glenn Brown and Kehinde Willey). Secondly, carrying out a thorough analysis of the underlying mechanisms of the existing work, which results in something more abstract (see Pietro Roccasalva and Matts Leiderstam, Pablo Bronstein and Willem de Rooij). And lastly but certainly not least, a conspicuous third category consisting of contemporary artists, like Riet Wijnen (Marlow Moss) and Jan Andriessen (Torrentius), who draw attention to precursors who were marginalised or neglected in centuries past.

Posthumous conversation

Whatever the angle or method used, the interaction between contemporary artists and those who preceded them often resembles an intelligent, 'bubbling and allusive' conversation, but one which goes beyond the limits of the grave.

A dialogue that may be far livelier than the conversation that actually goes on between artists of one and the same generation or period. In one of her many essays the writer Virginia Woolf wonders how and what role conversation played for writers (read artists here) in the eighteenth century.

> 'One cannot imagine that writers then retired to their studios or worked by the clock. They seem to have learnt by talk; their friendships thus were important and outspoken. Conversation was a kind of strife, and the jealousies and contradictions which attended the display gave it at least an eager excitement.'[2]

Woolf seems amazed that the 'talking' – which she herself so enjoyed as a hostes, in London society circles – did not get in the way of artistic production. Contrary to what Woolf describes, the silent dialogue between living and dead artists often looks like one-way traffic. Contemporary artists chatter away without any response, allowing their own work to be influenced by the work of the 'silent other' and that seems to be it. But appearances are deceptive, the contemporary view of the masters of the past changes their work irrevocably, not in the literal sense but in the figurative. The interpretation of the old masters is altered constantly and fundamentally by the creators of the present.

An example from the past – one that is close to home for me – is Frans Hals. In the seventeenth century he was highly appreciated as a painter. Yet in the eighteenth century critics and connoisseurs looked down on his rough and casual, semi-spontaneous style that conflicted with the prevailing academicism. However, the admiration, not to mention adoration, of nineteenth-century artists such as Courbet, Singer Sargent, Mary Cassatt and Van Gogh ensured that Hals's work was seen and appreciated as 'modern'. Suddenly, Hals was no longer just a messy dauber, but a forerunner of impressionism and naturalism. The view of his nineteenth-century successors influenced and even radically changed the work – or at least the reception of it. Hals was a source of inspiration, but his work was also posthumously influenced by the view of artists who lived after him.

The Anxiety of Influence

It is often dangerous – but nonetheless productive – to apply theories from one branch of the arts to another area of culture. I will happily take that risk for the unorthodox former Yale-professor Harold Bloom and his classic *The Anxiety of Influence. A Theory of Poetry* (1973). Bloom believes in the 'necessity of the peacock', just as Byatt does. His often acclaimed and dissected book is an interesting mix of theorising about the function of creativity (with a psychological slant) and an erudite study of the dynamics of the history of poetry. Bloom describes how every (great, white, male) poet is influenced by those who came before him and is occasionally overcome by a paralysing anxiety (the anxiety of influence) that he is not original and just reproduces the past. He describes artistic development as a process in three phases. Firstly, the admiration and imitation of a great predecessor, then rejection of the same inspirational fig-

Mark Leckey, *A Month of Making*, 2014
Gavin Brown, New York

ure and, finally, the crucial phase 'misprision' (misreading), where the writer transforms and 'misforms' his idol's work to create something new.[3] Edward Said wrote of Bloom's vision that

> 'Such a vision immediately plays havoc with the stability of texts and authors, indeed with the whole order of culture. The past becomes an active intervention in the present; the future is preposterously made just a figure of the past in the present. No text can be complete because on the one hand it is an attempt to struggle free of earlier texts impinging on it and, on the other, it is preparing itself to savage texts not yet written by authors not yet born.'[4]

In Bloom's eyes all literature is intertextual and there is constant productive strife in the work of the present, which is struggling with the past and engaged in work for the as-yet-uncompleted future. It seems natural, bearing in mind the peacock, to apply this loosely to art history and (visual) artworks too. Artists carry the past within them and change that past with every new work that is made. Regardless of whether artists actively reference their predecessors or are even aware of their existence.

The transhistorical museum

What role does the museum play in the polyphonic and posthumous conversations between artists? In fact, these silent dialogues take place mainly in creators' thoughts and feelings, in their studios and in their heads. Sometimes the expression of that exchange can literally be seen and felt in the work. More frequently the debate between the artist and what preceded him or her is hidden and encrypted in the work and therefore not immediately decipherable. In a very basic sense, part of the function of our museums is to make artworks accessible to those who do not have the privilege of being able to step into an artist's studio or workplace. Each artwork is essentially an accumulation of semiotic sediment. Museums that isolate artworks in their own period fail to explore and to expose for their visitors a whole spectrum of layers of meaning. Museums that think transhistorically, that facilitate a rendezvous between the old and the new, the artists of the past and those of the present, try to break through that isolation. This type of museum aims to link heritage and tradition to contemporary art and social questions (both contemporary and past), they question the traditional (art historical) categories and thereby develop new insights into the meaning and interpretation of objects (of art).

All artworks are essentially tran-historical. They are 'born' or created at a particular time and in a specific context. They survive that context and are shown and read years or even centuries later in a different era, a different setting, a different cultural context. In that sense all works of art are time travellers. 'They live in the present but in the company of the past', as John Berger put it. As a result, they always fall prey to *Hineininterpretierung* (eisegesis).

Museums that think transhistorically base their approach on the specific characteristics of the artworks. A transhistorical arrangement may mean that old art is combined with contemporary and modern art, but also that old works of art are subjected to a twenty-first-century interpretation that does not tally with the approach in their own period. Transhistorical does not necessarily mean that arranging works by period is censured or rejected. It means rather that alternative and additional narratives and possible interpretations of objects of art and art history are offered. It is a transition from one linear Western form of (art) historiography to a multiplicity of histories, which are not necessarily chronological but are associative visually or formally, or in terms of theme or narrative, and they do not necessarily respect the limits of the Euro-American sphere. In a world that is becoming increasingly monocultural and in which the interests of the individual are becoming ever more dominant, this is a countermovement. Other and elsewhere are as relevant as us and here.

Erwin Olaf, *Exquisite Corpses, Still Life with the Heart of Count Egmond*, 2012,
commissioned by Gaasbeek Castle (Exhibition: Exquisite Corpses / Hommage to Egmond (1522-1568). 1 july - 31 August 2018)
(original title: *Nature morte vanité avec le coeur de Sieur Lamoral d'Egmont*)

Transhistorical museums are, by definition, global. They are interested in reshuffling and rewriting current power relationships, in developing new configurations of meaning. Consequently, such museums always think about art – within the matrix of changing power relationships – politically. Including the Old Masters.

Until very recently, regardless of the type of collection(s) they housed, museums were unambiguous and important instruments in the canon-forming process. They perpetuated the fact that a more or less fixed group of artists, who were considered to be normative, dominated – and still dominate. This canonization is intrinsic to our need to classify, qualify and decide what merits the eyes and attention of our progeny. For a long time, museums claimed the role of guides and leaders in this, and allowed only one leading narrative. The museums of today benefit from being polyphonic, from allowing a multiplicity of sometimes conflicting or contradictory narratives. Museums used to be expressways that led straight to the truth. But times are changing, nowadays museums offer not only expressways but also meandering country roads and paths down which you can stray, exploring alternative scenic routes alongside the main arteries.

Anonymous artist preparing their version of Caravaggio,
Barthélémylaan / Boulevard Barthélémy, Brussels
© Ivan Put

Why is that desirable? In *Confronting Images. The End of a Certain History of Art*, the French thinker Georges Didi-Huberman maintains that visual representation has a downside, where apparently comprehensible forms lose their clarity and can no longer be understood intellectually. Furthermore, he claims, art historians have failed to engage with this downside. Their discipline is limited to the rational academic acquisition of knowledge and is based on the assumption that visual representation consists of interpretable signs, whereas images are actually full of contradictions and limitations.

Museums that *think* transhistorically try as a reaction to this not only to reason as art historians but also to think like artists. They complement their own museum methodology with an (artistic) way of thinking that cuts right through the constraints of time, space, culture and geography. In that sense, such museums do not simply respect the museum classification system but also complement their own methodology and frameworks (arrangement by medium, style and period) by embracing a way of thinking that goes beyond the limits of classification and is associative. A way of thinking that is not necessarily restricted by strict timeframes or national borders, but one that is eager and voracious, that scours a variety of different periods and geographical and cultural zones in search of inspiration. A way of thinking that is not tied to particular media or disciplines but is pluralistic and multifaceted, using forms that are appropriate for particular ideas at a specific moment. This kind of thinking encourages visitors to look at artworks – or read novels – and thereby to understand the world in a way that is not based on causal links but is more than anything else exploratory and associative.

Orhan Pamuk expresses this strikingly: 'Reading a novel (artwork) means understanding the world via a non-Cartesian logic – By this I mean the constant and steadfast ability to believe simultaneously in contradictory ideas...Novels (artworks) are unique structures that allow us to keep contradictory thoughts in our mind without uneasiness, and to understand differing points of view simultaneously.' ▦

Translated by Lindsay Edwards

NOTES

1   In Hans Ulrich Obrist, *A Brief History of Curating*, JRP | RINGIER & LES PRESSES DU REEL, 2011, p.74.

2   Stephen Miller, *Conversation. A History of a Declining Art*, Yale University Press, New Haven and London, 2006, pp. 183-84.

3   'Poetic Influence – when it involves two strong, authentic poets – always proceeds by a misreading of the prior poet, an act of creative correction that is actually and necessarily a misinterpretation. The history of fruitful poetic influence, which is to say the main traditions of Western poetry since the Renaissance, is a history of anxiety and self-saving caricature of distortion, of perverse, willful revisionism without which modern poetry as such could not exist.'

4   Edward Said, 'The Poet as Oedipus', 13 April 1975, *The New York Times*.

Copy of Pieter Bruegel, *Landscape with the Fall of Icarus*, c. 1600,
oil on canvas, 73.5 x 112 cm,
Royal Museum of Fine Arts of Belgium, Brussels

Musée des Beaux Arts

About suffering they were never wrong,
The old Masters: how well they understood
Its human position: how it takes place
While someone else is eating or opening a window or just walking dully along;
How, when the aged are reverently, passionately waiting
For the miraculous birth, there always must be
Children who did not specially want it to happen, skating
On a pond at the edge of the wood:
They never forgot
That even the dreadful martyrdom must run its course
Anyhow in a corner, some untidy spot
Where the dogs go on with their doggy life and the torturer's horse
Scratches its innocent behind on a tree.

In Breughel's Icarus, for instance: how everything turns away
Quite leisurely from the disaster; the ploughman may
Have heard the splash, the forsaken cry,
But for him it was not an important failure; the sun shone
As it had to on the white legs disappearing into the green
Water, and the expensive delicate ship that must have seen
Something amazing, a boy falling out of the sky,
Had somewhere to get to and sailed calmly on.

W.H. Auden, Brussels, 1938

The Africa Museum in Tervuren and Orhan Pamuk's White Gloves

[KOEN PEETERS]

Sunday morning, spring 2011. Black youths sat at a long, wide table in the coffee bar at Brussels-South station. They neither ate nor drank, but were doing something vague between talking and sleeping. There were TV screens in the station hall. Breaking news, the prime minister of Japan appeared in white overalls and talked about the nuclear threat. No one either heard or saw it. Or no, a Spanish poet did, looking for contact with passers-by and gesticulating broadly. The world might have come to an end in the meantime, but no one looked up or was concerned.

The train with the Turkish writer Orhan Pamuk was twenty minutes late. I waited patiently. Circumstances had led to me being asked to accompany the Nobel Prize Winner for a visit to the Royal Museum for Central Africa, or Africa Museum, in Tervuren. Pamuk was coming from Düsseldorf and would travel on to Istanbul the same evening. I was his chauffeur for the day, his guide, his travelling companion.

Suddenly, there he was in front of me, impatient. I took his suitcase and his thick, light brown leather briefcase. We walked to my car and drove onto the inner ring, then into the rue de la Loi and through the tunnels under the Cinquantenaire. During the car ride Pamuk took photo after photo. He photographed buildings, city vistas, but no people. Then suddenly photographed himself, casually, with a flick of the wrist.

I admitted to him that I did that too; that I took careless, unfocussed photos, wildly, almost endlessly documenting and researching. He immediately wanted to know whether I saved the photos to a disc or whether I deleted them.

'Both,' I said.

Pamuk looked at me from behind his large glasses, laughed and ran his fingers through his thick grey hair. He had visited Tervuren years ago, he acknowledged. He remembered the tram ride out there, 'just a short, melancholy quarter of an hour'. Now he wanted to know how we dealt in the museum with political correctness and the burden of history. He said that he had acquired a sharper, deeper insight over the years.

Pamuk was still interested in museums, despite the fact that his extraordinary novel *The Museum of Innocence* had been published two years earlier.

The novel, from 2009, is about an unhappy love affair. The main character is a sentimental collector who gathers objects in a museum.

While writing the novel Pamuk thought about actually opening a museum where he would keep all the objects that appeared in the book. He referred to these thoughts as a dream that brought him to a state of 'euphoria'. He would open his own museum the following year. He was busy working on it.

On the way to Tervuren, Pamuk asked me about the museum's operating budget, the size of the staff, the organogram, and what the museum had been called over the years. Pamuk wanted to know all about it. I was impressed by this writer, famous by now due to malevolent newspaper campaigns and the lawsuits filed against him in Turkey. In Istanbul he had to have a bodyguard to move around. Then he had fled abroad, but the death threats continued.

To change the subject we talked about relations between Congo and Belgium. Then Rwanda. 'You know the story of the genocide?' I asked him.

'Tell me briefly,' answered Pamuk.

From his nods and brief interjections I quickly understood that he knew all about this and other genocides.

We arrived at the museum, where we were met in the entrance hall by the director and two members of staff. We looked at the familiar racist statues, the slave driver, the leopard man, and 'Belgium bringing civilization to Congo'. Inside the museum, Pamuk took photos hungrily, without flash. He read every caption, took almost no notes but seemed to literally consume everything he saw and heard. He behaved earnestly, nervously, a little obsessed. Youthful and restless he trotted along behind the female guides, taking photos of all the display cabinets and the objects inside them.

In particular, it seemed, he took photos of 'everyday' Africa, the ordinary people. Their spoons and knives, their axes, aprons and shoes, masks and musical instruments. Was this a way of finding himself as an ordinary person? Is that why he photographed himself almost mechanically? I took some unfocussed photos of him too now.

We ate in the museum cafeteria. He laughed tiredly and ate from his plate with one hand. He told us how he had received an honorary doctorate from Brussels University. How he was driven around the city with motorcycle escorts, sirens blaring. 'And I sat in the car like a madman, taking photos of the furore.' He was dressed in a ceremonial toga, and then photos were sent round the world with the strangest of interpretations.

'Can we carry on with our visit?' he asked, defensively.

Objects communicate with each other

In his book *The Innocence of Objects*, published the year after our visit to Tervuren, Pamuk says, 'In the spring and summer of 2011, I stopped being a writer'. Under considerable political pressure following some controversial comments about the Armenian question, he found himself the unwilling focus of international attention, while all he wanted was to have the peace and quiet to write novels and visit museums. (Don't we all?)

It was during this difficult period that he set up his own museum, as he describes in the novel. 'Is it possible that by looking at objects we might see our memories as if they were a film?', he wonders.

'The power of things inheres in the memories they gather up inside them, and also in the vicissitudes of our imagination, and our memory', he adds a little further.

It is thanks both to the objects and to ourselves that museum visits evoke such rich experiences. Pamuk also claims that objects in a museum can communicate with each other. He admits to being an ardent fan of flea markets and second-hand shops, but refers to collectors as 'ill-tempered, jealous, and despondent [hoarders]'. He is talking about himself. 'For the sake of the objects they could not give up, many [hoarders] had become alienated from their families; they spent most of their time alone in dusty rooms that, as they filled up, came to resemble storage lockers', he goes on to explain. Collectors want, above all, to show an era: it is 'up to new generations to reconstruct the lives and histories of these people of the past through the things that they [...] left behind.'

Later, when I read this, I understood Pamuk's perplexity during our visit to the museum. It was the curiosity of the exile, shame for the neglect of things that had been left behind and an intense compassion for old objects. He had observed himself in the museum.

Caressing with gloved hands

After lunch we continued our visit. A guard opened a small door to the right, behind which dark stairs wound downwards. We descended into large cellars with old furniture and art-nouveau exhibition cases. In a trophy room there were masses of crates full of stuffed animals, shot long ago by big game hunt-

ers. The walls were covered with animal heads, most strikingly rhinoceroses without horns. Another room was full of elephant skulls, a cubbyhole full of elephant teeth, multitudes of stuffed birds, and – how sweet – stuffed okapis and an okapi foal.

We passed through a subterranean tunnel towards the Stanley Pavilion, the director pointing out secret passages on the way, and emerged in a small cellar where we climbed the stairs.

'Welcome to the Stanley archives,' said Mathilde, who was waiting for us there. She spoke polished English, and smiled broadly at Pamuk, who immediately pounced on her: 'Will you give me a thorough overview of your archives, with all the different sections?' It sounded like an order.

'May I faint here and now?' asked Mathilde affectedly, but she laughed again and quickly began pointing to objects. Boxes and trunks, books on shelves, the metal trunk on which Stanley's widow herself had noted the contents. Half hidden behind a cupboard a large framed photo looked at us: Henri Morton Stanley, legendary explorer of Congo.

We went upstairs, where Mathilde had already prepared various items for her important visitor.

'This is where I work,' she said conspiratorially.

Here she did what historians basically do: carefully dusting off, opening out and analysing objects and documents. Studying them almost caressingly and preparing them for the narrative. In other words, picking up and listening to the stories that objects themselves can tell. An old-fashioned word for it is magic.

Solemnly Mathilde passed a pair of white gloves to Orhan Pamuk, which he donned like an experienced surgeon. Gently they leafed through an old photo album full of fragile portraits. Then Mathilde spread, unfolded and unrolled valuable old maps. She pointed to the imaginary mountains, riverbeds and lakes, named the incorrectly situated, foolish or just invented place names. As we leafed backwards through ever-older maps, we saw the interior of the African continent become more and more unknown, blacker or whiter. Finally she showed us the oldest map of Africa. Pamuk took a selfie of himself and Mathilde with the map.

Then she showed us the *pièce de résistance*, Stanley's diaries. Pamuk bent lower and lower over the notebooks, hypnotised. Which version was the first, he asked. Show me a sentence, what was changed and by whom, how exactly had Stanley rewritten it?

Pamuk took more and more photos, asked for more and more details. He tried to spell the words out loud, asking Mathilde for help. They paid particular attention to the texts about Stanley's visit to Turkey. The explorer's breath was still fresh in the pencilled notes.

Almost gasping from all that knowledge we left the archive.

'Now I'll show you my diaries,' he said, pulling off the white gloves. I passed him his briefcase. He took out a Moleskine notebook, scribbled full with his minute handwriting, interspersed with colourful sketches of statues and landscapes in India and Istanbul.

We stopped at the model of the future museum. It glittered in the sun, transparent in glass and silver. The director explained it. Then Pamuk signed the museum's golden book, lying ready beside a glass of tea. The woman from the staff newsletter asked him some questions. She had read all of Pamuk's books and wanted to know, 'What did you enjoy the most during this visit to the Africa Museum? Will this short visit make a lasting impression? Do you intend to come back?'

'I'm not going to answer that,' said Pamuk with slight irritation in his voice. 'But I'm really happy,' he said, mischievous again. 'I love so much dedicated people.'

When we left, he took another photo through the car window of the museum staff waving, and showed it to me proudly as we drove. We were both tired. In the car we talked about the pleasure of in-depth research for the writer, the lure of details, and how difficult it is to kill your darlings. I dropped him off in front of his hotel on Boulevard Adolphe Max for the obligatory meeting with journalists. But first he politely signed my four Pamuk books, complete with dedication.

That evening, in the overfull Henri Le Boeuf hall in Bozar, Pamuk read from *The Museum of Innocence* and was interviewed. They were the classic questions and answers. It was a pleasant evening, with the scent of apple hanging in the air, I remember. There were no political questions. That had been explicitly agreed beforehand. He received the applause awkwardly, lingered a moment on the stage, and then the interviewer announced that people should queue in an orderly fashion for his signature. No chatting please! No dedications or dates!

Like a picture from another era. In *The Innocence of Objects* Pamuk says he has the impression that things communicate 'with one another' in museums, that the solitary objects even 'have spirits' and that they tell, above all, the story of simple people.

Pamuk does not like the 'big state-sponsored museums' (see 'A Modest Manifesto for Museums', at the beginning of this book). He prefers the collections of extraordinary individuals like Stanley. He allowed himself to be shown

Orhan Pamuk
© Koen Peeters

around the Africa Museum, but stopped to look mainly at small personal objects. I saw how he zoomed in on the soft-pencilled notes in Stanley's diaries. It was not the height of the rooms, nor the width of the entrance doors that Pamuk liked, but the ordinariness of the hero.

I saw him looking through greedy, literary eyes: what were the precious words jotted down next to the objects? Whose hands had once handled these objects so carefully, and whose hands had put them down here, in this academic manner? How had all these things found their places? How had their little spirits grown towards each other?

I looked at the man looking at the museum. He was looking for the love, the little anxieties, and the sadness in these objects. He was taking photos, but at the same time he was writing a book, a story, making a painting of this museum. Just as every visitor does in his head.

So can objects look at us? Yes, of course, they are constantly looking back, large numbers of them, tense. What we look at in a museum is the ancient desire to capture the world, to create a world.

In my copies of Pamuk's books I underlined special words and passages in pencil, so as to be able to find them again quickly. Objects in museums function like that too. They are uneasy signs that point backwards and forwards to ourselves, to our own lives. Beauty has to do with memory, says Pamuk. However ordinary they may be, objects tell us that their lives are complicated, unknown and unfinished, like history. By looking at them you become part of those lives.

Museums invite us to look at objects from an aesthetic point of view, so that they can communicate their messages like gleaming reflections, an ancient but ongoing process of oxidation. But it is a political viewpoint too. The story of these African objects is also that of the brutal, tainted colonial era, the story of Leopold II, and scientific conquest. This type of thing can only cause lasting controversy, as well as ongoing dialogue between the heirs on both sides.

Who were we? Who were they?

Two years after our visit the Africa Museum closed its doors for an extremely interesting, thorough renovation. It needed it. The old museum looked mainly at the broken Belgian heart of our own little Belgian nation, intimately and from the distorted, faded viewpoint of a View-Master. We looked there at an exotic world of animals, minerals and people. Who did we used to be? And, more to the point, who were they? Had it become the museum of guilt?

Later, in mid-2018, we will all visit the new museum together, happy and in celebratory mood. We shall see how everyday objects appear again: rough, incomprehensible, of sublime, unknown aesthetic. Once again it will be an invitation to look at unfailingly strange and colourful human behaviour, with a black, unknown side, both close to us and far away. ■

With thanks to the International House of Literature Passa Porta and Guido Gryseels, Sari Middernacht and Mathilde Leduc of the Royal Museum for Central Africa, Tervuren.

Translated by Lindsay Edwards

FURTHER READING

Orhan Pamuk, *The Museum of Innocence*, Faber & Faber, 2010.
Orhan Pamuk, *The Innocence of Objects*, Abrams Books, 2012.

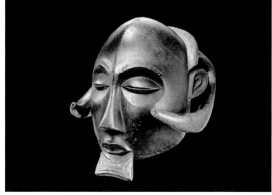

Candoia aspera: Jonathan Brecko
© KMMA Tervuren

Luba helmet mask, R. Asselberghs
© KMMA Tervuren

On Its Own Two Feet

Dutch Design in 2018

[JORN KONIJN]

In the 1990s, Dutch design took off internationally under the appropriate title of... 'Dutch Design'. It was fresh, full of humour and above all universal. In addition, it turned out to be an ideal emblem for the notion of positive progress and untroubled globalisation. It was also a standard-bearer that gave the Netherlands an excellent opportunity to establish its profile. Small but beautiful. Personal creative development rather than mass production, and above all a harmless way of taking a leading position worldwide. In this regard, the representatives who propagated the Dutch Design way of thinking proved themselves the best ambassadors imaginable. With the gift of the gab, full of bravura, and mediagenic, such designers as Marcel Wanders, MVRDV and the DROOG design collective became internationally renowned. But how much is left of the Dutch Design legacy? What sort of design emerged from it and how does the latest generation of Dutch designers handle the body of ideas that Dutch Design dominated for all those years? And what remains of the irony and bravura? In this essay, I will try to find an answer to these questions by outlining the present Dutch design landscape.

Knotted Chair

If there is one object that has come to symbolise Dutch Design it is Marcel Wanders's 'knotted chair'. It was a chair made of knotted cord that was then inverted and suspended in a bath of special coating which, when dry, enabled the chair to retain its shape. The function of the chair was secondary to its form: it is not really comfortable to sit in. The object plays with the user, who is challenged to reflect on what a chair actually is, what materiality is, and how it is possible that a number of cords knotted together can make up a chair. It introduces a tension between the object and the user, whereby Wanders had only one message: anything is possible. And in this way the chair embodied quite precisely the spirit of the late 1990s. The Wall had fallen, communism was dead and buried, and scientists were predicting the end of time. Anything is possible!

By means of this chair, Wanders indicated that he wanted to go back to the idea of the old crafts. 'I wanted to make a product that did not seem industrial, a design that shows that it is made for someone with love, with the same sort of air as an old worn-out wooden cupboard. Knotting is one of the techniques by which you can achieve this craftsmanlike feel.' An industrial product in a craft guise. A project intended to evoke the suggestion of being old, worn-out and handmade, but which fools the user. For some designers this went a step too far. They were trying genuinely to return to the old crafts and use them as a source of inspiration for the development of their work.

Tactility

Claudy Jongstra launched her practice in 1996, the same year Wanders's knotted chair was purchased by the Museum of Modern Art in New York. Jongstra studied fashion design and in her work with textiles tried to go back to such traditional crafts as carding, spinning and weaving. She wanted to bring every stage in the production process under her own control. From the herd of sheep whose wool she used to the colouring of her thread using dye plants from her biodynamic garden. Jongstra was one of the first designers to give priority to a sustainable production process: respect for nature, the use of exclusively local products and traditional craft production methods. In a clear break from the lightness, irony and globalisation of the Dutch Designers, Jongstra's tactile work radiated seriousness, contemplation *and* local sourcing.

This break, or perhaps it's better to say a turning away, from Dutch Design generated a lot of imitation. Nienke Hoogvliet (b. 1989) makes textile pieces based on the same sustainable principles, but adds a socially committed element by using her work to call attention explicitly to the vulnerability of man,

Iris van Herpen

society and nature. Nienke's designs are personal and poetic and are more than just a project. The products are traditional and sustainable, with a particular focus on natural materials and production processes.

Simone Post is another of these talented textile designers who dares to broach major social issues with considerable candidness. She uses a lot of residual material and waste in her designs, thereby imputing it with new value. But it is above all Jongstra's former trainee, Iris van Herpen (b. 1984) who has taken the most significant steps in the direction of the new tactility in Dutch design. Van Herpen became best known by taking Jongstra's sustainable methods as a basis, but combining them with modern techniques. Van Herpen has a pronounced urge to keep on experimenting, not shying away from the use of 3D printers, laser cutters and other modern techniques. Whereas Jongstra, Hoogvliet and Post remain close to the traditional design crafts, Van Herpen sees them rather as a stepping stone to continued and more contemporary experiments.

Innovation and techniques

This urge to experiment with new techniques also characterises another direction Dutch design has taken in recent years. Building on the tradition of technical innovation that was pursued for decades in Eindhoven, such young designers as Pauline van Dongen, Dave Hakkens and Marjan van Aubel have put this principle at the heart of their quest to shape the Dutch design of the future. In this regard, they fit perfectly into the prevailing trend in which innovation enjoys broad interest and is not reserved only for governments, industry and universities. Young, recently graduated designers can also be the driving force behind innovation. It is precisely their youthful zest, combined with high media sensitivity, that can turn ideas on the drawing board into actual designs.

Van Aubel has concentrated on the use of solar cells in everyday designs. Her 'Current Table', a simple table for the living room, is composed of special solar cells that generate energy out of light. 'When developing new technologies, it is often only the technical advantages that are considered, and much less how people use or want to use the technology.' Van Aubel tries not only to design clever innovative products, but also to bring about a change of mentality. In her designs, sustainability, aesthetics and social change actually combine very well. Like that of Marcel Wanders, her work has in the meantime been purchased by the MoMA in New York.

Dave Hakkens takes the same direction with his Block Phone, a 'telephone made of bricks' in which users can replace parts themselves. This modular telephone might provide a solution to the increasing amount of chemical waste caused by the short lifespan of mobile telephones. Even before he had graduated, Hakkens's design had been purchased by Motorola, and other tech-giants are also developing similar models. The young designers are not put off by this, nor are they simply swallowed up. Pauline Van Dongen is also moving in this direction and applies her technological innovation to the fashion world. Using laser cutting, Van Dongen develops fabrics that change as the wearer moves. She is fascinated by the interaction between designer and material, but also between the design and the wearer.

Social Design

The third significant direction that several Dutch designers have taken is that of social design: design that is emphatically socially committed. In contrast with the happy-go-lucky mentality of the Dutch Design creators of the 1990s, social designers focus on thorny issues. The design process – which itself takes an original form – is as important as the finished product. In many cases the

Dave Hakkens, Phonebloks   Marjan van Aubel, Current Table

process is itself the actual product. Christien Meindertsma (b. 1980) spotlights such topics as loneliness, poverty and animal suffering, usually by means of research projects focussing on products for everyday use. In her project *Loes' Pullovers* – a joint project with the Rotterdam collective Wandschappen – she sought out the vital DNA of the Charlois district in Rotterdam. In her quest she came across Loes Veenstra, an unemployed older woman who spent her days knitting pullovers, amounting to 550 in the course of her life. Meindertsma did nothing more than wash, repair, document and display the pullovers. This drew a huge amount of media attention, not only for the designer, but of course for Veenstra and the poor conditions in the district. The sale of the pullovers – among others to the Japanese designer Issey Miyake and Queen Maxima – were to the benefit of Loes and the neighbourhood.

In this instance, the designer developed nothing more than the process, remote from any aesthetics, innovation or irony. The designer effaced herself and was entirely at the service of the message and the ultimate socially committed goal. This is design as a solution for social injustice. The same principle is employed in the De Tostifabriek project by the young Amsterdam designers' collective Jansen Jansen & Bachrach. The basic principle is extremely simple: what does it mean to produce a toasted ham and cheese sandwich oneself, from beginning to end? The product appears to be simple: a slice of bread, a slice of ham, a slice of cheese, but is this the reality? The designers of De Tostifabriek planted a field of grain for the bread in the middle of Amsterdam, and reserved a piece of land for two pigs and two cows, thereby trying to produce all the ingredients for a toasted sandwich themselves.

The project made the news several times and set things in motion in the city. People living nearby lay awake for nights on end because the cow was lowing ceaselessly after being separated from her calf. And later there was a great commotion about the slaughter of the pigs. What the project did above all was to reveal perfectly how far contemporary society is removed from the production of its own food. It shows the impact that the production of a toasted sandwich has on our ecosystem and sheds a new light on increases in scale in the agricultural sector, on urban farming and relations between man and nature. Like Meindertsma, Jansen Jansen & Bachrach remain positive: the whole thing is presented with a smile. It is not an ironic smile, but one with a tragic undertone.

This tendency, which has become known as Social Design, has in the meantime firmly established itself in the Dutch design world. Even the original Dutch designers such as Droog Design and De Design Politie have launched large-scale social design projects. Droog has started the Socialcities.org project, an online platform that gives shape to the wishes of the city's inhabitants for the environment they live in. The accumulated data is intended to inspire the city's administrators themselves to take concrete steps. This project tacks between a bottom-up and a top-down approach to city building. Here again, the designer designs the process, not the finished product. The design studio under the name of De Design Politie, which achieved great renown in the late 1990s with its graphic work and its light touch, applies the same principle in its annual – since 2011 – international conference *What Design Can Do!*. Devised and organised collectively, and aiming at active participation, WDCD provides a platform for a large number of international speakers to talk about the social impact of design. Not design as frills, but as a way of thinking in order to tackle societal issues.

Social Design has taken off not only in the Netherlands, but worldwide too. It seems to have become commonplace for designers to be able to play a new part in society as game-changers. At the same time, critical voices are being raised that question this role. Can a designer actually play a social role? Isn't this idea too naïve in an era of religious terrorism and worldwide political instability? Aren't social designers claiming too much influence and isn't the whole movement little more than a case of the emperor's new clothes? After all, hasn't design always been social design?

What Design Can Do!

Yuri Veerman

Performative design

The real renewal in the design discipline is probably best expressed in the latest direction that Dutch designers have taken: performative design. In this case design is reduced to an action, something that is done, rather than what is seen. Even more than in social design, the emphasis is more on the design process than the artistic product. But whereas for the social designer the process is neutral, the performative designer actually seeks a dynamic process of dialogue in which the context, the technology *and* the spectators are seen as co-designers.

Yuri Veerman is originally a graphic designer and studies the representation of such large-scale phenomena as a country or population group. He focusses among other things on the significance and operation of symbols such as flags and currencies. For his work *Alarm Symphony* he transposed the Dutch national air-raid alarm sound into a composition for orchestra together with the composer Willem Bulsink. This work was a reaction to the culture cuts imposed by the cabinet of Prime Minister Rutten. The symphony was performed on the Hofvijver, a pool in The Hague, with the parliament building in the background. In addition to this performance, Veerman has previously made a name for himself with a play and a mini opera.

It seems that Maarten Baas is following a similar course. He made his name as a designer in the Dutch Design tradition with his luxury Smoke Chairs. However, in 2017 he surprised us at the annual Salone del Mobile with an art-like installation entitled *May I have your attention please*, in which he set up hundreds of loudspeakers, each in a different material and with different dimensions. The sound that emerged from them was of voices that were not quite distinct. The work was a critique of the concept of 'attention' and how it influences his work.

Although the work of the performative designers is definitely socially committed, the message (and the results) are less explicit than in the work of the social designers. The former are more like activists, but often with irony and humour. Their urge for renewal combined with a fairly light touch is actually very reminiscent of the Dutch Design of the 1990s. So is Dutch design returning to where it started?

There are distinct differences, however. Performative designers are constantly expanding the boundaries of the discipline, whereas the Dutch Designers of the 1990s were mainly concerned with stretching the limits of the product. When it comes to the current generation of designers you might wonder whether design is still the right word, when the designer may present a musical concert, an art installation or a mini opera. The traditional boundaries between the cultural disciplines are blurring fast, yet the mark of a Dutch designer is still distinguishable. What Veerman and Baas produce is very much conceptually driven and has a clear element of social commitment. Just like Dutch Design two decades ago.

So in spite of the various tangents and directions that have been taken, one can indeed say there has been a continuation of a specific body of ideas in the Dutch design sector. For two decades, Dutch Design has explored and developed. Such studios as Droog, MVRDV and De Design Politie are still engaged in free experimentation or have specialised in a single direction or theme. In the end it is Marcel Wanders who has remained most faithful to the original body of ideas found in Dutch Design. That said, he has gradually focussed more on the luxury market segment, but his designs are still characterised by a surprising and creative twist in the product. For several years in succession, he has been presenting his own versions of the classic Charleston sofa at the Salone del Mobile. He stood the whole sofa on end so that only one person could sit on it. A simple and amusing change which yields a seat that would be more at home in an art museum than in most living rooms. In Wanders's case, anything is *still* possible. ▪

Translated by Gregory Ball

Maarten Baas, Installation Salone del Mobile Milan 2017

'We Playact It Because We Mean It'

The Absurd Oeuvre of Annelies Verbeke

Annelies Verbeke (b. 1976) is a parade. She is a multitude of men, women, children and cross-dressers, all of whom are called Annelies Verbeke. This is what she said on the literary talk show *Winteruur* (Canvas). She transforms all these different selves into the series of remarkable figures who populate her pages: an author wakes up as a bear; after a failed relationship, Monique Champagne becomes stubbornly determined to save fish; a highly gifted boy called Hadrianus launches into the haka whenever the mood takes him. In that same conversation with talk show host Wim Helsen, the author declared her fondness for the short story, a genre for which she is happy to fight. In the short story, all the Annelieses get to have their turn. The short story is playtime and writing is a game, but one with serious stakes. By transforming facets of herself into characters, the author investigates the possibility of an alternative and often absurd existence. This makes the short story an ideal breeding ground for cultivating a wide range of outsider figures.

Verbeke's fascination with unusual types is evident even in her debut, *Slaap!* (Sleep!, 2003). This well-received novel carries the seeds of her later work within it and links her to the young Arnon Grunberg. Black humour and irony run rampant on the pages of both authors, although Grunberg's cynicism cuts more deeply. Verbeke is more gentle to her freaks. She makes fun of the absurdity of their existence, but always applies the comforting balm of familiarity. However unusual her characters' life choices might be, their emotions are our own. Picture the lonely gym manager who takes home the massively muscled Mehmet, whose use of steroids has made him impotent:

> *He goes to work, obediently and expertly, and you have complete confidence that it won't take long, until his breathing disturbs you, and you see that he is crying. There's a bodybuilder with his head between your legs, sobbing away. Just your luck.*

The derailment that constantly beckons

Annelies Verbeke
© Alex Salinas

In *Slaap!* the first-person narrator is Maya, a young woman with the unfortunate habit of not taking her severe insomnia seriously. She finds that at night she falls prey to an inescapable stream of thoughts, but she grants us no further insight into her mind. Maya plays down everything, including her lover's concern: 'Now he heard only my uncontrolled shaking, saw the hardness of my tears. He knew but he did not understand. Neither did I, but that was what was so funny about it.'

To dispel her restlessness, she goes for long walks at night, pushes her boyfriend away, wakes up forty-eight people and meets Benoit, who has been deeply scarred by his mother's death. He also features as a narrator, offering an emotional counterbalance to Maya's sarcasm. He does this right from his introduction, in which he talks about the imaginary whale Frederik, who would carry him to Morocco as an orphan. There is a gentle sadness simmering under his account. This balance between satire and pathos, between ruthlessness and compassion, quickly became Verbeke's trademark.

Slaap! set the tone. It is a taut, staccato debut, in which Verbeke immediately got to grips with her theme: escaping with nowhere to go, aimlessly fleeing everyday life.

Her next book, *Reus* (Giant, 2006), is also about characters who long to escape their daily life. Sisters Hannah and Kim hate the mother who abandoned them, celebrating this loathing every year on Mother's Night, and neither of

them knows quite what to do with their good husbands and beautiful houses. Just like Maya in *Slaap!*, Hannah shields her thoughts from the outside world. As a result, her actions seem extremely arbitrary. She eats Post-Its, shares a passionate kiss with her new stepmother's homosexual son, and breaks in to the house of one of her 'freaks', the people she interviews for her column in a weekly magazine.

Following Kim's breakdown, they end up in Australia, in search of another life, whatever that might be. 'The beginning of the end,' Hannah announces. There is a dark subtext in those words, which is undermined by her complete apathy:

> We waited patiently. Now and then I threatened him a bit more with the plastic knife.
> 'Hey, Hannah,' he said finally. 'I've had so much patience with you, but now it's over. It's done. I'm sorry.'
> Then we could finally leave.

In Australia, the sisters happen upon a trace of their vanished mother. Their escape develops a purpose, but the plot collapses in a concatenation of implausible twists and turns.

In her first collection of stories, *Groener gras* (Greener Grass, 2007), Verbeke is more successful at maintaining the focus. She weaves fifteen short stories around a central theme: winning and losing. With this as a starting point, she covers the entire range of human emotions: jealousy, pride, fear, joy. Her fondness for quirky characters, already seen in the freak parade in *Reus*, is now given full rein. At the same time, Verbeke moves away from a first-person narrator. She creates more distance and allows more room for alienation and gentle mockery, in which sympathy still resonates:

> [The young man] yelled a few insults, of which 'bald dwarf' hit Etienne hardest. Feeling rattled, he continued his walk through the night. When he got home, he kicked a cardboard box to pieces. He regretted it immediately. The box had been particularly suitable for waste paper. Now he would have to find a new one.

It is striking that these characters seem to move through life with just a little more direction. The eccentrics in *Groener gras* are saddled with a mission or have a goal in mind. The peculiarity of this mission or goal often plunges them into complete isolation: Steven wants to use his perfected skipping on the moon, Lola projects her affections onto an ox and kidnaps the animal, while Elsie founds her own state, Solemprium.

What unites them with Maya from *Slaap!* and the sisters from *Reus* is their fear of 'just any old life'. Verbeke's characters yearn for a compelling life and for escape routes, even when no escape is necessary. They burn bridges, go in search of something, without knowing what. They want to win. They create victims. Freedom beckons. But so does derailment.

We all live in fictions

With her accurate portraits, Verbeke makes these derailments believable. She focusses on abnormalities, capturing them with a fine brush, enlarging the image. Her characters, too, are excellent observers and are constantly interpreting, registering and reducing. They draw conclusions and make the complexities of reality more manageable. The sisters in *Reus*, for example, easily find proof of love in their shaky marriages: 'They loved us. You could see that. They did the vacuuming and bought salt when we'd run out.'

Her characters map out one another's weaknesses but disregard the beams in their own eyes. Hannah explicitly points out that they are not made for introspection:

> I realised that I no longer had a grip on myself, but it was not the right moment to go into that more deeply. It was actually never the right moment to go into it more deeply. Life was all about avoiding the moment to go into it more deeply until your very last breath.

Although they confirm their loneliness, they do not dare to delve into it. They hide behind a shield and make themselves unapproachable. The ways in which people avoid their pain is what Verbeke investigates in the novel *Vissen redden* (Saving Fish, 2009). For ex-writer Monique Champagne, her own salvation

involves saving fish. After a breakup, she fires off fanatical pleas against over-fishing. Her calling takes her to international congresses, where she serves as an emotional interlude between the academic lectures.

Monique Champagne, frequently referred to by both first and last name, bombards us with facts about species of fish, while refusing to confront her own sadness. It remains buried, revealing itself only in details:

> She turned on her laptop, ran back downstairs and unloaded the dishwasher. Most of the crockery was not originally hers, but it was now, it was now.

At the congresses, she makes friends with the aspiring writer Oskar Wanker and with Michaela, who mistakes her for her childhood friend Stefanie. While other characters by Verbeke move heaven and earth to begin a new life, Monique has a new life land in her lap. She plays the role of Stefanie with aplomb, but becomes more and more entangled in a web of lies. After a further rejection, this time from the fishing industry, the pain finally hits her with full force and the floodgates burst. In the central chapter, the sadness rolls at Monique Champagne in waves of memory; she is inundated by a host of separate paragraphs of no more than five or six lines. Every wave is an observation, which Verbeke captures in a new, poetic style.

> Finally he turns around between the sheets that she has soaked with her sweat. 'Look at me with those eyes,' she whispers urgently. When he stares at her, she trembles, shakes her head. Those are not the eyes she meant.

The bursting of the floodgates brings redemption, rebirth. Monique is a prophet; her goal assumes a religious dimension. Before long, other people's lack of understanding creates a new isolation, which Monique once again is unable to break through. So, for the length of the entire novel, she remains stuck in roles she has made up herself. She uses Stefanie's fake pain to suppress her own emotions. 'The child died,' Monique/Stefanie tells Michaela, before throwing herself into her arms, weeping. 'The comfort is real, she thought. The comfort is real.'

The communication skills of practically all Verbeke's characters actually leave a lot to be desired. In *Reus*, Kim falls into a stubborn silence for forty pages, while in the short-story collection *Veronderstellingen* (*Assumptions*, 2012), poor communication is elevated to a theme. Fifteen narrators remain stuck within their own frame of reference, do not express their assumptions and avoid confrontation. Or as one of the characters puts it:

> She once heard a guest on a talk show say that you should never ask about what you do not want to know. It was a casual remark, and maybe the guest had never attached much importance to it, but since then Samba has allowed that advice to silence her several times a day.

Rather than adjusting their own assumptions, the characters continue to live in their own fictions. Alex, for instance, is convinced that the author Dominique Favarque is feigning memory loss in order to be left in peace. This assumption is completely undermined by the story 'Feest' (Party), which is told from

Dominique's point of view. That happens throughout this collection: Verbeke has the various narrators wander into one another's stories. By doing so, she grants the reader a view into an alternative reality, one that often remains hidden to the characters themselves. 'We all live in fictions,' one of the characters in the collection *Halleluja* (2017) was later to confirm.

A typical element of Verbeke's work is that much is left unspoken between the characters. Only the novel *Dertig dagen* (*Thirty Days*, 2015) breaks this pattern to a certain extent: communication proves possible, but mainly between strangers. Clearly, a listener is needed who is far removed from the characters' own world and who suspends judgement. The sounding board in question is the Brussels-Senegalese Alphonse Badji, who works as an odd-job man in the Westhoek and receives an intimate glimpse of 'interiors'. While he hangs wallpaper and sands floors, the residents inundate him with their worries and fears. This is in contrast to his partner, Kat, whose fear of abandonment is so extreme that she fabricates a relapse of her cancer.

When current events intrude

Thirty Days is, in a number of ways, an odd-one-out in Verbeke's oeuvre. For the first time, we encounter a *happy* character who does not give way to the pressure of an alternative life. Alphonse is not tempted by derailment. In fact, he is the saviour who tries to prevent others from going off the rails. Alphonse is the man who takes Duran to the hospital with his chopped-off finger, who carries the ghost of a dead brother from the house of one of his customers, who sticks a newspaper article to the wall of his music room about Chen Si, the Chinese man who prevented 278 suicides all on his own. He is a Messiah figure and plays this role with bravura right to the end.

In addition, *Thirty Days* is a novel in which the outside world can no longer be denied and seriously damages Alphonse's happiness. Until that point, Verbeke's social criticism consisted largely of exposing the disease of a generation: an inability to settle in a normal existence. In *Slaap!* the outside world is completely absent. The setting matters little to people who are as focussed on themselves as Maya. *Groener gras* appears to indicate the first sign of change.

The opening story 'Naar de toekomst, waarin een reis gewonnen wordt' (To the Future, in which a Journey Is Won) is about war refugees dying in the back of a truck from a lack of oxygen. Elsewhere in the collection, the pressure to win, to be visible, becomes so great that Stefaan needs a shotgun to do it. 'Ste-faan is lord and mas-ter,' he screams, as he shoots people down. 'Stefaan is doing this because he can,' the narrator confirms. Then, in *Assumptions*, we meet the xenophobic Didier Van Ranst, who leaves piles of money all over the house in an attempt to catch his household help stealing. In spite of that handful of standalone stories with a socially critical approach, current events only truly entered the foreground of Verbeke's work in *Thirty Days*. The social issues that Verbeke raises in that novel are inextricably entwined with her main character and the setting in the Westhoek: latent racism, the refugee situation, the stubborn isolation of villagers in a region where death reigns supreme.

At the same time, it is the villagers who are the connection between *Thirty Days* and Verbeke's previous work. With the exception of Alphonse, the characters fit seamlessly among the people in her short stories. Take Duran, who runs a pita shop and, in his spare time, makes ice sculptures in his own image. Minor figures like this illustrate Alphonse's goodwill and prompt questions about the moral issues around the boundary between concern and interference. Their endless comings and goings disturb the rhythm of the book, however, which constantly shifts between a novel and a collection of stories.

Back to the beginning and the end

Her latest creation, the collection of short stories *Halleluja* (2017), is the most typical Verbeke and the highlight of her writing career so far. It is as if all the familiar ingredients have culminated in this collection: black humour, a sense of self-perspective, and eccentrics who are longing for a clean slate. This time the stories are held together by beginning and end, a thematic line that shines throughout her entire oeuvre. Every escape, in spite of its lack of direction, contains the promise of a new start.

In *Halleluja*, Verbeke takes her absurdism one step further. In order to provide an answer to the absurdity of existence, she explores the boundary of magic realism. Stylistically, she chooses to employ the metaphor. In the central story, 'De beer' (The Bear), it takes this form:

> *The author has become a bear. An old, brown bear. Of the male gender, but impotent, as he believes he discovers when carefully exploring with his bent paw.*

The author-bear, Verbeke's alter ego, is lying in bed beside his partner, who seems, just like everyone else, not to notice the metamorphosis. The only one who sees the change is a friendly gravedigger with 'a sixth sense for these things'. He tells the bear that you can begin something and end something. Sometimes, behind refusal, freedom beckons, the bear concludes before going to sleep. On waking, 'she is no longer a bear. And no longer an author either.'

'De beer' is a story about intense exhaustion. At the heart of the collection, Verbeke presents her alter ego as one of the characters who want to explore a different life. She refuses to play her role as author anymore. The stories before and after 'De beer' are an attempt to provide an answer to that central story. It is followed immediately by the disconcerting 'Bus 88', in which someone wakes up in another person's life and tries to make the best of it. This symmetry is the formal principle that lends structure to the collection. While the first story presents an omniscient wailing baby, the final one is about an elderly woman who wants people to love her. All of the stories pivot around the axis of 'De beer'.

In *Halleluja*, Verbeke demonstrates that she is an author who can continue to explore the same themes while finding innovation in form. In *Vissen redden* she goes in search of a poetic voice, in *Assumptions* she makes connections between all the stories, in *Halleluja* she applies a mirror structure. In this last collection, Verbeke adds a stream of header text in small capitals above the story 'Lente' (Spring), which can be seen as her credo and poetics:

WE LIKE BEING WHERE WE ARE. WE CANNOT DO WITHOUT OUR PARTNERS. WE WOULD GO CRAZY WITHOUT THIS BODY, THESE DAYS AND NIGHTS. UNDERSTANDING AND AFFECTION, EVERYTHING THAT IS PRECIOUS AND FAMILIAR TO US: WE CANNOT BE WITHOUT IT. SO THAT IS NOT IT. WE BELONG WHERE WE ARE. WE WANT TO STAY THERE. WE ARE NOT ALWAYS THERE. WE GET DISTURBED. WE DISTURB OURSELVES. [...] WE WILL DRIVE TO THE HOUSES OF OUR LOVERS AND CRAWL ACROSS THEIR FLOORS, SCREAMING THAT WE CANNOT CHOOSE. WE MEAN IT. WE PLAYACT IT BECAUSE WE MEAN IT.

Verbeke's characters want security and independence. They are restless actors. They take on the roles that are assigned to them and flee when that role stifles them. Verbeke herself also playacts it because she means it. Her writing is a play, a game with all those different selves, her absurdism is a way of capturing an illogical reality. That absurdism often springs from the way Verbeke observes the world. In her gaze – involved yet distant – lies the key to her oeuvre's irresistibility. ▪

www.anneliesverbeke.com

Annelies Verbeke's books are published by De Geus,
www.singeluitgeverijen.nl/de-geus.

Translated by Laura Watkinson

ENGLISH TRANSLATION

Assumptions (*Veronderstellingen*), translated by Liz Waters, published by World Editions, 2015.
Thirty Days (*Dertig dagen*), translated by Liz Waters, published by World Editions, 2016.

Two Extracts

By Annelies Verbeke

In the Bud

[...]

Mehmet and you are standing sipping apple juice among drunken people from another planet. It was your idea to go to a bar. Now and then a stranger comes and feels his biceps. He undergoes the touching passively, but something in his face makes one suspect that that will change.

'Shall we go?' you ask.

He puts his half-full glass on the bar and you follow him outside, to his car, which he scarcely fits into.

'So shall I take you home?' he asks.

'Will you stay over?' You've never asked that yourself.

'It won't work,' he says in alarm.

'Are you married?'

'No. Not anymore. But because of all the stuff I've taken' – he hits his ribcage hard – 'something's wrong.' His hands fall into his lap and start fiddling with each other's nails.

You understand.

'Just sleeping is fine too,' you say.

'OK then,' he says. 'But be careful, I can still fall in love. It happens more easily than it used to, actually.' He starts the car.

The city outside is your city, but you don't recognise it, you could be anywhere. The thin moon seems sharper than usual. Perhaps the bar wasn't your only bad plan of the evening. Perhaps the return of the monster and your desire for the man next to you do not coincide by accident. Perhaps no catharsis but a repetition will ensue.

To make matters worse, when you see his enormous body standing clumsily among the fragile things in your apartment, you are overcome by an excitement you have rarely experienced. Should a ray of sunshine come in now, a rainbow might appear between your legs. You decide simply to tell him.

'I can lick you or something,' he sighs.

On any other day your desire would have crumbled, but tonight you land on your bed with a jump and cry: 'Do it!'

He looks at the hummingbirds from close up. He puts his finger on one and says: 'Mehmet.' You are the other one. You are struck by this, but are mainly impatient because horny.

He sets to work obediently and expertly and you have every confidence that it won't take long, until his breathing disturbs you and it turns out he is crying. A

bodybuilder is lying between your legs sobbing. The things that happen to you.
'Sorry!' he says. 'I cry so easily these days. With Disney films, everything. Take my advice: don't mess around with your hormones!'
'Why are you crying *now*?' He is sitting bent forward on the edge of the bed, you've put an arm round him, you can just reach the other shoulder.
'Because I have no libidó anymore and at this moment I wish it were different.'
You feel a laugh coming on which in view of the situation you try to suppress. What you do come out with sounds nasty.
'Sorry!' you say to his indignant face. 'But you said "libidó", with the stress on the last syllable.'
'What should it be then?' He sounds rather pissed off.
'Líbido,' you say. 'Or libído. The last one is English, I think.'
'So you don't know yourself?'
'No.'
Meanwhile your own libido has also fled the room.
'Do you want a drink?' you ask.
'Do you have Aquarius?'
'Isostar.'
'That's fine.'
You each drink a bottle in front of the television. In the repeat of the news the newsreader discusses the new attacks. Mehmet bursts into tears again. You cry along with him. He puts a heavy arm round you, it must stay there.
'Can't be easy for you as a normal Muslim,' you say.
'It's not easy for anyone,' he says.
Fifty-three people have died.
'*Après nous le deluge,*' you say. It's an expression from a former life, it strikes you he may not understand it.
'No.' He looks at you, his arm remains, his freckles are stars, his eyes dry. 'No,' he says again. 'After the flood it's up to us.'

'In de knop' from *Halleluja*
De Geus, Amsterdam, 2017

Translated by Paul Vincent

Agreed, last night has something to do with it – not that I regret it, I have to live. Baron von Münchhausen was able to arrange a fix and my problem with MDMA – I've often noticed – is not the substance itself, but that I can go on drinking if I've taken some, I have the same thing with coke, no feeling of satiety as far as alcohol is concerned. OK, up to that point it's my responsibility, I should have left those cocktails alone, but in itself it was a great night: I kept weaving tiny dreadlocks in the baron's arm hair, and he kissed me on my temple, mouth and shoulders, as we embraced, as we danced, and there was a walk, after which we had to run back home fast because that woman was there, that Katja, I've forgotten what her fairy-tale character is called, the one with the ladle, is that Frau Holle? – but anyway she wasn't there last night, we all had time off and she was sitting as herself in a restaurant and nudging her husband and point-ing outside, at us, the Baron pissed a bubble on the asphalt, you couldn't see anything as it had rained. I could see it coming that I would sleep over with him, that wasn't the problem, or his paunch – he asked me if he was too fat for me – I love paunches, for a long time I lay across it on my belly, while he gently stroked my buttocks, that was nice, I remember, but then the sex itself, these things happen, I simply couldn't concentrate, I was sitting on top of him, but he seemed to be metres beneath me, after a while his head was no bigger than the head of a pin, really weird. I can't remember when I fell asleep but I do remember that in the morning the Baron kept pointing at me the whole time – that I now had to go to work with those ro-ho-ho-ho-hound eyes, I would have enjoyed that, if he had not laughed in a mean way. But I go off to Hamelin again, where I report and that Claudia, who says that I'm no need from next week, so, without any notice, I'm not needed any more, my input, it's over: das Ende! And she looks so bitter that I know there's been some sort of complaint, perhaps from Frau Holle, in that case the Baron could also forget it, but I don't call him because this morning was rotten, and I don't ask Claudia for a reason either, I don't ask what I'm supposed to live on, I don't even ask 'Und was ist mit meinem Deutsch? Ich bin doch hergekommen um Deutsch zu lernen!' No, I have one thought and it is very circumscribed, very clear: you don't promise a Pied Piper something you later renege on. So I've been fired and if I want those two weeks' wages, I've got to show up until the end of the week in the same stupid suit, play the same tune on my clarinet, this is a low point, this will leave a lasting mark on me. I consider sending a message to the Baron after all because I feel a Desire welling up in me, I am overpowered by Desire, but I won't get in touch and the Desire will turn into Longing and who knows I'll be able to cry a bit and there'll be something like a catharsis – I think, and I'll keep to two glasses of white wine to ward off a hangover. Less than half an hour later I see them coming in my direction, I'm sitting playing the clarinet on my step by the town hall. You can't hold it against a child like that, often it's the fault of the parents, in this case certainly. The way they come strolling up to me, family represents mood, one word, two syllables – boredom? Right! The father has shown the world how with very little cerebral activity and very little good taste you can become very rich and since that achievement all he fantasises about is screwing a Porsche, now too, in his mind, he unscrews the cap of the petrol tank, sticks his erection in and comes almost immediately. The mother looks around her disapprovingly, next year they must go to Disneyland Paris again. I can't really disagree with her, Deutsche Märchen Strasse, I'm pretty well sick of that kitsch at the moment, the language too, why did I actually want to learn it? *Hameln! Hameln! Rattenfängerstadt im Weserbergland!* Right through my headache I blow my clarinet, while every pore focusses on trans-mitting the telepathic message: Weitergehen! Lasst den Rattenfänger in Ruhe! Grimm-Grimm! But they don't, walk past me. They don't. They stand looking at me pityingly and the daughter is the worst of the three, I see that now, that child of nine who from hunger for attention sometimes plays a younger child, plays innocent while looking at you coldly, bloody kid, with a sharp voice asks: 'Mama, wer ist das?' And after the mother has shrugged her shoulders it is the father who answers: 'The Pied Piper'. And then that child again with her eyes latched even larger and colder onto mine: 'Aber Papa, der Rattenfänger von Hameln hat doch keinen Busen?' And they find that hilarious, the parents, both of them, the father laughs with his head thrown back, the mother tramples on the spot and hyperventilates in her hands. What a child they have produced, such a short time on this planet and already so corrupted, such a thing requires an effort, but they succeeded. Proudly the mother wants to say to her offspring that some people have to do the craziest jobs because they didn't pay attention at school, and the father wants to add that nothing like that will ever happen to his girl, but they can't manage it, I'm drowning the whole family! The whole of Hamelin! I make them clutch at their ears, the man, the woman and the child, I run on ahead of them blowing, until they realise they can't escape me, that I am leading the whole way back, past my steps, Claudia also charges out of her office, more people follow, a panicky procession whirls round and round but I am faster, I run past them till I am leading them again. Now I must lure them into a ravine or a river, a rock that closes, but spatial orientation has never been my strongest point, so I lead them to the staff toilets, to which I have the key. But then my lips contort, my mouth undermines me, my lungs slow down the blowing and here come the tears, there they are, just now, I think, not now, but at the same time I think: it's a start.

'In Hamelen' from *Halleluja*
De Geus, Amsterdam, 2017

Translated by Paul Vincent

Middelburg

The Town in the Middle

[DEREK BLYTH]

When I visited Middelburg for the first time, back in the early 1980s, the town was an old-fashioned, religious place. It was a Sunday and everything was closed, except for the churches, which were full. It felt twenty years behind Amsterdam.

When I returned to write this story in early 2017, it was clear that Middelburg had moved on, but not much, so it still feels a couple of decades out of date. Some shops are now open on a Sunday, but not too many. And the churches are still full.

The name means Middletown. And Middleburg does look like a middling Dutch place. It has all the usual details of a small Dutch town – dented bicycles parked outside the station, a shopping street with a Blokker and a Hema, a van on the main square selling *oliebollen*. You could be in any small Dutch town, I thought. But that's not really true, I found out later. Middelburg is far from average.

The town is called Middelburg because it sits in the middle of the former island of Walcheren. But it is nowhere near the middle of the Netherlands. The train from Amsterdam seems to slow down as it heads through Zeeland province, passing through a vast empty landscape dotted with cows, stopping at small places along the way, taking its time to get to its provincial destination.

I was staying in the Hotel aan de Dam on the former harbour front. It was a charming old place out of the Dutch Golden Age with creaking stairs, ornate carved doors and solid oak beams. Originally a private house, it was built in 1652, possibly by Jacob van Campen, the architect of Amsterdam's town hall. The bedrooms were furnished with old record players and a stack of vintage jazz records. The hotel did have wifi, so you could use a smartphone, but the owners seemed to assume guests would be happier listening to a slightly scratched Duke Ellington album.

Intriguing passages

The next morning, I went for a walk. The streets were strangely empty, apart from the occasional bicycle. I was struck by the scrubbed stoops, the potted

Middelburg Archives

plants on the street, the neatly parked bicycles. And something else I noticed. The bicycles were locked using a traditional rear-wheel clip lock, not the enormous reinforced steel locks you have to use in Amsterdam to prevent your bike vanishing in the night.

Most of the houses along the waterfront have attractive eighteenth-century white painted facades with straight classical cornices. But lurking behind the Empire-style facades, not quite hidden, were the older pointed gables from the seventeenth century.

The names painted on the houses in neat black letters offer some small clues about the identities of the previous owners. Some houses had biblical names. Others were named after foreign places like Antwerp or Edinburgh. And quite a few gave the names of the people who now lived in the houses. Here was where Tom lived with Ellen. And this is where the Van Rossum family lives.

I didn't notice at first, but the town has a network of secret lanes that run between the houses. I stumbled upon one lane called Kuiperspoort, where coopers once made barrels, hidden between the Dam and the Rouaanse Kaai. A low arch led into a seventeenth-century courtyard surrounded by mellow brick houses with step gables.

These intriguing passages are too small to be marked on the city maps. Some so narrow that only one person can squeeze through. Others so low that you have to duck your head. Yet they are fascinating to explore, leading you to overgrown gardens and hidden warehouses.

Facelift

There are other mysteries too, that don't get explained. The old town looks harmonious, well maintained, but then you sometimes notice an individual house or even an entire block that does not fit in with the rest. They look more like modern post-war Dutch houses. And you want to ask why they were built in these beautiful waterfront locations.

Fortunately, I was shown around town by John Louws, a retired teacher with a deep understanding of Middelburg's past. He told me about a forgotten episode in the early years of the Second World War, a few days after the bombing of Rotterdam. The Dutch government had already surrendered, but Zeeland refused to give up without a fight. There were French troops in the region who tried to resist the Germans. The town was shelled on 17 May 1940, possibly by the French, or maybe the other side. The population had already been evacuated to safety, and only nineteen local people were killed, but hundreds of old buildings were reduced to rubble, one third of the housing stock in all.

After they captured the town, the Germans almost immediately launched a reconstruction plan. They recruited architects trained in the Delft School to design modern houses to fit the scale of the old buildings. The new houses can often be identified by a little plaque showing a phoenix rising from the ashes, along with the date 1940. But the new buildings don't exactly blend in with the old. 'They look authentic, but they're not,' Louws explained. 'It's as if the town had a facelift.'

The beautiful Gothic town hall was one of the casualties of 1940. Eight members of the famous Keldermans family from Mechelen had worked on this ornate Late Gothic building, from the laying of the first stone in 1452 to the completion in 1520. But the building was destroyed in a matter of a few hours, leaving nothing but the outer walls standing.

The town was hit by another catastrophe in the winter of 1944 when the suburbs were flooded. For more than a year, the water remained more than a metre deep in places, turning farmland into lakes. Even now, Louws explained, anyone buying a house in Middelburg will ask if the property was under water in 1940. If the answer is yes, then the deal might be called off.

Rescued heritage

It took several decades before the town had fully recovered. The turning point came in the early 1970s when Dutch cities were beginning to realise the importance of restoring historic monuments. Middelburg was one of the first cities to rescue its dilapidated heritage. Despite the loss of several hundred houses in 1940, the town still ranked fifth in the Netherlands for the number of

historic monuments, after Amsterdam, Maastricht, Leiden and Utrecht. With some 1,150 listed buildings on its books, many of them in a poor state, the city launched an ambitious plan to restore its architectural heritage.

Louws took me down Spanjaardstraat to show me the results. Once a notorious slum, known mainly for its brothels, it has been transformed into an elegant cobbled street lined with renovated seventeenth-century houses.

We then walked out to the edge of town, where the Kloveniersdoelen, where the city guards once met, has been converted into an art cinema and restaurant. You can sit in the enormous banqueting hall, or, when the weather is good, find a table in the garden in the shade of a fruit tree.

The biggest surprise lies in the centre of town, where a modest gate leads into the Abdijplein, a huge open space enclosed by brick buildings. It once belonged to a Norbertine abbey founded in the twelfth century by monks from Flanders. Now it is surrounded by various buildings including a church, the Zeeland province offices and the Zeeland Museum.

One door leads into a hidden Gothic cloister enclosing a medieval herb garden. Some old stone steps lead down to a dark basement bar where you can drink Belgian and Dutch beers.

Eccentrics

The Zeeland Museum is located in one of the old buildings overlooking the abbey courtyard. It reopened in the summer of 2007 after an eight-year reconstruction led by the Brussels architect Christian Kieckens. The renovation

included a new entrance cut into the wall on the abbey courtyard and a bright, stylish café called ZMCAFE.

The original museum contained a dusty collection of oil paintings gathered in the nineteenth century. It didn't offer much of interest, apart from a portrait of Admiral De Ruyter in a splendid gilt frame and a paper model of a shipping disaster. But the museum has tried to bring some vitality to the collection by placing the focus on local crafts like chair making while adding playful touches based on Zeeland's traditional costumes.

The most inspired section comes at the end of the tour in the attic where three oversized crates are crammed with miscellaneous objects, like seventeenth-century cabinets of curiosities. Here you can admire dozens of odd items that have somehow ended up in the museum, like a waistcoat and breeches worn by skipper Verlinde at his wedding in 1820, a set of playing cards with faded pictures of the Battle of Waterloo and a tea box disguised as a stack of books.

It seems that Middelburg, far from being average, has more than its fair share of eccentric intellectuals, butterfly collectors and amateur scientists. One of the most interesting, Johannes Goedaert, was the subject of a small temporary exhibition. He was an amateur scientist, naturalist and illustrator. Fascinated by insects, he spent his time searching in the Zeeland sand dunes for rare species.

Outside the museum, a curious sculpture shows two metalworkers standing next to a cannon resting on two sandbags. Created by the artist Sjuul Joosen, the work commemorates the Burgerhuys family, who once cast ships' bronze cannon and church bells in a dark attic at the top of one of the abbey buildings.

A guilty secret

It took me some searching to find evidence of the trade that turned Middelburg into the second most important city in the Netherlands. It is still something of a guilty secret, but Middelburg grew prosperous from the slave trade. In the eighteenth century, ships of the Middelburg Commerce Company, the MCC, carried more than 268,000 African slaves across the Atlantic, returning to the home port with holds filled with sugar, tobacco, cotton and cocoa beans. But you find little evidence of this trade in Middelburg, apart from Hedi Bogaers's simple granite Zeeland Slavery Monument unveiled in 2005 on a little square close to the former headquarters of the MCC.

Yet the story of Middelburg's slave trade can be tracked down if you are persistent. It is preserved in the exceptionally detailed records kept by the company. These old logbooks, which cover 113 Atlantic voyages, are so complete that they have been added to UNESCO's Memory of the World Register.

An unknown island in the Pacific

The town also keeps strangely silent about its most famous explorer. At the advanced age of sixty-two, the local lawyer Jacob Roggeveen was sent to find the mythical continent Terra Australis. But on Easter Sunday 1722, his three ships stumbled by accident on an unknown island in the Pacific Ocean, which they named Easter Island.

You might have expected a statue of Roggeveen, but recently, when this idea was proposed, the council claimed it had no money. It could not even afford to put up a plaque on the house where Roggeveen was born, one local historian complained. It was left to the Zeeland archives to come up with an imaginative manner to remember Roggeveen. An extract from his diary is now carved onto a brick wall outside the Zeeland archive building on Hofplein. Other lines are inlaid on the polished floor of the cafeteria and there are even extracts from his account on the walls of the toilets. The expedition is also commemorated by a mysterious replica Easter Island *moai* head that stands outside a retirement home on Buitenruststraat.

Time is an empty bottle of wine

Middelburg's most notable contemporary artist, Marinus Boezems, has created some interesting works that are dotted around the town in unexpected locations. His most striking installation, the *Podio del Mondo per l'Arte*, is a replica of an old covered market where grain was once traded. Demolished in 1969, the market hall was rebuilt on the Damplein square as a platform for conceptual art. The art interventions are laid flat on the ground like gravestones, so they are easy to miss. 'This could be a place of post historical importance,' is carved on a stone set in the ground in 1976. Other works include Willem Breuker's 1998 iron manhole cover with the inscription 'Time is an Empty Bottle of Wine'.

St John café

Sint Jansplein

Next to an ancient stove

It's easy to miss the Sint-Jansstraat, a quiet lane off the main shopping street, which has a hint of Amsterdam's Jordaan. It leads to the Vismarkt, a hidden square where they used to sell fish from the North Sea. The market hall still stands on the square, along with a stone pump and several old chestnut trees, but the fish sellers have moved elsewhere.

I sat inside the St John café on Sint-Jansstraat at a little table in the back room next to an ancient iron stove. The café is a rambling place with a piano in the back room, old coffee tins and a wooden counter rescued from a Belgian bar. It's the kind of place where locals sit with the newspaper, tourists update their Facebook timelines and children are allowed a fluffy *Zeeuws bolus* covered with sticky brown sugar.

Years behind

Before leaving Middelburg, I rented a bike to explore the countryside. It doesn't take long to get out of the town. You cross a canal, then another, and – look! – there are cows. The cycle routes lead to pretty towns on the coast like Vlissingen to the south, Domburg to the west and Veere to the north.

With sea all around, the air is wonderfully clear. You can see the clocks on Middelburg's two towers from a long way off. Locals tell you that the clock on the town hall tower, known affectionately as Malle Betje, is always a bit slow, compared to the clock on the abbey tower, which they call Lange Jan. And the sundial is said to be slightly squint, giving rise to the notion of Middelburg time, thirty minutes behind Dutch time.

Someone recently sparked off an internet discussion on Middelburg time. 'The time is thirty minutes behind in Middelburg? More like thirty years,' he quipped. 'And that's the same for the whole of Zeeland.'

But maybe that's no bad thing. ■

© All photos by Derek Blyth

Nature and Woodland in Flanders

Policy in Times of Short-Term Thinking

[PIETER LEROY]

What is the state of the natural environment in Flanders? There are a few bright spots, but on the whole the situation is not good. And how about environmental policies? The so-called concrete ban, which is intended to preserve what is left of our open spaces, seems like good news, but there is every reason to be sceptical. After all, governments nowadays are rarely in a position to ensure that long-term policies are actually implemented. In contrast to fifteenth-century Venice which was able to do so through enlightened self-interest.

In 1713, Hans-Carl von Carlowitz, a German forester, published his *Sylvicultura oeconomica*, a comprehensive handbook on forestry based on the scientific insights of the time. Modern environmentalists know this text through its emphasis on sustainability as a leading principle of successful forestry. The book is a perfect example of mercantilist and early modern thinking on capital management. Forests are an important capital asset, and should therefore be treated by governments as an important national possession.

Of course, that idea goes back much further than the eighteenth century. The most striking example is Venice, which despite its vulnerable geographical position, was able to dominate the Mediterranean for a century and a half, between about 1400 and 1550. The Doge and his entourage were well aware of the importance of systematic forest management and practised it, not always very gently, even at great distances from the city itself. Venice appropriated forests deep into the Alps and as far away as modern Slovenia and Croatia. The city was heavily dependent on them. Wood was needed for building houses and ships, for armaments and trade, for water management, as a source of energy and so on. Archival research shows that the Venetians had a sophisticated system of forest management based on the careful recording of which types of wood had to be available, in what quantities, how often, and for what uses. Long-term thinking in the fifteenth century was inspired by economic, military and political needs and the defence of independence. And as Von Carlowitz was to write two centuries later, forestry should not only benefit the here and now, but should be long-lasting and sustainable, and should benefit future generations. That emphasis on sustainability was not inspired by ethical considerations, but primarily by enlightened self-interest. The utilitarianism of the here and now had to be reined in by self-restraint and long-term considerations. It

was perfectly acceptable to regard today's timber yield as a return on investment, so long as the base capital of that natural resource was preserved for the
future. After all, one was dependent upon it.

The minister and the entertainer

'The function of a tree has always been to be felled.' This observation by Joke
Schauvliege, the Flemish minister responsible among other things for Environment, Nature and Forestry as well as Agriculture, gave rise to widespread
critical comment. It was May 2016 and she had been under fire for a year. It
started in the summer of 2015, when forty-three academics published an open
letter expressing concern about Flemish environmental policy as a whole: its
lack of ambition, lack of money, and lack of performance. Then in September
2015, Wouter Deprez, a cabaret performer and not a conventional environmen-
talist, highlighted one particular event: the felling of eleven hectares of woodland in Genk for the expansion of a transport business. He was scathing and
to the point, he pulled no punches, he was scientifically accurate and he used
social media. Flemish ministers criticise each other on Facebook and Twitter
about everything but they are not very good at dealing with tweets directed at
themselves from outside government circles. Deprez, acting on his own, was
like the chorus in a Greek tragedy, passing comment, without mandate, dis-
interested, well informed and with surgical precision. While he was attracting
wide support, the minister faced mounting criticism for the proposed clearing

of the woodland, for a number of howlers in her defence of the decision, and subsequently for the failure of the fund that was intended to compensate for deforestation by planting new trees. An investigation by the parliamentary Audit Office revealed that the ministry's books were neither geographically nor financially in order. What fifteenth-century Venice had been able to do seemed to be beyond the competence of the Flemish government in 2015. Moreover, government spending on buying up forest and nature reserves in Flanders was in decline. Not surprisingly, minister Schauvliege found herself in the firing line. She avoided the media for some time but finally appeared in a TV programme in the middle of May 2016 where once again she was given a hard time, though this time less skilfully. Apparently, that's the trend in modern journalism. And then at the end of May 2016 came that controversial statement: 'the function of a tree has always been to be felled'. Factually it may be accurate, but Von Carlowitz would have added the proviso: so long as enough trees are left standing for the future. And the minister had added that more or less.

But the evil was done. For there was no suggestion of sustainability, of a vision beyond the here and now or concern for the future. The result was that yet again nature-loving Flemings laid into the minister. And things were soon to get even worse.

Ambivalent motives for protecting the environment

Protecting the natural environment as an end in itself is a recent phenomenon. Environmental historian Joachim Radkau rightly observes that only societies which have solved the problems of hunger and poverty can permit themselves the luxury of protecting a swamp for purely aesthetic reasons. Incidentally, aesthetics was only one of the motives behind the first wave of environmental

Lemberge,
Aldegondiswegel
© Michiel Hendryckx

protection, from 1860 in the USA and a few decades later in Europe. 'For the Benefit and Enjoyment of the People' has been hewn into one of the entrances to the Yellowstone Park, a quotation from the law which led to the establishment of the park in 1872. President Roosevelt unveiled the stone in 1903. There are many photos of the same Roosevelt, not necessarily in Yellowstone, standing proudly next to an animal which presumably he had just shot. It reflects the ambivalence of nature protection at that time which was prepared to protect it here and there, but primarily for the use and pleasure of human beings. Not everybody thought that way; the establishment of nature parks in the mid-West and West of the USA was accompanied by the compulsory and disruptive expulsion of 'native Americans'. Early nature protection was not only anthropocentric; it was also demonstrably ethnically discriminatory.

Similarly, the motives behind early European protection measures, say between 1880 and 1914, were ambivalent. In an echo of Jean-Jacques Rousseau, anti-modernism certainly played its part. Natural areas were seen as oases of authenticity and places of poetry and philosophy, as one can read in Frederik van Eeden. There was also scientific curiosity and, inspired by Alexander von Humboldt, great efforts were made to record and protect as much as possible against the rising tide of modernisation. What applied to Europe, applied even more to the exotic environments of the colonies. The arguments and strategies used by the colonial powers to set up nature reserves in their overseas territories reveal a remarkable mixture of high-minded motives of emancipation, academic interest, and crude economic and political repression of local populations.

The second wave of European nature protection was delayed by wars and poverty and developed more or less in parallel with the growing environmental awareness which took off around 1970. In particular, it was the damage to nature, landscape and open spaces caused by urban development, traffic and industry that aroused opposition. In Flanders, for instance, many a battle was fought over the proposed push-towing canal between Oelegem and Zandvliet and the A24 through Limburg. Nature, or at least its beautiful landscapes, had once more to be protected against advancing modernisation. Most of these battles were lost, but in some the outcome was deferred and something approaching an environmental policy began, hesitantly, to emerge.

Nature: what is it actually?

Meanwhile, across Europe it was abundantly clear that nature had long ceased to be 'unspoiled'. It was certainly true of Flanders: churned up by endless wars, hardened by centuries of urbanisation and transport, turned over to industry for two centuries, and to industrial food production for half a century. And what was left, in spite of great opposition, was being built over. There was no hint of environmental planning, let alone restraint on behalf of future generations. There is no more room for nature.

Elsewhere in Europe, attitudes towards nature and its protection have been changing during the past few decades. Just as in Von Carlowitz's time, science has played a crucial role in this. Three aspects deserve emphasis: space, quality and biodiversity, and then via a fourth, ecosystem services, we end up very close to Von Carlowitz's position.

Nature reserves remain very important. They are, after all, the location and storerooms of biodiversity and of specific species and habitats. Space must therefore be set aside for them. But even outside these nature reserves, where population density, intensive agriculture, industry and transport is putting great pressure on available space and the environment, it is essential to call a halt to further asphalting, urbanisation and fragmentation. To phrase it more positively, open spaces must be safeguarded and buffer zones and connecting strips for migrating species have to be laid down. Environmental policy is therefore to some extent also town and country planning. Secondly, these areas must be of such environmental quality, physically, chemically and biologically, that nature can thrive. Environmental policy is therefore also policy on

Below left
Warandepark, Brussels
© Michiel Hendryckx

Below right
Aalst © Filip Claus

the quality of air, water, and other natural elements. And thirdly, Nature as a gigantic, complex and delicate system is at its most robust and resilient when there are many different species, when there is great biodiversity. Environmental policy, therefore, is also partly a species policy for plants, animals and habitats. Not homogeneity, but variety.

Like many others, I am sceptical about the chances of success for an environmental policy that is only driven by ethical, aesthetic or scientific motives. Enlightened self-interest is a much stronger motive. After all, what is true of forestry is also true of nature in general. We need nature now and we shall need it in the future. We are dependent upon it and that realisation cuts across the presumption that modernisation can make us independent of nature, and that trees can simply be cut down. In direct opposition to such presumption is the relatively recent concept of ecosystem services which at its core is very factual and straightforward. Nature, the ecosystem, automatically provides at no cost to us all kinds of services such as oxygen, water, food, raw materials, a protective ozone layer and much more. These ecosystem services, just like Von Carlowitz's forests, are capital goods, which should be protected. The authorities of today must ensure that short-term interests are likewise constrained by the long-term protection of these essential ecosystem services. The hole in the ozone layer, climate change, and all the other current environmental issues show how essential and valuable they are. Perhaps we could set a price on them? Perhaps an economic and financial valuation of nature would in the long run prove to be its best protection?

Preserve nature? Yes, but not in my back yard

Flanders went through all this between 1990 and 2003 when under the so-called 'Main Green Structure' plan an attempt was made to establish a comprehensive environmental policy for Flanders. However, as soon as it was published, a coalition of convenience sprang up between farmers and landowners, Christian democrats, liberals and Flemish nationalists, hunters and developers, householders and speculators who viewed the setting aside of land for nature and the environment as a totally unacceptable limitation of freedom. Protecting nature was all very well elsewhere, but not when it came to their own back yard. Their terrain, after all, should be 'for the benefit and enjoyment of the people'. Open spaces and nature were given an exclusively private and short-term meaning and value. Neither the interests of the community nor long-term considerations were seen as sufficient reason for restraint, and the 'green spaces' element of environmental policy was torpedoed. Its political impact turned out to be too high.

Remaining ambitions

So, what is the current state of the natural environment in Flanders? The answer to that question depends on what is understood by the environment, which parts of it you want to protect and why. Farmers, civil servants, conservationists and scientists all have very different opinions, as do Sunday ramblers and

Ronse, 2005
© Filip Claus

pensioners on their electric bikes. Nevertheless, agreement has been reached in Europe and in Flanders on what is of value and how to preserve it. There is also international agreement on how to assess the condition of the environment and how to report on it. In Flanders, in addition to various inventories drawn up by butterfly lovers, bird counters and woodland specialists, the Research Institute for Nature and Forests plays a crucial role. Its Nature Reports contain long lists and time series for many dozens of indicators, including how ordinary people experience Nature.

On the basis of those lists, one thing has become clear: the natural environment in Flanders is not flourishing; on the contrary, it is in a bad way. Of course, one can qualify this assertion endlessly by citing the numbers of water birds, butterflies, and fresh water fish, the extent of managed nature reserves and accessible woodland, and the measures relating to defragmentation of the countryside or nitrogen deposits. But the conclusion would still be the same. Admittedly, the number of protected nature reserves and their surface area has increased during recent decades. Depending on which of the various conservation regimes one chooses and the degree to which they overlap, between about 100,000 and 120,000 hectares in Flanders are now subject to a regime of environmental management. Nevertheless, almost fifteen years after the date prescribed by law, only 74% of the Flemish Ecological Network, and a mere 3% of the connecting areas have been demarcated. Elements of the original Main Green Structure plan have meanwhile been renamed and watered down. In other words, the designation of the core natural areas, the original reserves, has been reasonably successful, but the sections linking them hardly at all. Beyond these spatial aspects of environmental policy there is little good news to report. Within the protected areas, the quality of the environment is extremely variable. Some species are flourishing but more than half of the 'species of European importance' are in a 'very poor state of preservation'. There is little natural diversity in Flanders. Outside those areas, the quality of the environment ranges from critical to negative. That has everything to do with a third aspect of environmental management: the admittedly improved but still poor quality of water and air. Flanders continues to breach European regulations particularly in the case of phosphates, nitrates and particulates. That is not only unhealthy for the environment but also for humans.

This regrettable situation is neither accidental nor ascribable to any one particular minister. Since 2004 Flanders has had a succession of governments none of whom has given priority to nature and the environment. It even appears in their policy statements, in such phrases as, 'we shall do no more than what is required by Brussels'. In fact, they have done even less than that. First of all, as we have already seen, budgets have been cut. Secondly, there has been a demonstrable failure to observe many EU regulations, for instance in respect of air quality, phosphates, nitrates and particulates. And whenever Brussels threatens to enforce them, complex and intricate covenants designed simply to keep everyone quiet, to maintain the status quo and obtain a deferment from the EU of between six and twelve years are sought out. The so-called Programmed Approach to Nitrogen (PAS), is the most recent example of this kind of manoeuvre. Thirdly, what lacks priority is usually badly administered. It is therefore not surprising that the regulations for forest compensation have still not been approved by the Audit Office and that the appropriate expertise, organisation and administration is lacking. The (non-governmental) forestry and environmental organisations, if only because of their contractual obligations, are better run than the Flemish government. All of which leaves any minister extremely vulnerable.

Ooidonk © Filip Claus

From short-term to long-term

Recently a fresh breeze has been blowing through Flemish town and country planning. Partly through the influence of the government architect, the Flemish government has decreed a future concrete ban. The civil servants in the Flanders Spatial Department have been busier than ever with inventories, studies and reports. The heart of their proposal is to safeguard, even expand the scarce open spaces in Flanders by discouraging and even forbidding the spread of new housing developments on, for instance, obscenely large plots of land outside existing built up areas. The counterpart of that policy will be to increase the density of housing within the cities and urban centres.

Most of the arguments in favour of a concrete ban have been familiar for decades. Flanders is messy and ugly; in Flanders there is no clear demarcation between town and countryside; the spread of housing leads to unnecessarily high levels of traffic and transport; it leads to needlessly high costs for collective infrastructure, from energy networks to sewers, from postal deliveries to public transport. But there are also two relatively new arguments. The first is climate change. Higher density housing would open up the prospect of lower and more sustainable energy use by households and traffic. It would also make it easier to adjust to the impact of climate change on, for instance, the risk of flooding and rising urban temperatures.

The second 'new' argument is not actually new, but is only now catching on. Open spaces are a communal good and important for the future. Only open spaces can provide ecosystem services. Encroaching on them therefore carries a price which has to be paid. Building in the countryside should ideally be banned and certainly be made far more expensive. That is Von Carlowitz in modern dress. I am surprised that that idea has proved more successful than all the efforts of well-meaning architects and planners, as well as the environmental movement, and has finally broken through to the highest government circles. At least, I am told that important ministers are attracted by it. So the recent Structure Plan for Flanders includes an ambitious plan to give the concrete ban proper form and content by 2040/2050. It has not shied away from imposing do's and don'ts, or using financial instruments. It is no 'soft policy'. The Flemish government is persisting, at least verbally, in its Jacobin mind-set.

From the long term back to that one map

It goes without saying that a concrete ban is most welcome, even essential, for the Flemish environment. Flanders would once again be able to enjoy open spaces, a more attractive social climate, and better living conditions. Nevertheless, I remain sceptical. For two reasons. Firstly, because of the length of time involved. Governments are hardly able to lay down and sustain a policy for ten years, let alone for several decades. Their attention is constantly distracted by the illusion of the day, the hype of the week, or the investment of the year. Furthermore, the cycle of elections and changes of government encourages discontinuity. The Dutch Scientific Council for Government Policy reported recently on the institutional, legal, budgetary and organisational conditions

Translated by Chris Emery

needed to pursue long-term policies successfully. Climate change was the example that they used, but the Flemish ban on concrete will require comparable conditions. From where I stand, none of those conditions have yet been satisfied in Flanders.

One of those conditions is the second reason for my scepticism. Just when everybody thought that the Minister for Environment, Nature, Forestry and Agriculture had survived her worst possible crisis, she faced an even greater crisis in 2017, with the so-called Forest Map. The intention, in brief, was to protect all woodlands, even those located in areas that had been designated for other purposes such as housing, business parks and so on. It affected about 12,000 hectares of woodland which did not fall within the regional planning guidelines. That in itself reflects the modernist pretension that we can impose a homogeneous order on nature. Whether it was much or little, the policy required an agreed and workable definition of what constituted a forest, or a woodland for that matter, a reliable inventory of where these were to be found, and the transfer of all that information on to a map. After much argument in the cabinet, as a result of ten times as much lobbying outside it, the map was presented in mid-May 2017. Opposition immediately broke out in a well-organised campaign. Obsolete data, factual errors, wrong geographical coordinates and particularly the threat of financial loss led to a coalition of convenience between employers' organisations, tradesmen, farmers, householders and others. The map was withdrawn straight away and the parties continued to squabble. The party disagreements were not particularly interesting. More important is to observe that the Forest Map protected a much smaller area than the Green Structure Plan had done earlier. Yet in spite of its reduced demands, the plan was still shot down because of the Flemish government's self-inflicted lack of expertise, administrative capacity and political will. That makes me sceptical about the concrete ban in 2050. 'And what about nature?' I hear you ask. What nature would be left by then? ■

Tradition as Scenario

On the Work of Ilja Leonard Pfeijffer

[LARS BERNAERTS]

'What happened to me may be assumed to be familiar as the material of the oldest stories.' The person talking is the narrator of *Peachez, een romance* (Peachez, a Romance, 2017). The man is at the end of his career as a professor in Latin studies and so knows a fair amount of narrative material from antiquity. He transmits it in his research and teaching. In the course of the novel this professor will both follow and betray tradition. The ancient story which he presents as a scenario, and which he knows through and through from his study of Tertullian, is that of conversion. But the old story is given new clothes. Through a Catphishing message, he encounters a certain Sarah Peachez. When they embark on an intensive exchange of emails, he neglects his university work more and more. Anyone following the intertextual trail of Tertullian, realises that the professor is leaving his subject for imaginary love just as the Latin writer converted to Christianity. 'The love that we know between people,' preaches the professor in a lecture, 'is like the human love of God an act of creation, which in modern psychological jargon is also known as projection.' What resounds in that statement is a well-known letter from St Paul to the Corinthians, as the reader of *Peachez* realises long before. In the words of the narrator: 'Faith, hope and charity, these three. And all things considered they are one and the same. You create a God in your own image.' On that level in the work of Ilja Leonard Pfeijffer great themes such as love, migration and literature are comparable: they are always grafted onto tradition, scenario and imagination.

Tradition is a treacherous protagonist in Pfeijffer's writing. The writer derives his mastery from 'Tradition and the Individual Talent', to quote T.S. Eliot. In his classic essay with that title the modernist poet argues in 1919 that the critics of his time are inclined always to emphasise what makes a poet new and hence individual. Tradition becomes a blind spot, although 'not only the best, but the most individual parts of his work may be those in which the dead poets, his ancestors, assert their immortality most vigorously'. Only when the poet is in touch with tradition can he really assess and assert the topical value of his work. A few decades later the German thinker Theodor Adorno goes a step further when he argues in *Ohne Leitbild* (1967) that poetry must at once embrace and repulse tradition: 'Poetry can only rescue its truth content, if in as close as possible a contact with tradition it rejects the latter.'

Ilja Leonard Pfeijffer
© Stephan Vanfleteren

Embracing resistance

This paradox definitely applies to Pfeijffer's work. It is imbued with a sense of literary tradition and it derives its uniqueness and contemporary character precisely from that hyper-awareness and the embracing resistance. 'Originality' is a misplaced term, because for that his brash dialogue with tradition is too crucial. To begin with Pfeijffer emphatically transmits literary tradition by making it accessible and comprehensible for a contemporary audience. In 2000, for instance, he publishes *De Antieken* (The Ancients), a history of Greek and Latin literature from antiquity, in which, with humour and decisiveness, he tells the story of literature from Homer (eighth century before Christ) to Quintilian (approximately 35 to 100 AD). Ten years later he retells the Greek myths in an even freer style.

De Antieken
Een korte literatuur-
geschiedenis
Ilja Leonard Pfeijffer

He is active as the erudite compiler of anthologies such as *De canon van de Europese poëzie* (The Canon of European Poetry; 2008, with Gert Jan de Vries) and recently *De Nederlandse poëzie van de twintigste en eenentwintigste eeuw in 1000 en enige gedichten* (Dutch Poetry of the Twentieth and Twenty-First Century in 1,000 and More Poems, 2016). By translating poets such as the Greek Pindar and the seventeenth-century writer Constantijn Huygens Pfeijffer also makes tradition tangible and topical. And in addition the writer, through creative and academic interpretations of canonical work, contributes to the transmission to posterity of the literary heritage. All these activities are extensions of each other. If the anthologist and translator are at first sight helpful transmitters, Pfeijffer shows that they are just as much creative renewers through the idiosyncratic choices that they make. It follows from his view of literature that the transition from anthologising, translating, interpreting and retelling to pseudo-translation, parody, pastiche, intertextual allusions and his so-called own invention is fluid. Each well-thought-out imitation is a creative gesture.

Pfeijffer's poetics are many-sided and always evolving, but the dialogue with tradition – often in the form of mockery and competition – is constant. The quote from Bertolt Brecht that precedes the essays and reviews in *Het geheim van het vermoorde geneuzel. Een poëtica* (The Secret of the Murdered Bunkum. A Poetics, 2003): 'Style must be quotable. A quote is impersonal. Who are the best sons? Those who make us forget the father.' Pfeijffer includes the quote in Dutch and without mentioning Brecht: the father is almost forgotten. So anyone wanting to show respect to his predecessors had better not pay them too much respect. In the poem 'firebird' from *Het glimpen van de welkwiek* (The Glimpsing of the WitherWing, 2001), which embodies a view of poetics, it is stated as follows: 'true revolution eats its fathers up and does not ignore them / but consumes and chews them'. In addition the writer constantly transforms tradition into a scenario: He openly appeals to old patterns for new stories and poems. We need only think of the title of *Idyllen. Nieuwe poëzie* (Idylls. New Poetry, 2015), a collection which at the same time refers to an old genre and announces a renewal.

Sublime acrobatics

The principal predecessors who echo in Pfeijffer's work are closely related to aspects of his poetics. The first is Pindar, the Greek poet of odes. In 1996 Pfeijffer obtains his doctorate from the University of Leiden with a study in which he examines three of Pindar's odes with a fine-tooth comb. Later he writes about Pindar in terms which since his debut collection *Van de vierkante man* (Of the Square Man, 1998) have applied to himself: 'Pindar is an experimental poet. His poetry is overfull, atmospheric and rich in sound. (...) The reader has to work hard to understand what he means. He subjects language itself to experiment.' In *De Antieken* (The Ancients) he notes that the Dutch poet and coryphee of the 'Movement of the Fifties', Lucebert, was inspired by Pindar via Hölderlin. Lucebert's poetry, of which Pfeijffer compiled an anthology in 2009 under the title *Er is alles in de wereld* (There is Everything in the World), is also an unmistakable reference point.

Pfeijffer follows the line of Pindar and Lucebert in *Van de vierkante man* (Of the Square Man), *Het glimpen van de welkwiek* (The Glimpsing of the WitherWing) and *In de naam van de hond* (In the Name of the Dog, 2005). The poetry in those collections is not aimed at accessibility, certainty and order, but celebrates difficulty of understanding, uncertainty and caprice. The programmatic poem that opens his debut collection already announces this vision: 'Serve me images baked in butter / and poetry with bulimia' are the final lines. The rhetorical and theoretical arsenal that Pfeijffer deploys in his work is overwhelming or 'bulimic'. With a great variety of metrical options, complex stanza forms and sound patterns, the poems can appear as tightly structured and comprehensible and only present at second sight obstacles to simply understanding. At other times they overflow with untransparent, playful neologisms and ungrammatical sentences without punctuation. One sees traces of Lucebert and poetry becomes sublime acrobatics. We see that for example in the collections *In de naam van de hond* (In the Name of the Dog) and *Het glimpen van de welkwiek* (The Glimpsing of the WitherWing; also at micro level in a palindrome like 'a te o poeta ateo poeta') or in the *Brieven uit Genua* (Letters from Genoa, 2016). In the Poetry Week gift publication *Giro giro tondo* (2015) the structural principle is present in the obsessive repetition required by the genre of the sonnet cycle and to which the title refers. The seventh and hence middle sonnet is the place where a happy love turns to disappointment. The beloved who is being addressed finds it difficult to accept that as a lover she is a figment of the imagination according to the I-figure. But he persists: 'We create those who love us in our own image.'

La Superba (2013) also shows the ineluctability of the mirror effect both in an embracing structure and in the story. The novel begins with 'The Most Beautiful Girl in Genoa' and ends with 'The Most Beautiful Girl in Genoa (reprise)'. In the last scene the character Ilja creates himself in the image of the other, and as a transvestite himself becomes the most beautiful girl. The novel demonstrates the complex inevitability of projection. That is not equatable with fatalism, but presupposes a recognition of mental models. Just as the author cannot escape tradition and so can better turn it expertly and self-consciously to his advantage, so man can better take control of the imagination that drives him.

While in the technical field Pfeijffer vies with old masters like Pindar, he determinedly gives tradition a new manifestation. A topos like the appeal to the muse sounds as follows: 'muse sing to me of the man with the many pressed sports jackets.' His modernisation of classical forms and motifs is not only reminiscent of T.S. Eliot, whose *The Waste Land* he integrated structurally in the novel *Rupert* (2002), but also of Martinus Nijhoff. In his 2016 anthology of modern Dutch poetry, Pfeijffer includes a maximum number of poems by Lucebert and Nijhoff, including poems that Pfeijffer makes echo throughout his oeuvre. Nijhoff's 'Awater' (which T.S. Eliot admired) is an important intertext in *Idyllen* (Idylls). With words and images from 'Awater' the collection with its fifty long poems in rhyming couplets makes it clear that the subject compensates for the experience of a sense of security in the present time with powerful illusions, such as the imagination of a travelling companion, an Awater.

In *Het geheim van het vermoorde geneuzel* (The Secret of the Murdered Bunkum) Pfeijffer clarifies the vision that guides him in incorporating his predecessors . What he considers bad poems at that time are poems that are determined to be about something, use authenticity as a credible criterion and aim at comprehensibility. Successful poetry is poetry that frustrates and disturbs, plays with sound and language, and is not reducible. The acrobat is not far

away when Pfeijffer says that poetry is 'a sophisticated fair attraction in which your own thoughts are yo-yoed. I want another go.' Acrobatics and fairs belong to the domain of risky games: although they appear to be separate from work and daily life, something is always at stake; they work directly on the body and elicit a response of being overwhelmed. That is what poetry can be like.

Illusion of love

A decade later Pfeijffer bids farewell to his poetics of uprooting. The requirement of risk remains, but is now defined differently. *La Superba*, *Gelukszoekers* (Searchers after Happiness) and *Idyllen* bear witness to that change of course. In a programmatic poem from *Idyllen*, which has the character of a manifesto (all the more because in 2016 Pfeijffer the anthologist includes it as the only poem of his own), the lyrical I pleads for committed poetry. However, the careful reader does not see a simple rejection of his earlier work. True, it says 'I was wrong in the past' and 'No more deconstructions, no cryptograms, no quizzes', but the fact that he criticises the exaltation of the incomprehensible, does not mean that poetry now has to be accessible and unambiguous. After all: the 'little poets of the Netherlands / and Belgium' must 'know everything / that googling fingers forget daily'. A poem must 'tell it like it is' by transcending this directly available and fleeting knowledge. We see how Pfeijffer presents the change of heart almost as a conversion and that is no coincidence. At the same period *Brieven uit Genua* (Letters from Genoa) and *Peachez, een romance* (Peachez, a Romance) testify to a new belief in the illusion of love alongside that turning point in his poetics.

Pfeijffer puts his changed view of literature into practice by directing cultural criticism at dominant modes of thinking, not only in the form of political commentaries or in a poem on Trump's election victory, but also through his literary reflections on migration, the media and virtual worlds. In a place where the reader may not expect it, these strands are strongly linked together, namely in the apparently nihilistic reportages of *Second Life* (2007). Here Pfeijffer assumes the form of Lilith Lunardi and with that avatar migrates to the virtual world of Second Life. That starting point is a striking reflection of what happens in *La Superba*: a man, who eventually becomes (the parody of) a woman, settles in another country and shows partly from an assortment of perspectives of other migrants that migration always draws on a reservoir of virtual reality. The migrant who wants a new place to live or the man who desires a woman; both cloak reality with imagination. The process is so strong that the world becomes virtual. In both works, the ontological boundary between fiction and reality is undermined, so that omnipresent claims to authenticity become problematical.

Illusion of fiction

In this area too Pfeijffer's hyper-consciousness shows through in his work: the writer is very concerned both to deflate and to cultivate the illusion of fiction. In the novels *Rupert, Het grote baggerboek* (The Big Dredging Book, 2008) and *Peachez* that is done through unreliable narrators who are out to mislead the

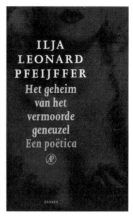

reader they are addressing, but finally mainly get lost in their own rhetoric. It is no coincidence that the narrators are placed in an institutional environment (a psychiatric institution, a legal environment), which elicits such manipulative language. What the novels make clear, however, is that every story misleads. Nowhere is the illusion of the novel so insistently, demonstratively and wittily undermined as in *Het ware leven, een roman* (True Life, a Novel, 2006), and that is achieved to a large extent via literary tradition. Not only does Pfeijffer parody the work of contemporary Dutch writers such as Connie Palmen, A.F.Th. Van der Heijden and Jan Wolkers, but he also alludes to the work of Goethe, Kloos, Tolstoy and many others. In most cases he presents the literary past as a hollowed-out pattern. In this way, the hyper-consciousness of tradition becomes a sign of critical distance.

Pfeijffer is not without criticism either for the contemporary world of the internet and social media. The awareness of the past sharpens his criticism and can help to relativise the novelty of current developments. In the same way as *La Superba* confronts the stories of migrants today with migration in the past, *Brieven uit Genua* (Letters from Genoa) and *Idyllen* (Idylls) recall historical changes that put the digital revolution and political changes in perspective. Where he attacks superficiality and emotive culture, which reign supreme in a time of internet and social media, the narrator says ironically: 'I feel nostalgia for the days when the Stoa forbade emotions and saw feelings as irrelevant.'

Tradition continues to operate not only in allusions, emphatic references, parodies of existing texts, but is evoked also in choices of genre. Anyone surveying Pfeijffer's oeuvre notices a fascination with genres as models. Besides the genres already mentioned, we find theatrical texts, a travelogue, a radio story, song lyrics, a TV documentary, a radio play, a self-help book and so on. In Pfeijffer's view, the literary interview and the poetry performance genres demand skill and deserve manipulation as well.

On the one hand, genres are firm moulds that make creativity possible. In *Harde feiten, 100 romans* (Hard Facts. 100 Novels), the writer imposes on himself the 'strict formal limitation' of writing 500-word micro novels. Such an exercise in narrative art is reminiscent of the regulated writing of OuLiPo, the Ouvroir de Littérature Potentielle or workshop for potential literature of writers like Raymond Queneau and Georges Perec. But Pfeijffer does not always keep to the rules he has set himself in *Harde feiten*. On the other hand,

Pfeijffer's work is constantly extending his models through parody, topicalisation and subtle genre transgressions. We can see that from the way he uses classical verse and stanza forms, but also in the story lines and characters. The first-person characters in his work sometimes parody the lonely heroes from popular genres: the romantic bohemian, the lonely cowboy, the bold knight or the exalted samurai.

Prescribed paths

Pfeijffer's texts then are particularly genre and tradition-aware, which links them to one of the central ideas: that life and literature cannot escape scenarios that are pre-existing and have a fictional nature. Finally, how does the reader fit into that image of Pfeijffer's literature? The reader too follows prescribed paths. Pfeijffer's narrators are generous in signposting: they deliberately send the reader in all kinds of interpretive directions. For example, the narrator of *La Superba* repeatedly describes the themes of the novel and comments on the structure and the characters. Because such a reflection is already included in the novel, however, the reader can never place himself *above* the text; he writes himself into a web of words, but does not precede them or rise above them. He can only interpret docilely or contrarily, feign understanding or plead incomprehension, but these are all scenarios that are known in advance. Like love, migration and writing, reading too is ironically characterised by trust and hope, tradition and scenario. ▪

Translated by Paul Vincent

FURTHER READING

Ilja Leonard Pfeijffer, *Rupert: A Confession*, translated by Michele Hutchison, Open Letter, Rochester, USA, 2009.
Ilja Leonard Pfeijffer, *La Superba*, translated by Michele Hutchison, Deep Vellem, Dallas, USA, 2016.

Two Poems

By Ilja Leonard Pfeijffer

Farewell Dinner

you can clear the table
the white-fringed nouvelle cuisine amuse-gueule
of chrysanthemums that are standing in the vase on the table by the window
but are not standing in the vase on the table by the window
vegetarian still-lifes sketched with the silver pen

bring in the well-filled roast game pierced by the larding-pin
and on a frank layer of dancing meat zap to shiny, lusty meat
like a clip in full-sized colour

serve me images baked in butter
and verses with bulimia

Afscheidsdiner

u kunt afruimen
de witomrande amuse gueule uit de nouvelle cuisine
van chrysanten die in de vaas op de tafel bij het raam staan
maar niet in de vaas op de tafel bij het raam staan
vegetarische stilleventjes geschetst met de zilverstift

laat met de lardeerpriem doorregen goed gevulde
wildbraad aanrukken en op een rondborstig banket
van dansend vlees zappen naar glimmend wellustig vlees
als een clip in grootbeeld kleur

serveer mij in roomboter gebakken beelden
en verzen met boulemie

From: *Van de vierkante man* (Of the Square Man), 1998

But friends, all you little poets of the Netherlands so dear
and Belgium, I really must talk to you. I fear
the weather has turned. Winter is coming. The nights
throw off their sweaty covers with tossing mental flights.
The days are rattled off. Otherwise
the right questions would arise.
Cold dishes are served with a shiver. Fear
is of fearful things what we most fear.
We can no longer make do with kitty pictures that
fit our profile, predictably unusual chat
on how the pancakes and the Moroccan's pals,
on how there are mirror bikes in the canals
on how the Vondelpark and then on your doorstep, a bit
about the past now, one day perhaps and dog shit
that's been accepted for a collection of art,
on the relativising of a broken heart,
on house plants in which Nietzsche's face is detected,
on the existence of suburbs unsuspected,
on shuffleboard referees, orange committee,
worries, puppy love. I say not me.
Whoever still dares to write has the solemn duty
to produce more than something passably pretty
that looks in amazement at feelings, which dazed
and very moved looks like everything amazed
that was once wrongly looked on as verse.
We must face up to the fact that it's quite the reverse:
our cosy niche threatens to get cosier still.
While at the fragile gate the hordes are out to kill
our debate is on how to masturbate.
We still have subsidies to fill our plate,
while we knit on spools like girls. But I'm telling you.
Because what we do is, put briefly or at length, not true.
It is untruth the truth to negate
while our own pastime we simply create,
and loudly thump our own breast and each other's nose,
artillery booms over the horizon. No cock crows,
though we have already betrayed each other at least thrice.
Wading through each other's swamps in pink wellies so nice
and blowing tender bubbles in the bath of balls and stuff –
we can do that and I have had enough.
A man is not made just eggs to lay.
Whoever thinks he has something to say, something must say.
The winter's coming and will last many years.
The poets will sing by the fires full of fears
or will no longer be poets. We must know everything

those googling fingers daily forget.
No more deconstructions, no cryptogram, no quiz.
We must learn to tell it like it is.
In the past I myself had erred.
Uprooter that I used to be. The false word
that I had to loosen the loose screws even more
and must passionately bury heaps of certainties galore,
did not do the business any good.
Someone with a good question wants to be understood,
since otherwise there'll be no one left to understand.
Gasping for air with too much air I stand,
being out of breath with wild coughing strangulate
while I underestimated how people calculate
and really need everything today
except what makes certainties ebb away.
The romanticism of épater la bourgeoisie
has gathered dust like a precious reliquary
that has lost relevance and urgency, it's plain.
Whoever doesn't know how to feel, should listen again.
Prophets don't stand in the sand on a rock,
to be unheard alone in their camelhair frock.
When the world goes crazy with madmen's chat
he will explain on prime-time just where it's at
and in the mud, high-vis jacket to the chin
will survive in harmony with the next of kin.
There's a storm. Or is it the hooves of the hordes
raising dust from the south to the fjords
and oceans with their rage will return
so that dry land will become calm sea and lakes in cities churn,
and automats will dispense ice and our cash amount
like constantly falling dust one can no longer count?
From our outposts I hear the strangest convolution:
we've been relieved by evolution.
The towers have long since fallen. The day after tomorrow
will most probably be even worse than tomorrow.
I don't want to sit here being apocalyptic.
But winter's coming. We must learn to read the skies, though cryptic.
So friends, great poets of all the Netherlands
and Belgium, where there is shouting language has no plans.
I ask nothing, want nothing, demand nothing, have nothing to explain.
But perhaps we can begin to say something again?

Maar vrienden, lieve dichtertjes van Nederland
en België, ik moet met jullie praten. Want
het weer is omgeslagen. Winter komt. De nachten
ontbloten zich bezweet met woelende gedachten.
De dagen worden afgeraffeld. Anders zouden
de juiste vragen aan de orde komen. Koude
gerechten worden rillend opgediend. De angst
is van de bange dingen wel het allerbangst.
We kunnen nu niet meer volstaan met poezenplaatjes
op ons profiel, voorspelbaar ongewone praatjes
van hoe de pannenkoeken en de Marokkaan,
van hoe er spiegelfietsen in de grachten staan,
van hoe het Vondelpark en daarna op je stoep,
van vroeger, nu en ooit misschien en hondenpoep
die in een kunstcollectie opgenomen is,
van het relativeren van een groot gemis,
van kamerplanten die op Friedrich Nietzsche lijken,
van het bestaan van onvermoede buitenwijken,
van sjoelbakcontroleurs, oranjecomité,
beslommeringen, poppenliefdes. Ik zeg nee.
Wie nu nog durft te schrijven, heeft de dure plicht
iets méér te leveren dan een zesmingedicht
dat met verwondering naar de ontroering kijkt
en zeer ontroerd verwonderd echt op alles lijkt
wat eerder al ten onrechte werd aangezien
voor poëzie. We moeten onder ogen zien
dat onze knusse niche steeds knusser dreigt te worden.
Terwijl de broze poort belaagd wordt door de horden,
gaat ons debat erover hoe te masturberen.
We kunnen nu nog even op subsidies teren
en punniken als meisjes. Maar. Er is een maar.
Want wat wij doen is, lang of kort gepraat, niet waar.
Het is onwaarheid om de waarheid te negeren.
Terwijl we slechts ons eigen tijdverdrijf creëren
en luid op eigen borst en elkaars smoelen slaan,
weergalmt geschut achter de kim. Er kraait geen haan,
al hebben we elkaar toch ruim drie keer verraden.
Op roze laarsjes door elkaars moerasjes waden
en broze bellen blazen in het ballenbad ---
dat kunnen we en daarmee heb ik het gehad.
Een mens is niet gemaakt om eieren te leggen.
Wie iets te zeggen meent te hebben, moet iets zeggen.
De winter komt en hij zal vele jaren duren.
De dichters zullen zingen bij de bange vuren
of niet meer dichters zijn. We moeten alles weten

wat googelende vingers dagelijks vergeten.
Geen deconstructies meer, geen cryptogram, geen quiz.
We zullen moeten leren zeggen hoe het is.
Ik heb het zelf in het verleden fout gedaan,
ontwortelaartje dat ik mij daar was. De waan
dat ik de toch al losse schroeven nog meer moest
ontregelen en hoopjes zekerheden woest
moest ondergraven, heeft de zaak geen goed gedaan.
Ook wie een goede vraag heeft, wil worden verstaan,
want anders is er niemand meer die het nog snapt.
Ik heb met te veel lucht naar lucht gehapt
om ademnood met woest gehoest te laten stikken,
terwijl ik onderschatte hoe de mensen wikken
en wegen en aan alles echt behoefte hebben
behalve aan wat zekerheden weg doet ebben.
De romantiek van épater la bourgeoisie
heeft stof verzameld als een dierbaar relikwie
dat relevantie en urgentie heeft verloren.
Wie niet weet hoe hij voelen moet, moet weer eens horen.
Profeten staan niet op een rots in de woestijn
om eenzaam kemelharig ongehoord te zijn.
Wanneer de wereld doldraait van de gekkenpraat,
zal hij op prime-time uitleggen waar het om gaat
en in de modder met een fluorhesje aan
met nabestaanden zeer eendrachtig nabestaan.
Het onweert. Of is dat de hoefslag van de horden
die stof opwerpen van het zuiden tot het noorden
en oceanen met hun woede zullen keren
dat droog land stille zee wordt en de steden meren,
de automaten ijs verstrekken en ons geld
als almaar vallend stof niet langer wordt geteld?
Ik hoor het raarste nieuws van onze buitenposten:
we zijn de door de evolutie afgelosten.
De torens zijn al lang gevallen. Overmorgen
zal hoogstwaarschijnlijk almaar slechter zijn dan morgen.
Ik wil hier niet apocalyptisch zitten wezen.
Maar winter komt. We moeten luchten leren lezen.
Dus vrienden, grote dichters van heel Nederland
en België, waar wordt geschreeuwd is taal vacant.
Ik vraag niets, wil niets, eis niets, heb niets uit te leggen.
Maar kunnen we misschien beginnen iets te zeggen?

From: *Idyllen. Nieuwe poëzie* (Idylls. New Poetry), 2015
Translated by Paul Vincent

An Extract from *Letters from Genoa*

By Ilja Leonard Pfeijffer

Letter to Europe

You sit in your flat in Brussels and watch the television. The news has been showing the same images for months. Thousands of Africans, setting off from the Libyan coast, where you were born, in rickety, crowded, barely seaworthy boats, risking their lives, driven by despair, with hope in their eyes, are trying to cross the sea you crossed. They are fleeing from wars, oppression and poverty that you yourself caused. Many do not make it. They were given too little water and too little petrol. There are too many of them. The boat lets in water. The waves are too high. There are too many waves. They had said it was not far. They had said they would be rescued. Sometimes hundreds of them drown at once. They had promised them the promised land and not the sea. But now they will forever see the sea with dead eyes. It is your sea. The sea that was there at your birth and to which you were always so happy to return on holiday with flowers on your summer dress and flip-flops, sipping at your cava, prosecco or retsina, has now become a mass grave.

Thousands of Syrians, Iraqis and Afghans, crouched on the axles of speeding lorries or hidden inside airtight containers or refrigeration units, driven by despair, with hope in their eyes, risking their lives, are trying to reach the coast from where they will be able to see Greece, the land where you were made a woman and became an adult. They are fleeing the wars that you yourself caused. Many do not make it. There are too many roads and too many borders and checkpoints. There are too many minutes that last hours. They hold their breath in fear and do not dare to move. There are too many bumps in the road. The cargo begins to shift. The pallets of tinned dogfood and crates of frozen fish that they hide behind press into their legs, backs and chests. There are too many of them and there is not enough oxygen. They suffocate on your roads, dozens of them at once. A dead toddler washes up onto a Greek beach. It is your beach, where you gave life to your three sons and to which you were always so glad to go back on holiday in your swimsuit with the flowers on, to lie in the sun, as an eagle flew by high above you, and not to have to think about anything for a little while and to listen to the splashing of the sea, the sea.

You might expect that those who do make it, those who succeed in reaching your coasts, would be welcomed as heroes, just as people welcome athletes who have performed arduous physical and mental feats. But they represent the wrong countries and the people here are not fans of their sport, the aim of which is to stay alive and to be permitted to live like the people who see them on television. It is all too serious. Feelings of fear and guilt are involved. It has to remain entertainment, after all. They are afraid that they are coming too close and wonder if there are enough televisions to satisfy all those foreigners.

They themselves had to work hard for their television and they are scared that the black people are coming to take it away.

You might think that those who have succeeded in escaping poverty, oppression and war, those who have been able to reach the Free West, would be embraced as brothers, just as we embraced as brothers the Hungarians in 1956, the Czechs in 1968 and the East Germans in 1989, those who had crept through the Iron Curtain or climbed over the Wall to flee communist dictatorships and finally join us in freedom. But they have the wrong names and are the wrong colour. They kneel to the wrong God. There are too many of them. No one can cope with so many brothers. New walls are hastily constructed and barriers of barbed wire are erected in an attempt to stop them.

[...]

You stand up from your chaise longue, turn off the television and hobble on your old, stiff legs to the windows of your flat in Brussels to close the shutters. If you do not see the pariahs, perhaps they will automatically cease to exist. All you really want is to be left in peace with your memories of simpler times when the world outside stayed outside. But you are old, Madame. I love you dearly and to me you are still just as beautiful as when you crossed the sea as a girl with a basket of flowers on the back of a bull and, face to face with an eagle, became a woman, or even more beautiful than that, as history has furrowed and adorned your face with character and sorrowful wisdom, but we have to recognise, you and I, that you are old. Your pale, thin hands are almost transparent. They can plough no more soil, thresh no more grain, and knead no more dough. You cannot even dress yourself anymore. Your gowns, negligees, handbags and boas come from China. Your fantasies are made in Hollywood and your telephone calls are conducted by someone in India. All you have now is your memories, which you can sell. But that does not bring in enough even to cover your doctors' bills. Your old age is costing more than you can make. You cannot carry on like this. Someone should take care of you.

And when you open your shutters again and look outside, I will tell you what you see. What has travelled from afar from the land where you were born and has come to you across the sea you crossed is your youth. See how broad their black backs are and how strong their black muscles. They are like bulls. See that look of hope and fighting spirit in their eyes. It is the look of an eagle. You must not be afraid of them. You need them. They are exactly what you need. There is nothing you need more than them. Open your windows, unlock your door, and welcome them. Bring them inside and embrace them. Hang garlands of flowers around their necks. They are your future.

From *Brieven uit Genua* (Letters from Genoa),
Arbeiderspers, Amsterdam, 2016

Translated by Laura Watkinson

Film as a Reflexive Medium and a Productive Space

The Artist Wendelien van Oldenborgh

[MIRJAM WESTEN]

'In the Netherlands, with its open and democratic society, inconvenient voices are cut short by the way other voices in society react to them.'
Katerina Gregos (2011)[1]

Wendelien van Oldenborgh (Rotterdam, b. 1962) has since 2000 been making her mark with remarkable film and slide installations in which she touches on topics concerning social relations, migration, racism and gender. Often these are 'neglected' topics from the past, lying dormant just below the surface of the present. One subject that has received her particular attention since 2005 is the influence of the Netherlands' colonial past on the present and on the self-image of the Dutch. With such film installations as *Mauritsscript* (2006), *No false echoes* (2008), *Instruction* (2009) and *La Javanaise* (2012), she is one of the few artists to have contributed to the 'faltering post-colonial discourse' in the 'colour-blind' Netherlands.[2]

Her film oeuvre is characterised by its considerable discursiveness: we see participants in conversation with each other, reading out a text or making music together. What is important is that no one single voice predominates. The artist is concerned with polyphony, enabling the different voices to be heard alongside one another. One of the essential principles of her method is the interaction between the invited participants, who sometimes hardly know each other nor have previously practised together, and their collaboration with the artist. Van Oldenborgh does not see herself as a director; she rarely uses a written script, does not give any directions, and at most steers them a little this way or that. She brings the people together, and what they say depends on who they are, whether young or old, black or white, individual or group, with all their different backgrounds. Sometimes she asks them to read out particular historical texts, after which they discuss the content. Though what is to be recited or discussed is considered on the basis of specific questions before filming. The participants do not play a particular role, but play themselves, and their dialogue unfolds on the spot. Van Oldenborgh aims to create a sort of 'aliveness', where the camera functions as a catalyst in these live moments. Everything is moving all the time and can be adjusted as it goes along; differences of opinion are heard and explored. Using the film medium, Van Oldenborgh creates an ac-

tive space that is built up by means of sound, text, image and recognition, and with which she 'enables visible and invisible connections between historical expositions and contemporary reality to unfold'.[3] According to the art historian Sven Lütticken, the way the participants play themselves 'not only makes history as tangible as the nagging tragedy of modernity, but also allows possible alternative histories and unwritten futures to show through.'[4] By means of the conversations between the participants, Van Oldenborgh creates a new view of the past, and thereby of the present, without otherwise drawing any conclusions.

Other voices on 'Dutch Tolerance'

In 2017, she exhibited three lenticular photographic works and two video installations under the title *Cinema Olanda* in the Dutch Pavilion at the Venice Biennale. The two-part *Prologue: Squat/Anti-Squat* (2016) consists of two films shot in the Tripolis office building designed by Hannie and Aldo van Eyck and built in South Amsterdam in 1994. In this diptych we see people of different generations talking to each other about their involvement in the Surinamese-Antillean activist movement, which in the 1970s organised squats on the Bijlmer housing estate and exposed the housing policy concerning Surinamese and Antillean people who moved to the Netherlands. The former activists talk to youngsters who were involved in the recent squatting campaign by the asylum-seekers' 'We Are Here' movement. *Prologue: Squat/Anti-Squat* is 'fuelled' by information from the *Vereniging Ons Suriname* (Association for Our Surinam) and by several archives at the International Institute of Social History. Her latest film, also titled *Cinema Olanda* (2017) was inspired by histories to be found in 'The Black Archives', a collection of documents on black history and culture in and outside the Netherlands.[5]

In their presentation in Venice, Van Oldenborgh and the curator Lucy Cotter wanted to shed a different light on the Netherlands. The rational, clear and transparent look of the 1953 pavilion designed by Gerrit Rietveld (acclaimed as the 'triumph of modernism') contributed to the image of the post-war Netherlands as a country of transparency, openness and progress. They adjust this image, which the Netherlands actively propagates, by bringing 'other voices' to the fore to expose a less rose-tinted side of the Netherlands' so-called progressive post-war modernity: the exclusion of 'newcomers' from Indonesia and Surinam and the distrust of socialist and communist movements which in the preceding decades had been closely interwoven with the ideals of the avant-garde.

Although Van Oldenborgh's work was until recently largely given a positive reception in art and opinion magazines and newspapers, the presentation in the Giardini was very critically received in the Netherlands, with the exception of the weekly paper *De Groene Amsterdammer*.[6] According to the art critic Rutger Pontzen, the artist is overestimating her own powers, and the film *Cinema Olanda* does not work at all. He condescendingly dismisses Van Oldenborgh and Cotter as '*Gutmenschen*'. His most serious complaint is that this latest film contains too much information – enough for five episodes of the TV series *Andere Tijden* (Other Times) – so that the intentions float around like 'loose scraps of ideas' in a 'revolting noncommittalism'.[7] Hilda Bouma characterises Van Oldenborgh's films as incomprehensible to the average Biennale visitor, but does give the artist 'marks for her good intentions', because she 'corrects the image of the renowned Dutch tolerance'.[8]

Unlike the foreign press, the reactions in the Netherlands were so disparaging that the young Dutch writer Frank Keizer published an open declaration of support in the online periodical *Rekto:Verso*. He accused Dutch art critics of taking a long detour around post-colonial history.[9] Although in general I endorse this, I nevertheless wonder whether this really is the crux of the matter. Is the criticism a consequence of a lack of familiarity with the stories, and out of irritation because it is not made immediately clear what we are watching? Is it because of the way of filming? Or 'did we Dutch not recognise ourselves' and 'did we look into a white mirror and see black nonsense'? as Roos van Lint, art editor of *De Groene Amsterdammer* wondered. Whatever the answer is to these questions, it is a fact that *Cinema Olanda* is indeed fuelled by a large amount of information and topics which, in contrast to all Van Oldenborgh's previous works, do not unfold *in relation to each other* from the beginning, but seem more likely to have been simply threaded together. The film raises a great many questions and discussions that touch on the complexity and stratification of modernity and the formation of images and which, indeed, cannot be grasped in the blink of an eye. What are these stories?

Cinema Olanda was shot in a single take and is set near Sint Bavo, the modernist church in the post-war district of Pendrecht in Rotterdam.[10] Even before we see a single image, we hear a conversation about the German-Dutch architect Lotte Stam-Beese (1903-1988) who designed this district. She was one of a generation of architects who combined *Nieuwe Bouwen* ('New Building') with social awareness and was active in movements that opposed fascism. In the 1930s she was involved in the construction of towns and cities in the Soviet Union and, as an urban development architect, played a major role in the reconstruction in and around the city of Rotterdam after the Second World War. Then a young black man (Mitchell Esajas)[11] appears on the screen, standing on the constructivist spiral staircase in the detached belfry of the church, and reads from the biography of the Surinamese-Dutch political activist Otto Huiswoud (Paramaribo, 1893 – Amsterdam, 1961). Huiswoud was a co-founder and the first black member of the Communist Party in America. Through their international contacts, he and his wife Hermine Dumont (1905-1998) were pivotal in anti-colonial movements. They contributed to the international magazine *The Negro Worker*.[12] In 1949 they settled in Amsterdam, where Huiswoud became the chairman of the *Vereniging Ons Suriname* (Association for Our Surinam).[13] The camera then moves from the belfry to a number of women standing at the side of the church: cultural historian Hanneke Oosterhof, cultural anthropologist Lizzy van Leeuwen and historian Maria Cijntje-van Enckevort. They are talking about the Indonesian migrants who came to the Netherlands after the Second World War.[14] When the young man joins them, they ask him whether he too would become a member of an international revolutionary movement. Together with a group of parishioners consisting mainly of local Antillean, Syrian and African residents, the group goes inside the church, where their conversation is drowned out by an indo-rock number by the guitarists Lode Simons and Remy Sonneville.[15] The camera then zooms in on a conversation about well-known freedom fighters and writers with whom Otto and Hermine had been in

Wendelien van Oldenborgh,
Cinema Olanda (film still), 2017

Wendelien van Oldenborgh,
Cinema Olanda (production image), 2017

contact. At the end of the fifteen-minute film, a woman (the Surinamese-Dutch artist Patrician Kaersenhout) reads out a text by the American poet Langston Hughes (1902-1967), who played a major part in the literary 'Harlem Renaissance' movement and who was a friend of the Huiswouds: 'I do not need my freedom when I am dead / I cannot live on tomorrow's bread // Freedom / Is a strong seed / Planted / In a great need // I live here too / I want freedom / Just as you.' Immediately after this, the local teenage band Addiction plays 'Labels', a number written specially for *Cinema Olanda*, which is about the way we dismiss others by 'labelling' them. As the credits begin, we hear Kaersenhout's voice continuing; the 'black struggle' always felt like someone else's history, until she heard about Huiswoud. She wonders how it is possible that she had never previously heard of the Surinamese-Dutch Huiswoud, while other Afro-Caribbean freedom fighters with whom he was in contact are still known today and play a part in the post-colonial debate. It is only when she poses this question that it suddenly occurs to me as I watch the film what the effect is of history written from a particular point of view, and which stories are out of place in the image of the open, tolerant and modern state that the Netherlands has made itself out to be – not only during the reconstruction period, but also in the present day. I was touched above all by the tone of her voice, in which sincere amazement and regret can be heard. And it was this that persuaded me of the power of *Cinema Olanda*. All at once, the various stories fit together like parts of a puzzle.

Wendelien van Oldenborgh, installation views from *Cinema Olanda*, 2017

Wendelien van Oldenborgh, installation views from *Cinema Olanda*, 2017

Slowness challenges the Netflix view

In an interview published in the voluminous publication *Amateur* (2016), Van Oldenborgh commented that she finds it nice 'to see that, outside their immediate context, certain topics are able to bring about something rich and full – that it is not necessarily about others, but that after seeing the work you can actually conclude, we now know something more about ourselves'.[16]

The artist does not make it easy for the viewer, however. It is typical of her filmmaking strategy: she does not present unambiguous storylines that are simple to follow. There is no traditional development with a clear beginning, climax or final conclusion with which you may or may not agree. There is no sign of a single leading actor, as the participants are all protagonists. Van Oldenborgh deliberately frustrates the viewer's desire to identify with or latch onto a single story; she presents numerous stories in parallel, letting them jump about in time, and all these elements are equally important. She also makes it hard for us to identify with the participants; they read something out and comment on it on the spot, so that there is a degree of alienation. This effect is increased by her frequent tendency to film from an annoyingly long distance; if she does zoom in, she rarely shows the whole face. And while I make an effort to listen to their voices I am quite regularly distracted by the movement of the camera, which wanders around and focusses on an insignificant detail of the wall, floor or staircase. I invariably wonder whether this has some meaning or is a matter of carelessness. In any case, the slowness of the images challenges the perverted Netflix view that is used to a change of image every three seconds. I find it hard to watch with concentration for a long time.

Mauritsscript, 2006. Stills from the video installation
Courtesy Wilfrid Lenz Rotterdam and the artist

Those who are speaking do not look straight at me, the viewer, and do not speak to me, but to each other. Yet I still feel as if I am being spoken to. I don't fully understand how this swing takes place, from the initial feeling of being kept at a distance to something that 'resounds' inside me. Van Oldenborgh has developed an ingenious way of making the viewer a partner in the process in which the participants are not directed, but give themselves the room to ask themselves and others questions and make connections between the past and pressing issues of the day, on the basis of their own knowledge and experience, and with all their hesitations and moments of silence.

Since 2005, Van Oldenborgh has made sixteen installations using this film-based approach.[17] The locations are also significant: the room, the building, the architecture – as in the case of Rietveld's pavilion in *Cinema Olanda* – are symbolic and sometimes form a historical reference. For instance, the filming for the installation *Mauritsscript* (2006), which is about the legacy of seventeenth-century colonial history, took place in the Mauritshuis in The Hague. Johan Maurits van Nassau had this 'Sugar Palace' built during his governorship of Brazil (1637-1644), with the money he earned 'off the backs of the enslaved Africans'.[18] The film material for the installation *Beauty and the Right to the Ugly* (2014), on the ideals and limits of the shapeable society, was shot in 't Karregat, a multipurpose community centre in Eindhoven which in the 1970s raised eyebrows with its large open space without walls. According to its architect, Van Klingeren, its users had to 'unclump'.

One factor in her oeuvre that is quite significant is the way she not only involves people of different cultural backgrounds in her work, but also brings together people of different ages to look back at history. One of the most moving films in this regard is *Instruction* (2009). We see four young soldiers during their training in a classroom at the Royal Military Academy modestly reading out texts relating to the violent 'politionele acties' (police actions) with which the Netherlands tried to prevent the independence of its former colony in 1946-1949. When the cadets then discuss the political and military analyses, a 1969 television script, the memoires of Captain Westerling and a 1981 travel report by Van Oldenborgh's mother, their struggle with such questions as the moral role of the individual and taking the law into one's own hands suddenly comes very close to home.

A major source of inspiration for Van Oldenborgh during her studies at Goldsmiths College in London was the South African-British theorist and curator Sarat Maharaj, who, with his 'ethics of difference', offered alternatives to the Eurocentric approach to art history. These 'ethics of difference', which he defines as 'the struggle to construct meaning together, across the border of cultural difference' can be traced as an important thread in Van Oldenborgh's oeuvre.[19] The urgency of the issues she broaches is already apparent from the furore that arose around the programme 'Cinema Olanda: Platform' that was held at the Witte de With Centre for Contemporary Art in summer 2017. A group of artists, activists and academics accused the arts centre of showing off in its discussion of decolonisation while its policy remained essentially the same: 'White institutions fortify themselves through the consumption of Blackness. Black people pass through them, seemingly without transforming them – they extract what they need from us to sustain their "criticality"'. In an open letter to the arts centre they also demand that it change its name: Witte Corneliszoon de With, often described as a 'hero of the seas' in the history books, was among other things involved in the siege of Jakarta (1618) and the plundering of the Moluccas.[20]

It looks as if the post-colonial debate in the Netherlands is now truly stepping up a gear and I expect it to become more intense, thanks in part to Van Oldenborgh.[21] ∎

La Javanaise, 2012. Production still by Barbara Wagner
Courtesy Wilfried Lenz Rotterdam and the artist

1   Speech Matters. Catalogue of the Danish Pavilion, 2011 Venice Biennale, p. 80.

2   Lizzy van Leeuwen, 'Voor wie het wil zien. Over de nationale herrijzenis en de Indische intocht'. *De Groene Amsterdammer*, 9 May 2017. Supplement to Vol. 141, No. 19, Cinema Olanda.

3   Interview in *Metropolis M*, issue 3, 2017.

4   *Amateur*, p. 45.

5   Delano Veira, director of *Vereniging Ons Suriname* at Amsterdam shared a lot of information. The artist also consulted archives at the International Institute of Social History, Amsterdam, such as Cineclub Vrijheidsfilms, LOSON and the 'Staatsarchief' (squat movement). 'The Black Archives' are an initiative by Jessica de Abreu, Mitchell Esajas and Miguel Heilbron. Their intention is to document and conserve the history of black emancipation movements and individuals in the Netherlands and make them visible and accessible to the public. The archives are housed in the building of the *Vereniging Ons Suriname* in Amsterdam.

6   This weekly is the media partner for the 'Cinema Olanda' project and was commissioned by the Mondriaanfonds to publish a special supplement on the Dutch entry on 11 May 2017.

7   Rutger Pontzen, 'Pijnlijk: Van Oldenborgh overschat zichzelf op Biënnale Venetië'. *De Volkskrant*, 10 May 2017. The 'Gutmensch' not only wants to do good, but also wants to be known for doing it.

8   *Het Financieele dagblad*, 25 May 2017. The Mondriaanfonds compares a number of reviews that appeared in Dutch publications with foreign newspapers. https://www.mondriaanfonds.nl/2017/06/13/reacties-op-cinema-olanda/

9   Available at: https://www.rektoverso.be/artikel/beste-wendelien-van-oldenborgh

10   The church was designed by H.N.M. Nefkens and was first used in 1960. Its construction is exceptional: the roof is supported by a structure of seven curved concrete ribs. The south wall consists of colourful glass-in-concrete by Bob Zijlmans.

11   Mitchell Esajas works at the University of Amsterdam and is a co-founder of the youth platform *New Urban Collective* and of The Black Archives.

12   As from 1930, the magazine *The Negro Worker* (1928-37) was financed by the *International Trade Union Committee for Black Workers*, an international communist organisation.

13   Huiswoud played an important part in the *Vereniging Ons Suriname*. He agitated vehemently against the Dutch policy on the independence of Surinam and invited influential Afro-American human rights activists to a talk in Amsterdam, including W.E.B. Du Bois. The esteem in which Huiswoud was held was still apparent years after his death; in Surinamese and communist circles in 1988, the 95th anniversary of his birth was commemorated with all sorts of activities. *De Waarheid*, 5 November 1988.

14   Oosterhof is engaged in doctoral research into Lotte Stam-Beese; Van Leeuwen is an expert in the position of Indian Dutch people in the post-colonial era; Cijntje-van Enckewort is doing her PhD on Huiswoud.

15   Indo-rock is mainly instrumental rock-'n-roll, performed by musicians from the former Dutch Indies. It provided the foundations for 'nederpop'.

16   *Amateur*, Frédérique Bergholtz, p. 368.

17   For her method, see: http://www.acertainbrazilianness.net/htmlpages/introduction.html#method.

18   When the Mauritshuis in The Hague reopened in 2014, it was followed in the online history magazine *Historiek* by a polemic between Zihni Özdil (lecturer at the Erasmus University) and Piet Emmer (Emeritus Professor of the History of European Expansion). Özdil criticised the omission of the Mauritshuis's historical connections with slavery on its official website and in its educational material. According to him, this history had also been 'pasteurised out of existence' in all the reports on the renovation of the Mauritshuis. According to Piet Emmer, Özdil wants to 'criticise the past by means of the values and standards of the present, and his aims seem not to extend further than that.' And:

'Özdil completely ignores the useful effect of what he sees as Johan Maurits's exorbitant lifestyle. Because, by taking countless artists and scholars to his colony, Dutch Brazil became the most studied and most illustrated exotic region of the seventeenth century. Botanists, ornithologists, historians and art historians if not more scientists are still reaping the fruit of this, while The Hague was enriched with a superb mansion, which is for that matter of very modest size by foreign standards.' http://historiek.net/het-slavernijverleden-van-het-mauritshuis/44119/. Emmer did not deal with Özdil's core criticism that the museum had deliberately erased this history of slavery. Özdil reacted to this in http://historiek.net/de-drogredeneringen-van-piet-emmer/44146/.

The Mauritshuis took this criticism seriously: on its website, there is now a reference to the historical connection with slavery dated 2/7/2017, at https://www.mauritshuis.nl/nl-nl/ontdek/mauritshuis/slavernij/. Under the heading 'history of the building', we read this: 'Some people also mockingly referred to the Mauritshuis as the "Sugar Palace". This was a reference not only to its light-coloured stone facades, but also to the source of Johan Maurits's income. In Brazil, he earned a lot of money for the West Indian Company, and for himself, through the trade in cane sugar. Its production was made possible by the use of enslaved men and women from Africa. So Johan Maurits was able to build his house in The Hague not only due to cane sugar, but also due to slavery.'

19 *Amateur*, p. 331.

20 http://www.metropolism.com/nl/news/31933_open_letter_to_witte_de_with. This arts centre thinks that a new name would clean up the link with the past, while it is precisely discussion of the topic that is so important. Since then, the website has given information on its role in colonial history under the heading 'Disclosure: Witte Corneliszoon de With'.

http://www.wdw.nl/nl/pages/acknowledgement_witte_orneliszoon_de_with.

21 But, as she emphasised in the conversation dated 25 April 2017, she is not speaking on behalf of 'others'.

Translated by Gregory Ball

The Dutch Revolt Began 450 Years Ago

William of Orange and the Wilhelmus Still Alive and Kicking

[HANS COOLS]

At the beginning of November 2017 the third Rutte cabinet took office in the Netherlands. One of its aims, according to the coalition agreement, is 'to increase knowledge of our shared history, values and freedoms.' It follows that the coalition partners have a pronounced opinion on that 'shared history'. 'Equality, regardless of gender, sexual orientation or religion; tolerance towards those holding different opinions and division of church and state. ... Those are values of which we are proud and which make us who we are.'

Obviously those 'values' derive from Dutch history. Indeed, the coalition partners believe they can point to the moment of their birth. Now that knowledge of them is under pressure 'in times of uncertainty and globalisation', they charge schools with the responsibility of 'teaching children the Wilhelmus, including its context.'

That is an odd diktat. The origin of the Wilhelmus is as a beggars' (rebel) song. It dates from about 1570, a few years after rebels in the Low Countries had taken up arms against their legitimate monarch, Philip II. In fifteen couplets the anonymous author describes the dilemma facing the leader of the rebels, Prince William of Orange: how to serve the Dutch, without failing in his loyalty to the king. Trust in God must provide the key. Because of its great propaganda value the song was never entirely forgotten in the succeeding centuries. In 1932, after a lobbying campaign by among others the celebrated historian Johan Huizinga, it finally acquired the status of the Dutch national anthem. Initially the choice of the Wilhelmus was anything but uncontroversial. Social Democrats and Communists were opposed to it. Only during the Second World War did the song grow into a widely supported symbol against the German occupying forces.

So the Wilhelmus is definitely part of the Dutch cultural heritage. But the song says next to nothing about the 'values' that the coalition partners, according to the coalition agreement, associate with Dutch identity. Such ideas were not yet current in 1570. Only two centuries later, in 'the period of wigs and revolutions', did some of them become common coin. Others were not generally accepted until the late twentieth century.

The idea of making knowledge of the Wilhelmus a compulsory part of the school curriculum comes from the Christian Democrat party. But it also reso-

William of Orange and
Marnix of Saint-Aldegond,
Antwerp, 2012
© Jean-Paul Laenen

nated with progressives. In the favourite publication of the left-wing intelli-
gentsia, *De Groene Amsterdammer*, influential voices like Herman Vuijsje and
Elsbeth Etty stressed that the text is first and foremost a call to oppose tyranny.
This, they argued, gave it enduring topicality.

The search for common ground in the past

The intensive search for their identity by the Dutch has been underway for a
good decade and a half. Pim Fortuyn was the first established politician to give
voice to the growing discontent with progressive European integration and continuing immigration. His murder, in the spring of 2002, deflated the myth of
an open, virtually non-violent society which had gained currency in the 1960s
and 1970s. Since then the belief that history gives meaning to the present has
been renewed, and fearing that knowledge of history is becoming lost the government is trying desperately to maintain it. In 2006, for example, a govern-
ment-sponsored 'national canon' was produced. If the new government has its
way, every Dutch citizen will henceforth be presented with a copy of that canon
booklet, and apart from that it will be an indispensable part of the naturalisa-
tion ceremony.

Almost axiomatically in this climate all kinds of groups appropriate history
for their own ends. For example, Dutch citizens of Surinamese origin have successfully drawn attention, both in the public arena and in academic research,
to the nation's slave-owning past and after an occasionally fierce debate
'Black Pete', the assistant of Saint Nicholas, is gradually disappearing from
the streets.

Taco Dibbits, the director of the Rijksmuseum in Amsterdam, has a sharp eye for such developments. In May 2016, in the knowledge that history can break or heal, he declared just before becoming director, in an interview for the *Art Newspaper*: 'The Rijksmuseum has the power to unite people... We must search for common ground in the past.' As a result in 2020 the Rijksmuseum will feature a general exhibition on the history of Dutch slavery. Before that, in the autumn of 2018 and spring 2019 the exhibition 'Eighty Years of War' will open. It looks as if that exhibition will anchor the image of William of Orange, and by extension the Dutch Revolt, in the national memory for at least one generation.

Eighty Years' War

Four hundred and fifty years earlier, in May 1568, the troops of Lodewijk van Nassau, William of Orange's brother, joined battle with the government forces led by Jan van Ligne, the local Habsburg governor, near Heiligerlee, in the extreme north-east of the Low Countries. That battle is regarded, somewhat arbitrarily, as the start of the Eighty Years' War, since in it the rebels had gained their first (Pyrrhic) victory on Dutch soil.

In reality there had been unrest for almost two years in the Low Countries. In August 1566 the Iconoclastic Fury was unleashed in South-West Flanders and had subsequently spread like an oil slick to large parts of the country. Ham-

Frans Hogenberg, *Mechelen Sacked by Spanish troops in 1572*, engraving, Rijksmuseum, Amsterdam

Erwin Olaf, *Exquisite Corpses. The Last Tribute to the Counts Egmond and Horn*, 2012
('Re-enactment' of the painting by Louis Gallait, 1851)

pered by the great distance – messages from the Low Countries took a month to reach Spain – Philip II reacted as if in slow motion. The expeditionary force under the command of the Duke of Alva charged with quelling the uprising, arrived only a year later in the Low Countries. When it subsequently became clear to William of Orange that he, like Counts Egmond and Horn, would be held responsible for the troubles and would pay a high price, the prince fled to his ancestral estates in order to direct the resistance from there. The battle of Heiligerlee was a part of an invasion plan coordinated by him. That plan failed dismally. But the revolt continued, gradually turning into a war and finally lasting eighty years.

Two very different states emerged from the war: the Republic of the United Provinces in the north and the royal, Habsburg Netherlands in the south. The former was the forerunner of the present Kingdom of the Netherlands, the latter, after various historical vagaries, became the Kingdom of Belgium.

North and South, then, share the past of the Dutch Revolt. But in the collective memories of the two nations the episode is housed in different places. In Belgium, anti-clerical activists presented themselves in the mid-nineteenth century as rebels (*geuzen*). They saw the *reconquista* by Philip II's regent Alessandro Farnese who between 1579 and 1585 had wound up the Calvinist city republics of, for example, Antwerp, Bruges, Brussels and Ghent and in so doing had reestablished Habsburg authority in the south, as a horrific scenario. For them the triumph of the counter-reformation church heralded a period of deep decline. A similar scenario threatened to repeat itself if the Catholics gained the upper hand over the Liberals in the party conflicts that flared up violently from time to time. Those sentiments were expressed in a masterly way by Charles de Coster in his *Légende … d'Ulenspiegel*, first published in 1867. The book, in fact the first important historical novel from French-speaking Belgium, soon achieved cult status. In the following century the hero Ulenspiegel appealed to much wider groups, from Flemish Nationalists collaborating with the German occupying forces to the Soviet director Aleksandr Alov, who filmed De Coster's novel in 1976.

So De Coster's *Ulenspiegel* was part of the historical culture of the young Belgian state. Meanwhile that shared historical culture has disappeared almost completely as a result of Flemish emancipation. French speakers can scarcely relate any longer to the past of the Dutch Revolt. Even as a *lieu de mémoire* this episode has disappeared from the collective past.

Adriaen Pietersz van de Venne, *Fishing for Souls*, 1614, oil on panel, 98.5 x 187.8 cm, Rijksmuseum, Amsterdam

Cover of the first impression of Charles de Coster, *La légende et les aventures héroïques,*
joyeuses et glorieuses d'Ulenspiegel et de Lamme Goedzak au pays de Flandres et ailleurs,
Paris (Librairie internationale), 1867. Engraving by Hippolyte Boulenger

A vulnerable hero

In Flanders the Revolt persisted longer as a living memory. Following the example of Charles de Coster at first mainly anti-clerical activists referred to it.
For example, in the mid-1870s, the Liberal Antwerp town council originally
named many streets in the newly developed Zuiderkwartier after heroes from
the Revolt. Where Alva's oppressive fortress had once stood, Graaf van Eg-
montstraat and Graaf van Hoornestraat were full of splendid mansions for the
rapidly expanding Antwerp bourgeoisie. Almost 150 years later, in 2012, they
were joined at the back of the Royal Fine Art Museum by statues of William of
Orange and Marnix of St. Aldegonde. They are surrounded by seventeen blue-
stone columns: one for each province. This stresses the sadness at the division
of the Low Countries and hence the (relative) decline of the south.

At the end of the 1970s best-selling author Louis Paul Boon still belonged to the old Belgian anti-clerical tradition. In his posthumously published *Geuzenboek* he described: 'how the South had gone under in blood and bitter tears... Having been misled the rebels, although they had been able to seize power, had stalled in their charge against the Roman Catholic church walls.' Driven by their own interests the high nobles, with William of Orange at their head, had like cynical power-brokers used the rage of the people for their own ends. Although *Het Geuzenboek* had been written quickly, was carelessly edited and became a very thick tome, the compelling style made up for all imperfections. Once he had come to himself again the influential Catholic critic Kees Fens stated in *De Volkskrant* that he 'had never been so anti-Catholic for seven hundred pages.'

The positive reception of Boon's *Geuzenboek* in the Netherlands too reflected the growing interest there in Flemish literature. Four years later Hugo Claus was to enjoy if anything even greater success with his *Sorrow of Belgium*. Meanwhile performing arts did not lag behind: in 1981 the Flemish cultural centre *De Brakke Grond* opened and from 1985 on the so-called 'Flemish wave' inundated Dutch theatres. Hence it was no surprise when in 1984 the Dutch and Flemish public broadcasting companies, exactly 400 years after the death of William of Orange, jointly produced a large-scale drama series. The William of Orange who emerged, convincingly played by Jeroen Krabbé, drank a lot and committed adultery. In brief, though plagued by doubt, he lived to excess. Only the influence of his parents made the prince realise that his instinctive dislike of the persecution of heretics, if it was not to become hypocrisy, required a break with the sovereign Philip II. The William of Orange of the television series was therefore a vulnerable hero, one who was far from achieving all his aims.

Monumental traces

The professional historians who focussed on William of Orange on the occasion of the commemorative year 1984, also mainly highlighted his limitations. They stressed, for example, that the prince's decision to begin the Revolt in 1568 was born of necessity, that his military understanding was minimal, that his stubborn clinging to French support led to a miscalculation and that in the last years of his life he increasingly became the hostage of Calvinist hardliners. The Revolt, his Revolt, had not united the Low Countries, but torn them apart. In this way the Revolt degenerated from an illustrious war of liberation against a foreign invader into a vulgar civil war.

Such a vision of the Revolt did not cause friction since meanwhile for the baby-boomer generation the Second World War had come to serve as the nation's moral benchmark. In the resistance against the German occupying forces and the securing of safe addresses for persecuted Jews, the modern secular Netherlands was born. In that vision the Eighty Years' War and its outcome were just a reminder of that wretched religious division and for the inhabitants of the meanwhile heavily urbanised southern provinces, the old Lands of the Generality, mainly of centuries of backwardness.

That development saddened Edgar Nordlohne (1922-1999) greatly. This erudite Liberal of Polish origin began as a journalist with the *Nieuwe Rotterdamse Courant* (NRC) and in 1968 transferred to the Ministry of Education and Sciences, where he became successively director of communications and senior advisor. In the latter position he was responsible for dossiers relating to the Dutch Language Union. Previously, in 1984, Nordlohne had represented his ministry on the committee coordinating events surrounding the 400th anniversary of the death of William of Orange. Even then his personal commitment was striking. He devised a television quiz, wrote a lesson plan for primary education and advised the creators of an educational exhibition. But Nordlohne felt something was missing. In the public realm there were virtually no monumental traces of William of Orange.

True, the Father of the Fatherland had as early as the early seventeenth century been given a splendid monumental tomb in Delft and in The Hague there were two nineteenth-century statues close together, one on Noordeinde and one on the Plein. But apart from that there was nothing. Nordlohne wanted to change all that. Successive ministers did not believe in his plan and so Nordlohne finally took the initiative himself. In 1989 he commissioned the Frisian sculptor Auke Hettema to produce a bronze portrait bust of William of Orange, which he then presented to the castle of Vianden in Luxemburg. The result was positively received and so Nordlohne set up a foundation in his will and generously bequeathed funds. The foundation is charged with the task of keeping alive through 'monumental historical instruction' the memory of William of Orange as 'an icon of freedom and tolerance.' Since then with funding from the Prince William I Foundation monuments have been erected in Delft, Dillenburg, Leiden, Middelburg, Antwerp (see above), The Hague and Paris. Negotiations are still continuing on the placing of a statue in Dordrecht.

Context please

So Nordlohne's statues restore William of Orange's heroic status and in the meantime fit seamlessly with the zeitgeist. 'Freedom and tolerance' were obviously the ideals that the prince embodied and in the name of which he began the Revolt against Philip II. They are also values with which the Dutch cabinet and by extension Dutch society identifies. But they say more about the present than the past. The cabinet seems to realise that, witness the addition that the Wilhelmus should be taught 'including the context'. Precisely for that reason one is so eagerly waiting for the exhibition that opens in the Rijksmuseum in autumn 2018. It seems to be just up Taco Dibbits's street. The fact that the same coalition agreement of Rutte III promises that all schoolchildren will have the chance of visiting the Rijksmuseum at least once during school hours, is for that reason alone a cause for rejoicing. ◾

Translated by Paul Vincent

Poetics of Postcolonial Art

The Installations of Ana Torfs

In Simon Schama's *Rembrandt's Eyes* (1999) we read how Rembrandt acquired a rare stuffed bird of paradise from New Guinea near the Spice Islands in the Moluccas, then part of the Dutch maritime empire. Schama describes it as 'not only an eye-filling wonder of dazzling plumage but the object of intense debate [....] as to whether the creature had legs'. To Rembrandt, the beautiful bird in his curiosity cabinet was an irresistible riddle, and in his studies in ink of the late 1630s, now in the Louvre, he drew it twice - once exactly as it was, without legs; then once more with legs added, supplying the missing detail by his art and imagination.

Equally, in 1644, when Johan Maurits of Nassau-Siegen, governor-general of Dutch Brazil, returned home, he was accompanied by a tribe of Tapuyas, his Native American allies against the Portuguese. In August that year, in his palace in The Hague (today the Mauritshuis museum), they gave a performance of their ceremonial music and dances. Then in May 1652 they appeared in Johan Maurits's reenactment at Cleves of the decisive battle between Rome and Carthage at Zama in 202 BCE, as captured and shackled barbarians in Scipio's victory parade after his annihilation of the enemy under Hannibal.

In both these cases of colonial contact and exchange we encounter what today is known as an installation – in Rembrandt's case, an anatomical experiment on one of the curiosities displayed in his cabinet; and in Johan Maurits's palace, the theatrical mise-en-scene of those 'Indians' in an imperial celebration of his dynasty. Both were part of a wider cultural innovation in early modern Europe. For, as we know from Stephen Greenblatt's *Marvelous Possessions* (1991), the discovery of the world brought along new and transforming ways of seeing, thinking, (re-)presenting and handling those exotic new realities.

Today, this fascination with people and objects from outside Europe continues, while being reinvented by artists working in a global context of critical postcolonial discourse. In 1992, for example, in a re-enactment of the colonial realities underlying Greenblatt's thesis, the performance artist Coco Fusco put herself on display as a captured Native American woman, held in a cage on a square in central Madrid - a bitter counterpoint to the lavish Spanish celebration of the discoveries of Columbus in 1492. And in The Hague in 1994 - inspired by Maria Dermoût's novel *The Ten Thousand Things* (1955), which is set

in the former Dutch East Indies - Renée Green produced *After the Ten Thousand Things*, an ethnographic installation exploring the dynamics of gathering and collecting but also the dispersal of objects and people, as well as the vicissitudes of colonial memory and its traces, which today can be as scattered as the collections that Johan Maurits brought with him as *souvenirs de Brésil*.

Echolalia

Against this historical and cultural background of colonial memories - beyond the horizon, half forgotten, fragmented, often contested - we will now take a closer look at the Belgian artist Ana Torfs and her eye-opening installations which, in their imaginative exploration of earlier globalities, are amongst the more interesting works of art to come out of the Low Countries in recent years. In particular we will consider the following four of her installations exploring (post-)colonial themes – *Family Plot* of 2009-2010; *[....] STAIN [....]* of 2012; *TXT (Engine of Wandering Words)* of 2013; and *The Parrot & the Nightingale, a Phantasmagoria* of 2014.

In 2016 the four were shown together in her solo exhibition, *Echolalia*, in the Centro de Arte Moderna of the Gulbenkian Museum in Lisbon. An interesting reference here is to the eponymous work by Daniel Heller-Roazen, quoted on the back cover of Torfs´s artist book of 2014, where he describes echolalia as 'the memory of the indistinct and immemorial babble that, in being lost, allowed all languages to be'. In his view, in growing up we humans lose the unlimited babbling capacity of newborn infants, which may resurface later on when our echolalic brain engages in parroting and repetition, with soundplay, shifts of meaning and playful transpositions, exploiting the ambiguities and polyvalence of language.

The exploration which Ana Torfs undertook in these installations pursues what happens in and through such babbling - the new meanings and imaginings it enables, the new potentialities of art it may trigger. The work of Oulipo writers such as Georges Perec and Italo Calvino is a key reference here, and the process has been described by her Lisbon curator, Caroline Dumalin, as 'worlds unfolded by word', reflecting how Torfs's creations often emanate and evolve from an initial, central word or text.

Acts of naming

Family Plot (2009-2010) presents two different series of elements - twenty-five small black-and-white silk screens (on glass) of tropical plants, with their pedigree in Linnaean nomenclature and a portrait of the important, usually European individual whose name was thus eternalised; each coupled with a larger frame showing a reversed engraving of a world map from the time of those

Ana Torfs, *Family Plot*, 2009/10
Installation view, Museum Kurhaus Kleve, 2015
© Photo: Ana Torfs

Ana Torfs, *Family Plot*, 2009/10
detail
© Photo: Ana Torfs

individuals, surrounded by other reversed engravings and woodcuts from many different sources covering the colonial era, and text fragments in speech bubbles – the whole displayed in a sequence of uniform sets along the four walls of the room.

In a striking counterpoint to this calm, eighteenth-century museum-like order, one of the engravings presents the black writer Olaudah Equiano, also known as Gustavus Vassa (circa 1745-1797), who in his 1789 autobiography spoke up for his fellow slaves and advocated the abolition of slavery. This is a reminder that *Family Plot* and its Latin plant names have a history in the colonial past. There are other images like the one portraying Equiano, and they raise disturbing questions about that past.

Take, for example, the ambiguity of the title *Family Plot*. Since 'plot' can mean a piece of land in a cemetery but also a plan or intrigue, which family can she mean? That of tropical plants, as domesticated in scientific botanical taxonomy? Or rather that of the dead white males who appropriated those plants with their nomenclature? Or perhaps both – the history of colonial botany intertwined with the global history of European expansion? But where then does Equiano fit into their dialectic of naming and exclusion, with his aching question of a slave: *Am I Not a Man And a Brother*?

Questions such as these continue to occupy Torfs's viewers long after visiting this installation.

The world of colour

With her second installation, *[...] STAIN [...]* (2012), we enter the world of colour - here the subject of an experimental investigation using four white tables, each holding five differently coloured frames featuring coloured goose feathers and numbered images of all kinds of objects and persons; plus two loudspeakers relaying English notes and comments spoken by Diana Weller in a random loop of ninety minutes.

Ana Torfs, *[...] STAIN [...]*, 2012
Installation view, Centro de Arte Moderna (Gulbenkian Museum), Lisbon, 2016
© Photo: Ana Torfs

The effect on visitors of the diverse visual and auditory input from this installation is to disrupt their perception and shift their understanding of colour. For one thing, *[....] STAIN [....]* suggests that there are no colours without language - although, as it turns out, words are far too indeterminate for an exact identification of colours, so today numbers are used for this purpose. But equally, as this installation suggests, colour does determine perception. Each of the installation's twenty frames comes in a different colour, which affects everything we see - almost as in Rimbaud's poem 'Voyelles', in which each of the vowels A, E, I, O and U adds a distinctive colour, meaning and symbolism. In *[....] STAIN [....]* we find the same evocative power, not least because of its beautiful colours and their exotic names, such as Congo red, Paris violet, Indian yellow, Sudan black, Rose Bengal, Prussian blue, Malachite green, Bismarck brown and so on.

More on these colours and colour names comes from the spoken notes on their history – a history of art and artifice, of human industriousness and technology, of coining words for the new dyes invented in the nineteenth century, but also of competition and profit hunting. As *[....] STAIN [....]* makes clear, the industrial revolution of colour production was at the origin of many of today's chemical and pharmaceutical multinationals, such as BASF, Bayer and Agfa. And part of this process was what happened in the colonies – for example, the war over indigo production between the German chemical industry and Gandhi's indigo workers in India; and the comment about the human cost of this dye from a member of the Bengal Civil Service in 1848: 'Not a chest of indigo reaches England without being stained with human blood'.

Unfolding the double meaning of this installation's title – 'stain' is not only a 'dye' and a colouring technique, but also a 'blemish, flaw or smear' - Ana Torfs brings to light, for her viewers to ponder, how seemingly natural and innocent colours, which delight our eyes, turn out to have a disturbing colonial and political history.

Majestic tapestries

In her third installation, *TXT (Engine of Wandering Words)* (2013), Ana Torfs takes a rather different tack. This installation consists of six large Jacquard tapestries focussed on colonial produce - coffee, sugar, ginger, tobacco, saffron and chocolate. Each of these six key words is shown backwards, upside down and between brackets, above a quote from Swift's *Gulliver's Travels*, which runs along the bottom of the tapestry. The centrepiece in each tapestry, meanwhile, is a large block of images – five across by five vertical – woven into its fabric, picturing Swift's text engine complete with handles for moving the images inside those blocks. With each of these tapestries thus unfolding into a series of pictures, *TXT* turns into an image machine, making us see what is behind those six key words – indeed, what we need to see if we are to understand anything at all of the meaning of these words.

The 150 images in this installation (and many more if those handles could be turned) are presented without caption or annotation. They are just that: vivid images, of ancient maps, wonders of the world in far away countries, cities, islands, colonial atlases and travelogues, caravans, camels, slaves and ships,

Ana Torfs, *The Parrot & the Nightingale, a Phantasmagoria*, 2014
Installation view, WIELS Contemporary Art Centre, Brussels, 2014
© Photo: Sven Laurent

imperial postage stamps and advertisements. Colonial produce is everywhere, and the coffee tapestry carries a picture of *Max Havelaar* (1860), the Dutch anticolonial novel on the human cost of the coffee produced in its colonies. Taken as a whole, it is a mesmerising installation – six magnificent wall hangings, in a striking and colourful composition, rich in images, woven together into a pictorial history of European colonial expansion and exploitation of the world outside.

Past and present meet here in *TXT*'s link to the longstanding Flemish tradition of weaving imperial tapestries. A display similar to *TXT* can be found in the Museo Capodimonte in Naples, in a large room with seven Flemish tapestries depicting the battles over the city of Pavia in 1525 between the French king Francis I and Holy Roman emperor Charles V, the first to rule over both the old world and the new. These tapestries were presented to Charles by the States-General in Brussels in 1531, and later transferred to Naples by the family of Francesco de Avalos, who held Pavia for the emperor. In other outposts of Charles's empire, in Seville and in Middelburg, there are similar palace rooms with Flemish tapestries which depict, in wool and silk, silver and gold, the story of his victories. Memories of this imperial tradition live on today, reworked and critically interrogated, in works of art by contemporary artists – the 2009 photograph by Candida Höfer of that Capodimonte tapestry room; and the large

Ana Torfs, *TXT (Engine of Wandering Words)*, 2013
Installation view, Sharjah Biennial 11, 2013
© Photo: Ana Torfs

woven wall map of the Kingdom of Naples in 1786, reconfigured by William Kentridge in 2009 and also in the Museo Capodimonte, its red frontiers over-written by thick black brushstrokes depicting Don Quixote with an enormous Gogol nose.

In *TXT*'s majestic tapestries and their images the colonial past is met head on. The images are left unexplained, the six colonial key words obscured, their message hidden in plain sight, their impact as strong as Maya pictorial signs. In view of these Oulipian techniques the question at the heart of this installation is: How exactly are words and images related within *TXT*'s engine, with its enormous potential? It is here that the *wandering word*s in Ana Torfs's subtitle come into play, beginning with the multilingual etymologies of the nomadic words we use with our everyday consumption of chocolate, sugar and other colonial produce. *TXT* does not offer a static picture book in the word-and-image tradition of Comenius, and it also rejects the view of language in Swift's text engine, that words are only names and labels for things. Instead, this monumental installation insists that, without the primordial impact of those images and without the memories and connections they generate, the meaning of those six key words will continue to elude us and remain beyond our ken.

Web of language

Ana Torfs's last work to be discussed here, *The Parrot & the Nightingale, a Phantasmagoria* (2014), is a multi-sensory installation which combines three components – first, two large projection screens showing a series of black-and-white slides of translucent tropical nature in a loop – second, three LED

Ana Torfs, *The Parrot & the Nightingale, a Phantasmagoria* (Detail), 2014
© Photo: Ana Torfs

displays featuring a video of the interpreter Lissa Zeviar as she translates into American Sign Language a series of fragments selected by Torfs from the travel journals of the 'Admiral', Columbus – and third, we hear a succession of voices giving different English renditions of those fragments. The emission of these visual and auditory streams serves to weave together images, sounds and associations, wrapping the viewer into a complex web of language which recounts and deconstructs the historical realities involved.

Here, Torfs's installation calls to mind Rachel Berwick's *Humboldt's Parrot* of 1997, an installation with parrots who were taught to speak the extinct Maypure language, from the phonetic notes written down by Alexander von Humboldt on his travels along the Orinoco river in 1800. But while Berwick's parakeets are parroting a dead language which nobody knows, Torfs has added a few extra layers of alienation, and so questions abound: Could the parrot and the nightingale be singing to each other? Or is their birdsong being drowned out by those English-speaking voices? But there were no nightingales in the Caribbean. So why then are those fragments translated, and why those different renditions? Is the marvellous new world which the Admiral keeps evoking an echolalic masque for his all-modern, all-consuming lust for gold, riches, possessions and slaves?

In this intriguing set-up, it is as Caroline Dumalin put it: 'The Admiral looks, but he doesn't see. He listens, but he doesn't hear the Other'. The multiple garbling going on in this installation represents an echolalic experiment as opaque as the hieroglyphic performances in the theatre of Antonin Artaud. A real phantasmagoria, that is, a sequence of images as in a dream, a fantastic assemblage of things seen or imagined – as if only such incomprehensibility could do justice to the unknown beauties and realities of that other world which the artist puts before our eyes.

Is that what art – or at least, Ana Torfs's art - is and does with its imaginings, precisely when one cannot decode them?

As we see, all four of Torfs's installations evoke a new and unexpected artistic reality, driven on by an echolalic creativity, through allusion, transposition, hint, footnote, riddle and other triggers of the imagination, and seeking to retrieve the oft-forgotten, only half-remembered events, images, memories and ways of seeing of past globalities. These four postcolonial installations delve deeper and deeper into the colonial past, and scrutinise crucial but little known episodes - ranging from eighteenth-century European labelling and appropriation of tropical nature alongside the unsettling issue of slavery; via nineteenth-century imperialism and its industrial subjugation of the world, including even our colours and their production; through the tradition of imperial wall hangings, reworked in *TXT* as a never-ending pictorial history of colonial exploitation; down to Columbus and the absences and obsessions in his narrative of discovery. Their central theme is how, today, the colonial past is making its presence felt, through Torfs's eye-opening narratives linking plants, colours, conquest, colonial production and enslavement - in a complex artistic language which examines our inability to capture in words or images what actually happened in colonial history.

The point which these installations drive home is to what far-reaching extent the language we use shapes reality around us. The front cover of Torfs's *Echolalia* book features Saussure´s well-known diagram of the human communication circuit, but no longer does she subscribe to the view that language is a closed and static labelling system. Instead, we see her cutting out a space in art for new modes of language use - discursive, poetic, learned, metaphorical and imaginative, as the case may be - for coming to terms with the colonial past, whilst simultaneously generating a disrupting view of its heritage in the world we are living in today.

Ana Torfs´s beautifully crafted, enchanting, experimental installations start out from established European conventions of art and reality, but then step outside and present us with a multimodal *Gesamtkunstwerk*, made with full use of anything that may serve to evoke what one cannot simply see - whether it is the meanings and insights produced by this echolalic art, the unresolved presence of the colonial past, the shackles of our language, or the legs of Rembrandt´s bird of paradise. ▩

See also: www.anatorfs.com

REFERENCES

Caroline Dumalin, *Ana Torfs, Echolalia*, Lisbon, 2016.

Coco Fusco, *English Is Broken Here: Notes on Cultural Fusion in the Americas*, New York, 1995.

Renée Green, *After the Ten Thousand Things / Na de Tien Duizend Dingen*, The Hague, 1994.

Stephen Greenblatt, *Marvelous Possessions. The Wonder of the New World*, Chicago, 1991.

Michiel van Groesen (ed.), *The Legacy of Dutch Brazil*, New York, 2014.

Daniel Heller-Roazen, *Echolalias. On the Forgetting of Language*, New York, 2005.

Simon Schama, *Rembrandt's Eyes*, New York, 1999.

Ana Torfs, *Echolalia*, Brussels, 2014. This artist book accompanied her first *Echolalia* exhibition, in WIELS Contemporary Art Centre, Brussels.

Tension in Controversy

The Cabaret of Hans Teeuwen

[JOS NIJHOF]

The stages on which he performs have grown over the years, but he can still make do with a couple of square metres. His last show featured a piano which was only used briefly for one song. There are no accompanying musicians. The decor is austere, if not lacking in imagination. His body, voice and facial expressions have to suffice, and so they do: his arms and legs resemble those of a ragdoll; even without a microphone his voice has an enormous range; his face is a landscape on which improbable vistas unfold.

Hans Teeuwen is a theatre wizard for whom the right term has yet to be coined. The term 'cabaret artist' does not do him justice, as the concept is still attached to a mixture of diverse stage genres such as narrative and poetic art or song, whereas with Hans Teeuwen these disciplines combine to form a completely unique theatrical grammar, far removed from existing theatre conventions, with controversial content and an absurdist style. Any attempt to copy him is doomed to failure: Teeuwen's cabaret is best described as 'typically Hans Teeuwen'.

He is a stage animal, an entertainer and natural comedian. Shortly after the start of his career, speaking about the ease with which he moves before his audience, however massive, the way he has so magically fused with his craft, he himself said, 'From the moment that I set foot on the stage, I was successful, because what I do is right. I'm at home there. The public sense that it's good, that I'm present. There are cabaret artists for whom it isn't right. They weren't born to it, but by working really hard they've managed to win a place. They fight their way to it. I've never had to learn that fight.'

Personal tragedies

Hans Teeuwen was born on 3 March 1967 in Budel, a small village near the border between the province of North Brabant and Belgium. After secondary school he attended drama academy in Eindhoven, but he soon decided to swap theory for practice. In 1991 he joined forces with guitarist Roland Smeenk to take part in the prestigious cabaret festival Cameretten. The duo won both the press and the audience prizes.

The chemistry between Teeuwen and Smeenk was unprecedented. Seldom has a jury been so unanimously full of praise for a performance or the public so wildly enthusiastic. However, a collaborative future in cabaret came to a sudden end a year later, before *Heist* went on tour as an evening show, when the two were involved in a car accident in which the thirty-five-year-old Smeenk lost his life. It was a first personal tragedy in the life of Hans Teeuwen, a sudden, tragic violation of the special connection he had formed, not only with a cabaret partner, but also with a very close friend. A 2007 TV documentary about the duo makes it clear how much Teeuwen owes to Smeenk and how many years it took before he finally dared to enjoy his success as a solo artist.

That success started straight out from his first show, *Hard en Zielig* (Hard and Pitiful, 1994), with which he achieved a fast breakthrough to a large and steadfast audience. Ingredients which were to prove characteristic of his entire oeuvre can already be found in this show: when it comes to form, flitting between very diverse sketches, and in content, a lack of inhibition which sometimes astonishes the audience and makes them uncomfortable, especially where it comes down to recurring themes such as sex, violence and religion.

Hans Teeuwen & The Painkillers,
Popstukken

This dream debut was followed by *Met een Breierdeck* (With a Breierdeck, 1995), a show with an endless playlist. Teeuwen threw himself into his craft with so much energy that he paid the price with exhaustion and lack of inspiration. False rumours even did the rounds that he had ended up in a psychiatric clinic with suicidal tendencies. In actual fact Teeuwen was busy with a number of projects outside the world of cabaret, including film and radio work.

The year 2000 marked his return to the stage. In his third show, *Trui* (Sweater), more than previously, he sought out confrontation with the audience and practised with gusto what the Austrian author Peter Handke termed *Publikumsbeschimpfung*. In a provocative, ironic game he entered into a trial of strength with the viewer, persisting with it until the end of the show. Finally he spurned the customary applause, adding power to his refusal by addressing the audience with a rage which balanced on the edge between reality and pretence. At the end of his fourth show, *Dat dan weer wel* (On the Other Hand, 2001), he did precisely the opposite, refusing to leave the stage, causing the audience to continue whooping and clapping for minutes on end, eventually edging their way slowly out of the hall, still labouring under the anxious assumption that an encore might yet follow. After that, *Industry of Love* (2003), which would be Teeuwen's last show for the time being, became notorious for the scene in which he imagined himself in word and gesture sexually pleasuring the queen of the Netherlands. The sketch has come to belong to the collective memory of Dutch cabaret lovers, because the shock factor achieves a sense of embarrassment in even the most hardened viewer.

After this period of around ten years, Teeuwen acknowledged that an 'incredible fatigue', as he put it, had taken hold of him. He lacked the energy for a new show and a long tour, and proceeded to withdraw from the limelight to focus on making films. He wrote and directed various productions, including the TV film *Masterclass* (2005), a pseudo-documentary about an insane theatre guru, and he contributed to the scripts of two films by his friend Theo van Gogh, whose murder by a Muslim extremist on 2 November 2004 signified a second personal tragedy in his life. The death of Van Gogh was to have a lasting influence on Teeuwen's subsequent career.

This turned out to be a temporary period of respite. Teeuwen would not be Teeuwen if he had permanently turned his back on the world of entertainment during this period. In 2006 he returned to the theatre, this time to everyone's surprise not as a cabaret performer but as a jazz singer, joining a growing list of pop artists – Robbie Williams, Bryan Ferry, Rod Stewart – who dress in sharply tailored suits and put their talent to the test as crooners of the standard glamour repertoire. After a time, in addition to covers, Teeuwen increasingly sang songs he had written himself in English. Although he was endowed with a magnificent, sonorous voice and a strong theatrical feel for timing, Teeuwen (like the others) lacked the vocal quality of a figure like Frank Sinatra, whom he admired. By interspersing his performances with odd runs, comic asides and nods in the direction of famous cabaret texts he had written, he put into perspective the seriousness of a craft in which he was only an overconfident passer-by. A fantastic band and his grandiose charisma did the rest.

Adventures over the border

An aversion to tired-out conventions and hypocrisy, as well as grief and anger at the violent murder of his friend Theo van Gogh, have made Teeuwen a fanatical champion of the free word. Without a doubt his performance on 30 August 2007 in the programme *Bimbo's en Boerka's* (Bimbos and Burqas) belongs to the iconic Dutch TV moments of recent times. Here he was interviewed by the 'Meiden van Halal' (the Halal girls), three TV presenters from a conservative Moroccan background. Earlier that year Teeuwen had made a speech at the unveiling of a monument to Van Gogh and sung a song ('Het vrije woord', The Free Word) in which he unambiguously placed the 'Meiden' in a sexual context. A fierce discussion arose about the sensitivities of believers and non-believers, about freedom of expression and the right to cause offence. The statement from that interview most characteristic of Teeuwen as a cabaret artist is this: 'I don't just call people names, I make jokes, and sometimes those jokes are about things... because it's precisely the subjects which are sensitive or controversial that are funny, or exciting. That's where the tension is, and as a cabaret performer that's precisely what you work with, otherwise you'd have to abolish the entire genre of cabaret or satire.' It says a great deal about him and no less about his cabaret style: offence to him is a form of humour; Teeuwen seeks out the tension in controversy.

The English-speaking world became acquainted with Teeuwen in 2007, when he appeared at the Edinburgh Fringe Festival as part of an occasional group with the temporary name, the Amsterdam Underground Comedy Collective. The performance consisted of translated excerpts of previous shows. His fellow comedians enjoyed warm interest from the British press, but Teeuwen clearly stole the show. *The Guardian* labelled him 'the most thrilling find of the festival so far', characterising his performance as, 'Nonsense it is, but performed as if our lives depended on it.'

The positive experiences of this adventure led just a year later to a return to the United Kingdom. Teeuwen performed in the Soho Theatre in London and at various festivals. During a performance at the Latitude Festival in Suffolk he was booed by some of the audience: the cabaret artist's style of humour appears to come across more harshly in Great Britain than in the Netherlands, and apparently politically, religiously and sexually 'incorrect' jokes will take some getting used to with audiences on the other side of the Channel. Another year on, at the Greenwich Comedy Festival in London, he again clashed with some of the audience. On this subject Teeuwen later said in an interview, 'Once I was really seriously booed, yes... In the early days it happened in the Netherlands too, you know, people walking out. It's just that here there's no tradition of expressing the sentiment verbally, they just leave. In England they want the artist to leave.'

At the end of 2010, Teeuwen announced that he was embarking on another cabaret tour. There was a rush for his new show, *Spiksplinter* (Spic and Span), but the press reactions were rather stingy to say the least. Many critics observed a lack of innovation: 'Hans Teeuwen is repeating himself,' was the general tone. For a cabaret artist just starting out, reviews might still be significant, but what the critics have to say about Teeuwen has long ceased to matter. His performances have become events for which the biggest halls in the Netherlands are insufficient, where technical aids such as broadcast microphones and mega-screens now form part of the necessary entourage.

Variety versus causality

Tickets for his most recent solo show, *Echte rancune* (Real Rancour, 2016), sold out in no time. Again the critics were divided, although reviews here were dominated by admiration for the craftsmanship Teeuwen displayed, particularly in the first half of the performance. The discussion in the prominent daily newspaper *NRC Handelsblad* concludes, 'amoral, confrontational theatre, terrifically cleverly acted and extremely spirited. In Teeuwen's seventh solo show he reveals himself once again as belonging to a genre, a world and a class of his own.'

In October 2016, Teeuwen performed an adapted version of his latest show in London under the title *Real Rancour*. Press and public at the Soho Theatre were more enthusiastic than ever. The review in *The Guardian* described Teeuwen as follows: 'His wild-eyed commitment, aggressively odd behaviour, and his oblique, vaguely malevolent facial expressions all work to scramble significance, and demagnetise whatever moral compass you thought you'd brought with you to the theatre.' After London he went on tour through a number of cities in England and in November he spent an entire month at the Leicester Square Theatre.

Once again in *Echte rancune* Teeuwen ridicules viewers, for instance when he criticises their lack of loyalty during his recent forays into music. Apparently audiences want to see the joker and are less interested in the singer, he observes with affected bitterness. While such gibes are still said with a cheerful, ironic undertone, at other moments there is a definite sense of unease, because with Teeuwen it is sometimes far from clear where the satire ends and seriousness begins.

Cabaret was once the privilege of a left-wing vanguard, but Teeuwen's arrival in particular appears to have broken through that tradition. A progressive viewer might labour under the naive impression that he is surrounded by kindred spirits, but Teeuwen does not allow himself to be pigeonholed and as soon as he makes a statement a rather further to the right of the spectrum, such progressive types can feel extremely lonely in a packed auditorium. I must admit it has happened to me once or twice, especially when I have heard roaring laughter around me and exuberant encouragement for what to me seemed terribly 'wrong' statements. Teeuwen, as stated above, is unfathomable and from sketch to sketch the artist's opinion can shoot off in completely different directions.

Teeuwen's performances follow a tight rhythm, but there is hardly a hint of a consistent train of thought or causality to the content. When he finally seems to be on his way to a point, he effectively picks up a pair of scissors and snips it off with a nefarious grin. This fragmentary style makes Teeuwen, more than

Hans Teeuwen © Tom Bertels

his fellow performers, an ideal YouTube artist. Countless Dutch viewers – and now British audiences too – know Hans Teeuwen from attending one or more of his shows or through TV broadcasts and DVD recordings, but that consumption takes place more than ever through the video site YouTube, a factor which should not be underestimated in the consumption of cabaret in our time.

Particularly for young people, for whom digital media form an inexhaustible source of learning, and even more of entertainment, who barely derive any knowledge of cabaret from attending shows, which is exorbitantly expensive, or from DVDs or TV broadcasts, which take far too long and always happen at the wrong moment. Flicking between YouTube clips is the new way of being entertained and Hans Teeuwen's cabaret certainly eminently lends itself to this style of watching.

The most popular acts have been viewed tens of thousands – sometimes hundreds of thousands – of times. A sketch about world religions from *Dat dan weer wel* now has almost 1.5 million hits and there are even excerpts dating back to the period in which Teeuwen still performed with Roland Smeenk. Teeuwen's constant availability on YouTube also explains his undiminished popularity as a cabaret artist, while in real time he follows sidelines as a singer or cineaste.

In this context, it is striking that in the autumn of 2017 Teeuwen set up his own online platform with recordings of all his theatre productions. In return for signing up to *Hans Teewen World*, fans gain access to videos of his programmes with a new clip each week, special live broadcasts, and for example, priority booking for shows.

Hans Teeuwen and Roland Smeenk

In service to the free word

Echte rancune is more austere than all Teeuwen's previous shows. His message is the focus, and variety elements involving hand puppets, mouth acrobatics and piano medleys remain absent, while what Teeuwen does, says and sings more than ever serves a single purpose: the proclamation of the free word. He is profoundly convinced that it must be possible to say and show everything, and he follows through on that too, explicitly and authentically, not with the resolute intention of antagonising people, although that can happen at any moment.

Fellow craftsmen with a similar status produce content with greater power or less abstraction than Teeuwen's. The oeuvre of Freek de Jonge, now the grand old man of Dutch cabaret, contains a hefty dose of morality and sometimes tends towards the issuing of practical tips for a better life. The rather younger Youp van 't Hek sinks his teeth into a society which enjoys greater prosperity than ever before, but which at the same time increasingly wallows in dissatisfaction. Teeuwen's contemporary and relative match Theo Maassen merrily rebels against everything that irritates him along the spectrum of self-importance and arrogance.

Engagement with cabaret has slowly but surely come to be a thing of the past, in part due to innovations in the 1970s for which Freek de Jonge was in fact one of the pioneers. Thanks to De Jonge, Van 't Hek, Maassen and other Dutch celebrities from the entertainment world, the public is now beginning to expect a more activist attitude from cabaret performers. Those who look to the art form as a moral guide will not be disappointed. Two years ago, Freek de Jonge leapt into the breach for the residents of the northern province of Groningen who in recent decades have suffered earthquakes as a result of gas extraction in the region; Herman Finkers, a celebrated cabaret artist from the eastern region of Twente, started a broad protest against the reopening of a military airport for civil aviation; Dolf Jansen has worked for more than ten years as an ambassador for Oxfam Novib, and there are plenty more examples. It goes without saying that such cabaret performers eagerly participate in talk shows and other TV programmes on the side to give their activism an extra boost.

Anyone who follows Teeuwen's work knows that he will never be conscripted into a cultural or social institution which strives for a particular goal on the periphery of his art. You will not encounter him as an activist who attaches himself to the fate of compatriots in distressing circumstances, nor is he the man to put on a New Year's Eve show, which in the Netherlands is the highest platform available in the media world for any cabaret artist. Such a show requires a retrospective look at the social and political developments of the past year, precisely the kind of terrain on which Teeuwen does not wish to embark. In such a show the cabaret artist is challenged to take a stance, but thus far no one knows what Teeuwen actually stands for or what he thinks, as a cabaret performer or as a public figure. This masked position has come to be his trademark. He does not hold any points of view with which he might please one or other half of the population, only revealing himself to be a fundamentalist when it comes to the free word. His defence of freedom of expression is deeply rooted and tolerates no concessions whatsoever.

The rare moments when Hans Teeuwen nevertheless appears in a talk show take place when that free word is at issue. Sadly, this is still in question in a time when the public debate is struck dumb by the mutual denunciation of left and right and by the ever-sharper oppositions between the values of east and west. Where necessary Teeuwen enters the debate on that subject, as he has shown on various occasions, undoubtedly with the memory of his good friend Theo van Gogh in his heart. ▨

Translated by Anna Asbury

Looking for Leeway

K. Michel as Alice in Wonderland

In the course of the 1980s, a new generation of poets emerged in the Nether-lands. Their appearance was accompanied by a great deal of tub-thumping and polemics, with Joost Zwagerman as the most important voice, in the magazine *De Held* (The Hero) and the anthology *Maximaal* (To the Maximum, 1988): work by poets who set the tone at the time like Rutger Kopland, C.O. Jellema and T. van Deel was dismissed as introverted and shrivelled up, as hermeticism that had outlived itself. Their own poetry on the other hand, which was labelled 'vital' and 'extrovert', was presented (in a famous quote from Lucebert) as an expression of 'the space of the fullness of life'.

Elsewhere this new generation presented itself more playfully and on the sidelines in the magazine *AapNootMies* edited by Arjen Duinker and K. Michel. Their rejection of recent Dutch poetry was more implicit: they drew their in-spiration from the broader international tradition of William Carlos Williams, Fernando Pessoa, Octavio Paz and others.

The core group of the Maximalists, to be found in trendy artistic circles in Amsterdam, was very concerned with the 'image' of poetry, created by grand gestures and stories surrounding the poem. Michel and Duinker on the other hand, who in the period of *AapNootMies* were studying philosophy in Groningen, were more interested in what Walter Benjamin called the 'aura' of art, the fas-cination generated by language.

Yet it is not surprising that several poems by Michel (1958), to whom I shall restrict myself in what follows, were also included in *Maximaal*. Like 'Code', which later found its way without a title into his debut collection *Ja! Naakt als de stenen* (Yes! Naked as the Stones, 1989). With its ecstatic exclamation marks and imperatives, this poem testifies to lyrical entrepreneurship:

> *Poet!*
> *Comb your hair, shine your shoes!*
> *Put on your inner life!*
> *We're going to shake hands with the wind.*
> *We're going to greet the horizon.*
>
> *So much to see! So much to do!*

With hindsight, it is easy to see that in fact it is only the externals of open form, exclamation marks and verbal dynamics with which this early poetry of Michel's fits in with that of his Maximalist contemporaries. His poetic enter-prise (with combed hair and polished shoes – not the cliché of the maladjusted artist, but rather like someone applying for a respectable job) is principally a search for the inner self and the 'freedom of movement in the etiquette of language, in the codes that prescribe the way to do it,' as he formulated it later. The title of his collected poems, *Speling zoeken* (Looking for Leeway, 2016), is the short summary of this aim.

The search for the inner self is given a clear shape in the long poem 'De weg van het water' (The Way of the Water), with which *Ja! Naakt als de stenen* concludes. In this high point from his early work we hear of a strange kind of journey along various European rivers, made by an I-figure 'to investigate / whether rivers live like people'. Like Wallace Stevens, one of the godfathers of Michel's early work, who in his poem 'The Idea of Order at Key West' gives the sea a voice, whose words must be ordered by a poet, the I-figure in Michel's poem sets himself the 'problem of ordering' and also finds the solution to this problem mainly in poetry. The Meuse at Charleville, the Guadalquivir at Seville, the Svratka at Brno; with one river it is Arthur Rimbaud who gives him an in-sight, with the other Federico García Lorca, with the third Velimir Chlebnikov, the Russian sound poet. He takes something for the journey from each one. But only in the Drowned Land of Saeftinghe, not a flowing river, but an area of salt marshes that is periodically flooded, does he realise that he has been barking up the wrong tree:

And I suddenly saw
that man's inner self is not a river
but a drowned land
that consists of channels and mud flats
worn away by time and silted up
covered with marram grass and samphire
[...]
The inner self has no essence
that can express it.
It is a form that fills and empties
and in seasons like autumn and spring drowns.
No, not form but matter
where nothing would grow without the tide.

There are no sources, there is no kernel, everything is liquid. Thales of Milete, the Ancient Greek, would have nodded in agreement, as would the postmodern philosopher Zygmunt Bauman.

Philosopher, pataphysicist, poet

One can deduce from this one example that studying philosophy has left its mark on Michel. Yet he emphatically denies that he is a philosopher: 'I can't think and argue well enough to be able to call myself one', he maintains. For that reason the poet Rutger Kopland has called him a pataphysicist, the practitioner of a poetic science that has the characteristics of a good joke. Embarking on a trip through the whole of Europe to find out whether rivers live like people is one such joke: something totally irrational is given a semblance of rationality. In its comic seriousness, this logic is akin to that in *Alice in Wonderland*.

That is, for example, also the case in 'Daaag' (Hi-i-i) in the collection *Bij eb is je eiland groter* (Your Island's Bigger at Low Tide, 2010), in which Michel tells us that he is unable to say anything substantial about the hereafter as long as he has not been there. At the same time he is aware that true endings do not exist, and that everything just continues. Whereupon, to solve this dilemma, he conjures up a splendid image, in which the poet easily wins out over the philosopher:

a traffic sign
(at a junction near Han-sur-Lesse)
with two forceful bossy arrows
under the one pointing left
it says toutes directions
under the one pointing right
autres directions

With Michel two signs at an arbitrary junction give a greater insight than systematic thought. In this poetry insight always comes incidentally: the world is full of interference and the poet wants to let the reader experience that. Because although his ultimate objective is to filter signals that offer an insight from this noise, Michel likes to leave the noise intact in his poems. As in 'Zijn oude vriend Norman Malcolm kijkt terug' (His Old Friend Norman Malcolm Looks Back) from the recent collection *Te voet is het heelal drie dagen ver* (On Foot the Universe is Three Days Away, 2016), based on a biographical essay by Norman Malcolm on the philosopher Ludwig Wittgenstein. In five successive stanzas, we learn that Wittgenstein was a good whistler, loved fairs, had a blooming pot plant in his room, as a guest was keen to help with the washing-up, etc. All interference, that is, amusing but of little importance for our knowledge of the philosopher – this Wittgenstein could have featured in a children's story.

As if he has not yet made the philosopher everyday enough, the poet lays it on even thicker in a final, extra-long stanza, by informing us that Wittgenstein, Malcolm and his wife once went for a walk together. Only then does the philosopher the reader had been waiting for loom up: during the walk Wittgenstein proposes representing the motion of the sun, earth and moon. Wittgenstein, who plays the part of the moon, has to run for all he is worth (around Malcolm, the earth, who himself moves in turn around his wife, the sun, calmly advancing in a straight line), with the result that he becomes dizzy and sees the horizon waving up and down. The poem ends with a question that puts what precedes it in a different light: 'Did that line then belong as a contour in the immense field / or in the plane of the sky? And our life does it know no end as our field of vision knows no limit?' In this way the poem finally forces its way, through all the anecdotal interference, to one of Wittgenstein's central assertions: 'The limits of language are the limits of the world.'

Unlike for many modern artists for Michel limits are not in the first place there to be overstepped, but to be explored. He is fascinated by places where one thing touches on another, both in the everyday world and in a much wider context. For example, the prose-poem 'Ontmoetingen' (Meetings) from *Bij eb is je eiland groter* offers a series of visual observations on borderline situations such as 'the [suit]case is a cross between there and here', 'in the revolving door the lobby draws breath' and 'when you are asleep you are somewhere between present and far away': ingenious, spiritual, often comic, in a natural tone and focussed on the ambiguity of language.

In addition, a poet in the twenty-first century doesn't necessarily have it any easier than primitive man. At least you can infer that from 'Uit de bomen afgedaald' (Descending from the Trees) in *Kleur de schaduwen* (Colour the Shadows, 2004), a poem about the evolution of language. That evolution goes from cries such as 'Ow', 'mmm' and 'brr', via simply formulated observations as 'ape stares we not' to our capacity to say 'garden furniture cushion storage bag' and 'fluctuating interest rate'. However, in stretching the limits of language the chance of losing oneself in the increased language interference or getting stuck is proportionally greater.

An exploration of limits in a wider sense is implied by the title 'On Foot the Universe is Three Days Away'. This is an allusion to the Kármán Line, at a height of 100 kilometres, which is regarded as the border between Earth's atmosphere and space. The idea that one could go there on foot is of course absurd, but it is true that someone who walks at a fast pace can cover a hundred kilometres in three days. As he frequently does, just like Carroll's Alice, Michel here too reduces the thought of what exceeds our comprehension to the proportions of daily life.

(In parentheses: if there is a Dutch-language tradition into which this poetry fits it is that of K. Schippers and Gerrit Krol, both poets with a lightness of touch and a sharp eye for the chance, odd and often fairly arbitrary connections in life.)

In other poems someone has an insight while singing in the shower or while waiting at a raised bridge watching a ship sail past ('The Skinny Bridge Miracle', *Waterstudies*, 1999), when listening to the royal speech at the state opening of parliament or when a child submits a language puzzle answer to him. All the information, pronouncements or images present in everyday reality are usable for Michel. There is no question of any hierarchy. If something is tracked down, that is anyway often by chance. As in 'De meeuw van Treytel' (Treytel's Seagull) from *Boem de nacht* (Boom the Night, 1994), in which disparate events count as 'souvenirs of a lost connection':

As my life unfolds
and disintegrates into increasingly capricious patterns
I receive such signals all the more
eagerly; souvenirs of a lost
connection; the suggestion that round the corner
happiness waits for a collision

Bewilderment and astonishment

From the very beginning Michel's poetry met with considerable appreciation, from readers and from critics. Of the collections in the omnibus edition *Speling zoeken*, *Ja! Naakt als de stenen* and *Boem de nacht* are each in their third edition, his most successful collection, *Waterstudies*, in its seventh and both *Kleur de schaduwen* and *Bij eb is je eiland groter* in their fifth. Prize juries also show appreciation for his work. *Boem de nacht* was awarded the Herman Gorter Prize, *Waterstudies* both the VSB Poetry Prize and the Jan Campert Prize, while *Bij eb is je eiland groter* won the Awater Poetry Prize and the Guido Gezelle Prize.

Critics value him for the wittiness of his observations, his ability to put the everyday in a new perspective, his eye for the mysterious, his hidden melancholy, his lucidity. The critic Rob Schouten talked of a 'pleasant and intriguing kind of poetic freedom' and Mustafa Stitou of 'light-footed bewilderment'.

Bewilderment and astonishment often go hand in hand in Michel's work. In his prose collection *Tingeling & Totus* (1992) he introduces two characters, each of which embodies one of these reactions: Tingeling, who moves through life 'like the clouds through the sky' and whose attention is drawn to 'the rhythm of things', feels only bewilderment and optimism at the constant changes in reality, while in Totus dismay and astonishment are given form. By separating and then confronting these two sides of his writer's personality, Michel is able constantly to surprise the reader.

Both the Tingeling and Totus sides feature in 'Vers twee' (Verse Two, *Waterstudies*), in which Michel comments on the Hebrew text of the second verse of the Book of Genesis, 'tohu wa bohu'. To begin with he limits himself to the sound of the words, their suggestiveness, the landscapes evoked by, let's say, 'the rhythm of things'. But after he has translated them ('the earth without form and void'), he realises how astonishing and unimaginable their meaning is. Subsequently this Totusish heaviness is lightened by a Tingelingian insight: 'Perhaps the sudden convulsion which shudders / through your body just before you fall asleep / is a distant aftershock of that original violence'.

In this way Michel is able to lighten his heavy subjects in all kinds of ways, now by the choice of a particular perspective, now by consistently maintaining an absurd image. In 'Vlinderverhuizing' (Emigration of the Butterflies, *Bij eb is je eiland groter*) he presents the disturbance of the natural balance through global warming as a newspaper report that he reads to the puss sitting at the window. In 'De lach van Rutte' (Rutte's Laugh, *Te voet is het heelal drie dagen ver*) his anger at the lack of vision of those in power, politicians and journalists takes the form of a verbal cartoon. In it the prime minister Mark Rutte, after years of 'smiling / smirking, giggling, grinning / chuckling, sniggering, joking / guffawing, exploding with laughter, laughing his head off, thigh-slapping [...]' suddenly loses control of his laugh, which consequently detaches from his face, crashes to the ground and runs away. At that moment all journalists turn away from Rutte and follow his laugh. The message is clear: what the prime minister has to say has long ceased to count. What people are after is his image.

K. Michel

SPELING ZOEKEN
ALLE GEDICHTEN TOT NU

Squeezed into a confined space

Michel has frequently given voice to his concern about political and social developments. As early as *Boem de nacht*, his second collection, he sketches himself as someone who 'after the fall of the Berlin Wall / [...] / and the invasion of Grenada and Panama / and the hijacking of the currency market' sits in his attic room pulling his hair out 'over the dust storm of news facts / and the ubiquitous lack of vision'. At the same time, he is aware that the resistance of a poet is always paper resistance – see the poem 'Paris / Charlie 7-1-15' (*Te voet is het heelal drie dagen ver*): from bookmarks and pious pronouncements which after the news of the slaughter in Paris he shakes out of the holy books ('matter seeking for purity'), the I-figure kneads a paper snowball, after which he sits and waits helplessly 'for the uncontrollable melting'. Obviously poetry offers him no more leeway than this. The search for leeway assumes a very literal form in 'En zo ging het' (And That's How It Went, *Te voet is het heelal drie dagen ver*). In it the I-figure is given 'a box-like thing in cardboard', but as it grows larger and larger, he cannot get a grip on it. Finally he is able to squeeze inside it, in 'a space where you can't stand / can't lie or sit.' Just as the expanding Alice gets stuck in the White Rabbit's house, he has to look for 'an attitude / for leeway'. That search is not a game, it is the position in which the poet finds himself: squeezed into a confined space. ■

Translated by Paul Vincent

FURTHER READING

Speling zoeken. Alle gedichten tot nu, atlas contact, Amsterdam, 2016 (Collected poems).

Four Poems

By K. Michel

Treytel's Seagull

Through the open window a starling
flies into Hans Broek's studio
and on its way shits on the painting
in the blue area top left
'Finished' growls the painter

Three metres behind the car the bridge collapses

We walk late in the evening through
Verversstraat and stop to
inspect a courtyard
From a window come waves of panting
o's and a's from two, no three voices
and only then do I see the sign
Bianca Castafiore Square

'Reality goes far too far'
complains my friend the poet and grins
'we couldn't make it up'

God used to live, I kid you not
around the corner from us, on Bosscheweg
His initials were J.H.L.
He was a bailiff by profession

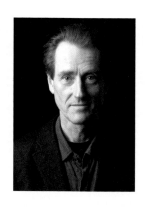

See also Rust Garage on the Zeeburgerdijk

'On Saturday evening a cyclist waited
three hours at the opened Caland Bridge in the Europoort
After midnight the man heard from patrolling
policemen that the bridge was closed until Sunday afternoon
for maintenance work'

And then that bird that in the 1960s
in thick fog in the Sparta-Feyenoord match
lost its way and in a goal kick by goalie
Treytel was hit by the ball

As my life unfolds
and disintegrates into increasingly capricious patterns
I receive such signals all the more
eagerly; souvenirs of a lost
connection; the suggestion that around the corner
happiness waits for a collision

Complex processes: if I walk barefoot
over the tiles to the balcony,
I start sneezing

From: *Boem de nacht* (Boom the Night),
Meulenhoff, Amsterdam, 1994

De meeuw van Treytel

Door het open raam vliegt een spreeuw
het atelier van Hans Broek binnen
en kakt onderweg op het schilderij
in het blauwe vlak linksboven
'Klaar' bromt de schilder

Drie meter achter de auto stort de brug in

We lopen 's avonds laat door
de Verversstraat en staan stil om
een binnenpleintje te bekijken
Uit een raam golven hijgende
o's en a's van twee, nee drie stemmen
en pas dan zie ik het bordje
Bianca Castafiore Plein

'De werkelijkheid gaat veel te ver'
klaagt mijn vriend de dichter en grijnst
'dat zouden wij niet mogen verzinnen'

God woonde vroeger, echt waar
bij ons om de hoek, op de Bosscheweg
Zijn initialen waren J.H.L.
Hij was van beroep deurwaarder

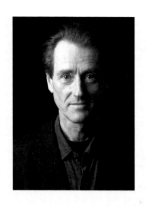

Zie ook Garage Roest op de Zeeburgerdijk

'Een fietser heeft zaterdagavond drie uur
voor de geopende Calandbrug in de Europoort gewacht
Na middernacht hoorde de man van surveillerende
agenten dat de brug tot zondagmiddag
wegens werkzaamheden was gesloten'

En dan de vogel die in de jaren zestig bij dichte
mist in de wedstrijd Sparta-Feyenoord
verdwaalde en bij een uittrap van doelman
Treytel getroffen werd door de bal

Naarmate mijn leven zich ontrolt
en ontbindt in steeds grilliger patronen
ontvang ik dit soort signalen des te
gretiger; souvenirs van een vergane
samenhang; de suggestie dat om de hoek
het geluk wacht op een botsing

Complexe processen: als ik op blote
voeten over de tegels naar het balkon
loop, begint mijn neus te niezen

From: *Boem de nacht* (Boom the Night),
Meulenhoff, Amsterdam, 1994

K. MICHEL
Water-
studies

Gedichten

MEULENHOFF

Verse Two

On rereading it sounds like
a postcoital feeling of melancholy
tohu wa bohu, tohu wa bohu

If you repeat this aloud
you see landscapes unfold
a November sand bank in the Waddenzee
the desolate plains southeast of Glen Coe
and you start smelling peat, slate
two hanging hares in the barn

Five syllables heavy as lead
with more weight than all the elements combined
tohu wa bohu, the earth without form and void
in the Hebrew text of Genesis one verse two

What they are supposed to mean is unimaginable
the beginning before the beginning, a condition so primeval
that my suburban imagination has
only inadequate comparisons to hand

Even Hollywood-style earthquakes
tidal waves, hurricanes and volcanic eruptions
must be peanuts compared with the horror back then

Perhaps the sudden convulsion which shudders
through your body just before you fall asleep
is a distant aftershock of that original violence

A convulsion that says:
there is sleep, there are dreams
languidly floating, swaying under water
but there is no ground to carry us

Vers twee

Bij herlezing klinkt het als
een postcoïtaal gevoel van droefenis
tohoe wa bohoe, tohoe wa bohoe

Als je het hardop herhaalt
zie je landschappen zich ontvouwen
een novemberse zandplaat in de Waddenzee
de desolate vlaktes ten zuidoosten van Glen Coe
en ga je turf ruiken, leisteen
twee adelende hazen in de schuur

Vijf loeizware lettergrepen
met meer gewicht dan alle elementen tezamen
tohoe wa bohoe, de aarde woest en ledig
in de Hebreeuwse tekst van Genesis een vers twee

Wat ze moeten aanduiden is onvoorstelbaar
het begin voor het begin, een toestand zo oer
dat mijn buitenwijkverbeelding slechts
tekortschietende vergelijkingen voorhanden heeft

Ook Hollywoodiaanse aardbevingen
vloedgolven, orkanen en vulkaanuitbarstingen
moeten peanuts zijn vergeleken met de horror van toen

Misschien is de plotse stuiptrekking die
vlak voor je in slaap valt door je lichaam schrikt
een verre naschok van dat oorspronkelijke geweld

Een stuip die zegt:
er is slaap, er zijn dromen
loom drijvende, onder water wiegende
maar gedragen worden wij door geen grond

From: *Waterstudies* (Waterstudies),
Meulenhoff, Amsterdam, 1999

K. MICHEL

Water-
studies

Gedichten

MEULENHOFF

The Skinny Bridge Miracle

The first two boats passed smoothly
but the third was a deeply laden barge
which approached so slowly that (present for Karin
pasta, cream, beans, call plumber)

Suddenly the barge looms up close
and I see that it is completely filled
with water that flows in jaunty waves
from the dark hold over the sides

Above the waiting people
the fatigue of the working day has grown
into an almost visible bunch of text balloons

Wrapped in thoughts and concerns
we do not see that from the barge
all the water in the Amstel wells up
Incognito the source of the river floats past

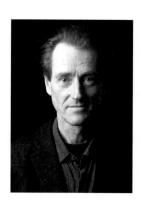

Het Magerebrugwonder

De eerste twee boten passeerden vlot
maar de derde was een diep geladen aak
die zo traag naderde dat (cadeau Karin
pasta, room, boontjes, loodgieter bellen)

Plotseling doemt de aak dichtbij op
en zie ik dat hij geheel gevuld is
met water dat in springerige golfjes
uit het donkere ruim over de boorden stroomt

Boven de wachtende mensen
is de moeheid van de werkdag uitgegroeid
tot een bijna zichtbare tros tekstballonnen

Verwikkeld in gedachten en beslommeringen
zien we niet dat uit de aak
al het water van de Amstel opwelt
Incognito drijft de bron van de rivier voorbij

From: *Waterstudies* (Waterstudies),
Meulenhoff, Amsterdam, 1999

Bij eb is je eiland groter

K. Michel

Gedichten

Augustus

Butterfly Removal

Puss sits at the window, looks with
nervous movements of its head
at the birds on the balcony.

Yes Puss, islands move
birds migrate, woods advance
tectonic plates shift, icebergs float
souls transmigrate, finches mutate and
paperclips relocate from desk to desk.

Listen Puss, I say, unfolding the newspaper
'Climate change is forcing many butterflies
towards the cooler north, but they do not fly
fast enough to keep up with the warming process.
British biologists have come up with a solution:
they ferry the butterflies by car.'
And it works, Puss, they report here.
Populations of small skippers and
melanargia galathea are given a smooth lift
in soft cages and have successfully
established themselves a long way north.
Imagine: clean fresh air
white nights, blooming heathlands.
Puss gives me a searching look, ears pricked.
'Because the method appears to work the biologists
want to transfer populations more often.
Species that cannot keep up with the warming process
should be given a hand.'
I look up and close the newspaper.
Fine mess, says Puss's look, if we go on
this way, the North Pole will soon be in sight.

Vlinderverhuizing

Poes zit voor het raam, kijkt
met nerveuze kop beweginkjes
naar de vogeltjes op het balkon.

Ja Poes, eilanden wandelen
vogels trekken, bossen rukken op
aardplaten schuiven, ijsbergen drijven
zielen verhuizen, vinken muteren en
paperclips migreren van bureau naar bureau.

Luister Poes, zeg ik, de krant omvouwend
'De klimaatverandering dwingt veel vlinders
naar het koelere noorden, maar ze vliegen niet
snel genoeg om de opwarming bij te benen.
Britse biologen verzonnen een oplossing:
ze brengen de vlinders per auto.'
En dat werkt, Poes, schrijven ze hier.
Populaties van het geelsprietdikkopje
en het dambordje kregen in zachte kooien
een vlotte lift en hebben zich met succes
een flink eind naar het noorden gevestigd.
Stel je voor: schone frisse lucht
witte nachten, bloeiende heidevelden.
Poes kijkt mij vorsend aan, de oortjes gespitst.
'Omdat de methode lijkt te werken willen
de biologen vaker populaties verhuizen.
Soorten die de opwarming niet bijhouden
zou je een handje moeten helpen.'
Ik kijk op en vouw de krant dicht.
Mooie boel, zegt de blik van Poes, als we zo
doorstomen, ja dan komt de Noord pool snel in zicht.

All poems translated by Paul Vincent

From: *Bij eb is je eiland groter* (Your Island's Bigger at Low Tide),

Augustus, Amsterdam/Antwerpen, 2010

The Cuckoo in the Artistic Nest

The Work of Jef Geys

[ERIC BRACKE]

The Flemish art-tsar Jan Hoet is said to have once called him 'more a social worker than an artist'. It seems that after that relations between Hoet and Jef Geys (Leopoldsburg, 1934-2018) never really recovered. The fact is that, throughout his long career, Geys tried to erase the boundary between art and everyday life.

Whether they paint, take photographs or make films, artists 'question the representation of reality, the status of the artwork, or the mechanisms of the art world'. These are stopgaps that recur frequently in writings on contemporary art, so often in fact that the word 'question' has lost all its bite. But if there is one Flemish artist who has made 'questioning' – raising things for discussion – his hobbyhorse, it is Jef Geys.

Following the example of his father, who was a soldier, the young Jef Geys initially opted for the army too. But after only a few years he brought his military career to an end and enrolled at the art academy in Antwerp. This young artist was a thorn in the side of the artistic world from the very beginning. His work did not match the expectations of the art circuit, but criticised the institutions and undermined the convention of the uniqueness of the work of art.

Geys was keen to interact abundantly with his local surroundings in Balen, a village in the Campine region: the school, the neighbourhood committee, the local committees with the ability to influence local decision-making, the cafés, the clubs and so on. This often resulted in a presentation of all sorts of documents, cuttings, drawings, objects, photos and letters. You might call it an unstreamlined, eclectic communication of knowledge.

The fact that, throughout his career, Geys was an art teacher in Balen, at the same school where his writer-friend Walter van den Broeck and the socialist politician Jef Sleeckx also taught, probably helped shape his open and unstructured method. In the classroom, instead of giving pupils an academic initiation into the plastic arts, he entered into conversation with them. He hung up original works by well-known artists at the back of the room, curious to hear the pupils' reactions. It was also during discussions in these classes that his list of 'Women's Questions' took shape, which was often to be seen in his exhibitions. 'A woman in politics. How does that work?' is one of at least 150 questions that Geys collected in his lists.

Working-class and rebellious

Geys also liked to incorporate popular culture into his unruly work. A good example is the project with a young local racing cyclist in 1968-69. Geys super-
vised and coached the fifteen-year-old cyclist during his races. In exchange,
the boy told of his experiences, which Geys incorporated into a number of letters to friends. Geys also followed Eddy Merckx in the Tour de France and from
there wrote letters to his protégé in which he described the great champion's
cycling technique and lifestyle. The result of this project, consisting of framed
photos, letters and cuttings, is kept in the collection of the M HKA, Museum of
Contemporary Art, in Antwerp.

It was at about the same time that allotments first began to appear in his work, and later they frequently recurred as a full-blown subject. In 1969 Geys suggested to the then Minister of Culture, Frans van Mechelen, that the Middelheim sculpture park should be dug up and turned into a kitchen garden for the people of Antwerp. Several years later he himself planted cabbages ('edible art') in the park in Ghent, and for the bicentenary of the French Revolution, in 1989, he suggested to Jacques Chirac, the mayor of Paris, that vegetables be grown on the Cour Royale.

In some cases his early work also had a rebellious side. In 1971 Geys proposed blowing up the Royal Museum of Fine Arts, KMSKA, in Antwerp. The weak points in the construction of the building were marked on the plan. The artist confronted the artificial world of art with its own pretensions, its self-determined demarcation and its irrelevance.

In his early years, his field of action also included the Socialist Meeting House, especially when the wildcat strike broke out at the Vieille Montagne zinc factory in Balen in 1971. Regarding this period, Geys said that it was the only time in his life that he had felt useful as an artist. In that same Meeting House he had also once taken part in a hobby exhibition organised by the 'association of socialist women'. It was at this exhibition that his painted packets of flower and vegetable seeds made their appearance.

Every year since 1962, Geys painted a large panel in which he copied the illustration of vegetables or flowers on a seed packet. In 2001, this series of paintings, a continuous thread running through his oeuvre, was shown at the Kunstverein in Munich, the place where the Nazis had exhibited the *Entartete Kunst*, or Degenerate Art Exhibition, in 1937. On the wall opposite the painted panels of flowers and vegetables was a countdown from the year 1962 to 1928,

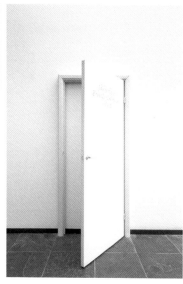

written in chalk. Next to this hung a list of ethnic population groups. Associations with the dark chapters in German history and with the issue of refugees were quite plain to see even at that time.

Chambres d'Amis, Ghent, 1986
© Dirk Pauwels,
S.M.A.K. Ghent

Geys's social commitment was also expressed in his contribution to *Chambres d'Amis* (1986), Jan Hoet's controversial project in which artists showed their work in the homes of Ghent residents. This artist from the Campine region selected a number of small, shabby houses inside which he installed a false door with the slogan of the French Revolution: Freedom, Equality, Fraternity. When you opened the door you came up against the wall. One of these doors can now be seen at the S.M.A.K., the Municipal Museum of Contemporary Art, in Ghent.

In the catalogue, the artist included accounts given by the inhabitants of these houses. Ingrid Verdonck, for example, said: 'As an unemployed single mother with two children who has to manage on an allowance of 9,000 Belgian francs a month, I no longer feel much need to go and look at art in the museum. As I watch my children growing up in this small, damp house, I often think "what will become of them later?"'

Figurative art

Geys prompts us to look for the meaning behind his experiments and presentations, without leading us by the hand. Inevitably, the viewer sometimes sees intentions that the artist probably never had. In *Kunst in België na 1975* (Art in Belgium after 1975, 2001) we read: 'With his painted copies of *Seed Packets* (as from 1962) and above all *Culture HQ* (1969), *Edible Art* (1967-68) and *Cabbages* – which he installed as sculptures in the flower beds of the South Park in Ghent in 1969 (and which were promptly removed by the council) – he parodied figurative representation in painting and in addition took aim at the notion of the artist as the individual maker of an artwork.'

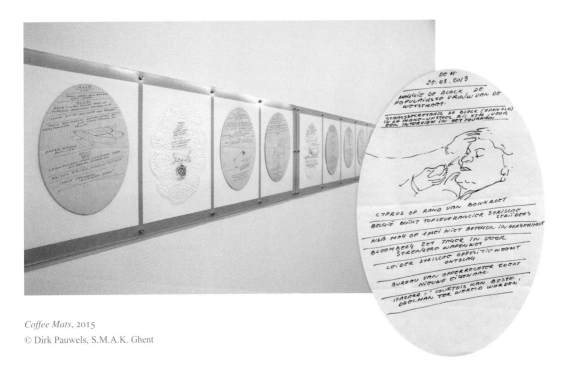

Coffee Mats, 2015
© Dirk Pauwels, S.M.A.K. Ghent

I am quite sure that it was never Jef Geys's intention to denounce figurative representation in painting. Geys guarded against pushing art in any particular direction, and even joined in exhibitions by so-called amateur artists. In the popular Flemish newspaper *Het Laatste Nieuws*, for example, we read that Jef Geys also took part in the first exhibition by the Balense Kunstkring KUBA (an art club) in September 2016. He wanted, rather, to accuse the artistic bastion of unworldliness and expose the dominance of commerce and marketing.

After being awarded the Flemish Culture Prize for Visual Art in 2000, Geys told the writer Walter van den Broeck, a kindred spirit, in a rare conversation: 'It's my opinion that significant images can still be made using pencil and paint.' According to Geys, this no longer happened because it was no longer taught. 'And it is no longer taught because the schools believe there's no money in it.' This does not really sound like someone who reviles figurative representation in painting. On the contrary, according to this former teacher of art, drawing is a matter of true seeing. He himself collected a series of his drawings in 'colouring books for adults'. And in November 2011 he gave every year six pupil at Leopoldsburg's schools one of these colouring books.

Archive

Jef Geys almost constantly reincorporated themes and elements from earlier work into his projects. He kept his reserves of material and ideas neatly archived in Balen: from drawings he did as a thirteen-year-old boy to a Super-8 film of a concert by the crooner Zwarte Lola in a roadside café in the Campine region, and even police tickets, all arranged tidily and chronologically. These archive items frequently turned up in various combinations, as was the case in the *Retrospectieve-Introspectie* ('Retrospective-Introspection') exhibition at the Erna Hecey Gallery in Brussels in autumn 2007.

Earlier, at the 2002 Documenta in Kassel, Geys projected the negatives of all his photos onto a screen. This really means every single one of his photos, from snapshots of his private life to photos documenting one or other project. This is typical of Geys, since he made no hierarchical distinction between the items he used to compile his artworks. It took thirty-six hours for half a century's worth of photographs to pass across the screen. The majority of the negatives had previously also been published in a tiny but thick 500-page book entitled *Jef Geys – Al de zwart-wit foto's tot 1998* (Jef Geys: All the Black-and-White Photographs up to 1998).

In the newspaper *De Standaard*, Johan de Vos wrote that 'a real photographer would never do such a thing'. 'The art lies in the selection, quite literally.' And he concluded: 'We outsiders can only look on in wonder, guessing, searching. In the end the images will make a different impression on everyone. And these impressions will have little to do with Jef Geys, but plenty to do with the viewer himself. That's what makes it an odd, incomprehensible, but delightful book.'

Het Kempens Informatieblad (The Campine Newsletter)

Geys's whole oeuvre was a gigantic work in progress, always branching off in new directions. The younger shoots largely fed on the same humus as fifty years before, reflecting the artist's consistent position in the world. Geys always sided with the weakest party.

He considered the social reality more oppressive than the art world, which he appeared to want to unmask as elitist, mercantile and artificial, sneaking everyday things into his art that do not have the exalted aura of an artwork. He replaced the usual exhibition catalogues with his own issues of *Het Kempens Informatieblad*, the name of a regional newspaper that used to be delivered door to door. If ever prepared to take part in a group exhibition, he would ask for his résumé to be omitted from the catalogue. But in his own modest publications he gave a detailed account of his sources and offered his views on socially relevant topics.

Geys had always been interested in how mass communication works. As a student at the academy, he took the course in advertising because he was interested in the publicity machine used to reach the masses. It was clear from his exhibition at the Middelheim Open-Air Museum in Antwerp in 1999 that advertising had continued to fascinate him. He turned his fire on 'corporate image-building'. At the time, Geys told the journalist Christine Vuegen: 'There is a type of logo being made that carries out a subliminal campaign... For example, cigarette advertising is banned; a colour is then linked to the brand. A colour is appropriated, just as political parties do. Will a time come when one will not be able to paint one's house yellow?'

At Middelheim, Geys used an advertising strategy himself. He copied pornographic drawings ranging from Ancient Greece to the nineteenth century. Geys planted the drawings on stands in the museum park and linked each one to a different product logo.

Geys had already incorporated logos into his work in the 1960s. At that time he was mainly interested in their form, the simplicity of which was overshadowed by their weighty symbolism. One striking example is the stars and triangles the Nazis used to stigmatise Jews, Gypsies and homosexuals. These geometrical figures appeared in his paintings and the Star of David turned up again in his entry for the São Paulo Biennial in 1991. In a series of photographic self-portraits, Geys, in a black overall, shows several of these highly charged geometric forms. But their meaning is obscured by the fact that they are given the colours of a local football team. Jef Geys called this 'image wear'.

Recognition

For the last couple of decades, Jef Geys has been receiving international recognition, ironically enough even from the major art institutions. Having taken part in Documenta 11, he was given a retrospective at the Van Abbemuseum in Eindhoven (2004) and was later a guest at art institutions in Finland and

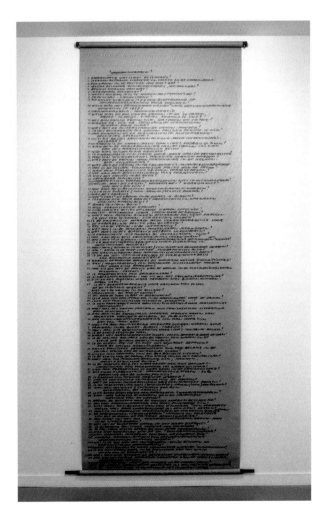

Women's Questions, 1965
© Dirk Pauwels,
S.M.A.K. Ghent

Outlines of a Wing of the Museum of Fine Arts, Ghent
© Dirk Pauwels, S.M.A.K. Ghent, 2015

France. They have also discovered him over in the United States. Dan Graham invited him to take part in the *Deep Comedy* exhibition (2007) at Marfa in Texas and a year later Geys's work was shown at the International Center of Photography in New York (*Archive Fever: Uses of the Document in Contemporary Art*).

In 2009, when he was already seventy-five, the Flemish Community also sent him off to the Venice Biennale, where he carried out the *Quadra Medicinale* project. He asked four acquaintances to look for twelve wild plants between the paving stones in a square kilometre marked off in their own city – Villeurbanne, New York, Moscow and Brussels. What was found in these four 'terroirs' formed the starting point for a richly documented study that was presented in the Belgian Pavilion.

In 2015, Geys was also finally given his own solo exhibition at the S.M.A.K. in Ghent. It turned out that the artist still had a bone to pick with Jan Hoet, the former director of the museum. Geys applied coloured lines to the floor of several otherwise empty rooms. They turned out to be the outlines of a wing of the neighbouring Museum of Fine Arts (MSK), where Geys had been promised an exhibition long before. Geys had already prepared everything when Hoet cancelled that earlier exhibition, supposedly because he didn't have the money for it. This unsettled account was now settled at the S.M.A.K.

The question remains whether Jef Geys was 'more a social worker than an artist' who made arresting art. One thing is certain: that with his uncommon attitude he kept the art world and his audience awake. And although the visual impact of his work is often subordinate to its content, an almost moving, poetical beauty lies dormant in many of his works. A recent example of this was the presentation of a series of so-called coffee mats in the S.M.A.K. exhibition. The artist went to a café to read the paper every morning. On the paper mat the coffee was served on, he wrote down the headlines and topics that struck him that day. Together these kitschy mats form an enthralling diary of current events that had troubled the artist. ▪

Translated by Gregory Ball

Individual in an Undivided World

Charlotte Van den Broeck, Maud Vanhauwaert and Ellen Deckwitz
as New Romantic Poets

Dutch poetry's progressive narrative has come to a halt. At least that is what Bertram Mourits claims in the literary journal *De Gids*, edition 2012. Mourits describes the history of Dutch-language poetry over the last two centuries as a series of caesuras. Again and again small groups of avant-gardist authors have rejected their predecessors and grasped at eternity. But in Mourits's opinion the Romantic paradigm whereby poets are prophets who can give us a glimpse of eternity has become jaded. He pleads instead for an assessment of the state of poetry based on the authors 'who quietly reinvented themselves'.

He himself does that in this essay by quoting poems by five contemporary authors who, in his opinion, show reality rather than the unattainable. Without actually saying so, but undoubtedly deliberately, Mourits chose only female poets' work. That makes his article implicitly a story about the quiet revolution that has taken place in recent Dutch-language poetry. Noisy groups of men – because that is what the avant-gardist movements were – have made way for individual voices, of whom a growing number are women.

A glance at debut prizes awarded recently in the Dutch language area shows that the rise of young female poets is impressive. Between 2010 and 2017, six of the eight winners of the C. Buddingh' Prize were women; the Herman de Coninck Debut Prize went to women in 2015, 2016 and 2017; while the Liegend Konijn Debut Prize has been awarded five times now – and always to a female author. Yet prior to 2000, hardly any women poets were active in Flanders.

I certainly agree that these women – and the young male poets – operate in a far more individualistic way than twentieth-century poets. But I find Mourits's idea that there has been a break with the heritage of Romanticism unconvincing. In fact, I think there is a deeply Romantic longing in the work of many young poets.

In-dividual

You can see that, for example, in the way these authors deal with individualism and commonality. On the one hand, many poets write highly egocentric poetry, which is itself a Romantic characteristic. More importantly though, they

also place themselves emphatically in the world, which is an interpretation of the 'individual' that is completely in line with the Romantics. A person is 'in-dividual', a literally 'un-divided' whole that is one with the world in which he or she functions. What is more, contemporary poets are inspired by texts from the environmental movement and certainly by feminist authors like Chris Kraus and Rebecca Solnit, who demonstrate that the personal is political.

Poets like Hannah van Binsbergen and Dominique De Groen reveal how individuals are one with the *political* and *economic* systems in which they are embedded. In recent anthologies Astrid Lampe, Marwin Vos and Maartje Smits opted for an *ecological* focus, showing that all beings and objects in the world are constituent parts of an ecosystem. And still other poets, including Char-lotte Van den Broeck, Maud Vanhauwaert and Ellen Deckwitz, concentrate mainly on the *social* systems and public spaces in which people live with each other. These poets can certainly not be neatly divided up into different groups. Vanhauwaert's portrayal of social alienation in the big cities, for example, is reminiscent of Marwin Vos's impossible longing for a nature untouched by mo-dernity. What the poets share is – well, a rather Romantic unattainable longing for purity.

Left
Charlotte Van den Broeck
© Koen Broos

Middle
Maud Vanhauwaert
© Noortje Palmers

Right
Ellen Deckwitz
© Merlijn Doomernik

The performer as prophet

Deckwitz, Vanhauwaert and Van den Broeck, three of the leading poets of their generation, can be labelled modern Romantics not only because of their themes but for other reasons too. All three quite naturally combine work on paper with poetry performances, which is a response to the nineteenth-centu-ry-type desire to see poets speak in flesh and blood.

That desire for the physical presence of the poet seemed to have died out in the first half of the twentieth century, in the slipstream of paper-oriented modernism. Since the 1960s, however, poetry readings have been back in the Netherlands and Flanders, with popular poetry festivals like Nacht van de Poëzie, Saint Amour and Poetry International. In the 1990s poetry slams appeared on the scene too and have grown from a poetic niche into an iconic phenomenon. For countless young poets, poetry slams have become the ticket to success in the 'paper' circuit, as they were, for example, for Deckwitz. She won the NK Poetry Slam in 2009, but ceased to be an active slammer two years later when she debuted on paper. For Vanhauwaert and Van den Broeck, success on festival stages and in poetry films came more or less simultaneously with their success on paper.

The fact that I refer to these poets as Romantics is not only because they operate in a system that attaches special significance to the spoken word. Their work also deals with themes familiar from the nineteenth century. If we look more carefully at the question of individuals in their social environment, which I have already introduced, we will see that these poets deal with themes – changeability, parallelism and flow – that look very like Romanticism.

Changeability

The title of Charlotte Van den Broeck's debut, *Kameleon* (Chameleon, 2015), immediately expresses the idea of changeability. This first anthology is about becoming adult and Van den Broeck relies a lot on haunting stand-alone images. Take 'Flamingo', for example, in which the I-figure compares her sleep position to that of a flamingo: 'I sleep like flamingos stand, / with one leg stretched and the other one / bent at the knee against the abdomen / like a folded blindman's cane.' In one verse she introduces two apparently unrelated images: the flamingo and the white cane. But later in the poem the birds reappear in one verse with the theme of visuality: 'Flamingos conquer each other synchronously / a courtly mating dance, at least twelve / eyelash flutters and a monogamous life long.' In the final verse, the speaker makes it clear that she and her beloved have undergone some development. Initially, like young flamingos, they were grey in colour, but now they are 'almost pilots / almost an ode to birds.' The crux is the word 'almost'. The I and her beloved are not as perfect and monogamous as flamingos, but are actually poor imitations of flying creatures or people. And that failure is there already in the opening of the poem, because while 'eyelash flutters' are crucial for a successful monogamous flamingo relationship, the image of the white cane suggests that the I-figure has no eyes for her partner.

In *Kameleon* we see the development of a (feminine) identity. The final section, for example, reflects on the process whereby mothers and daughters slowly grow apart, but at the same time remain enclosed in each other forever, as in a process of fossilization. 'Slowly we fossilized into two separate beings. / Uncertain which of us // was becoming insect / and which amber.' *Nachtroer* (named after an all-night shop in Antwerp, 2017) deals with a similar theme, namely the fragmentation of the I into a large number of temporary identities and bodies, but the reach of this anthology is much greater than the debut. The poems are 'more flowing' due to the lack, on the whole, of interpunctuation. They are more emotional, and are more concerned with sustaining a consistent theme than highly poetic lines. That is clear in the first section, 'Eight, ∞', in which the demise of a relationship is told backwards. In the first poem we see how the duality of the relationship is broken. The poem goes back, step by step, to the beginning, that moment of endless promise and limitless absorption with each other. But that moment is not actually accessible anymore, because it is only available to the I-figure in retrospect: 'In the field lie a boy and girl reminiscent of days gone by / I imagine they are us, eight years ago, yet they look so unfamiliar / that I don't run over to them saying they've not remembered right'. The moment experienced has immediately become a(n unreliable) memory, however much the boy and girl think, in their 'abandon' in 'the blinding light of the afternoon', that they only have eyes for the moment itself.

In this way Van den Broeck's poetry illustrates the essentially Romantic view that identities are not only in permanent evolution – there is no such thing as a 'crystallized I' – but that they are always formed in the world. Several poems play in the big city, for example, where the I must constantly define her position vis-à-vis her fellow human beings: 'It's too narrow here / in the fluid dot that just happens to be my hesitant body / on other people's photos'.

Parallelism

That urban context plays a crucial role in the poems of Maud Vanhauwaert too. She is particularly interested in simultaneity, in the complexity of events that make up the world and the 'parallelism' with which people live alongside yet separate from each other. In her debut, *Ik ben mogelijk* (I Am Possible, 2011), she portrays that in the image of a city like 'united streets' that are stuck 'to each other with chewing gum'. In one of the sections there is a collage of simultaneous events all over the world that have nothing to do with each other, yet that can be connected to each other purely by their simultaneity: 'The woman in Paris crosses the street but is not / run over, whilst a man in Kinshasa is / run over.'

Maud Vanhauwaert

Ik ben mogelijk

Like Van den Broeck, Vanhauwaert relies, in her debut collection, on powerful and often amusing artifice ('a light is something you can dim / but you cannot slightly jump off a cliff'). However, in her second anthology, *Wij zijn evenwijdig_* (We Are Parallel_, 2014), she takes an important step in terms of theme and form. The anthology has an unusual 'horizontal' form – it is wider than it is high – and consists of ninety-eight unnumbered pages, with two short 'texts' side by side on each page, concluded by an underscore. This character is reminiscent of the cursor on a computer, so the anthology gives the impression of having been written on the spot and being forever 'unfinished' – an element many nineteenth-century Romantics played with in their work. The symbol also creates the idea that the anthology is one flowing whole, which is confirmed by the fluid way in which the first 'poems' flow into each other grammatically. 'We are parallel_', 'Touch each other in infinity_', 'And we run_'. Further on the poems are mainly *thematically* linked to each other, as we see in a sequence about the interactions between people on an underground train. Another series combines associative images around motherhood, physicality and illness.

First the I-figure says she's carrying a 'hollow doll' inside her ('Deep inside I'm not a mother'), after which a man starts to explain black holes and clusters of milky ways. A little later the I-figure seems to respond to the man by giving him another definition of a milky way ('a path (...) through the meadow you follow to go and milk the cows'), after which an association is made between milk and breasts when a surgeon makes a wry joke about breast amputation. Immediately after that there are poems about 'a lump' which, because of the text about amputation, make one think of a tumour. Then the touching of the lump is compared to the exploration of a landscape.

*Wij zijn evenwijdig_* (We Are Parallel_) is a radical continuation of the technique of simultaneity and chains of associative meaning which *Ik ben mogelijk* (I Am Possible) contains. An ever-present element in the book is the assumption that people barely understand each other. They are insensitive to each other's weaknesses and cannot fathom what drives other people. But at the same time they want nothing more than to make contact, driven by the impossible desire to be able to touch each other 'in eternity'. Just as Van den Broeck opens *Nachtroer* with the infinity symbol or lemniscate (∞), Vanhauwaert ends with it. 'Then fits her self into mine, makes a / lemniscate. Come. We're late already_'. In physical proximity there apparently lurks a (utopian?) possibility of reaching infinity and breaking through the fundamental boundary between ourselves and others.

Flow

ELLEN
DECKWITZ
**DE
STEEN
VREEST
MIJ**

Ellen Deckwitz debuted with *De steen vreest mij* (The Stone Fears Me, 2011), in which she used oppressive images of nature to symbolise a family relationship. It is a grim book in which quasi-sweet images of the relationship between a girl and her brother are set in the blackly romantic light of a disintegrating family. The anthology is crawling with images like 'The moon / a child's nail ripped right off' and 'All tucked away, neatly like the cellars that are hidden in daughters'. In the final poem the brother is dug up. It is not clear whether he is dead, undead or alive: 'My brother coughs up clods, / sinks back well I can stand / digging, the stone fears me / for I shall strike till it is broken.'

Its thematically related successor *Hoi feest* (Hi Party, 2012) consists of a number of sections that are called, respectively, 'Hands', 'Others' and 'Hands/Others', in Dutch 'Handen', 'Anderen' and 'Handen/Anderen'. The poet exploits the fact that the Dutch words sound very similar. In this anthology hands symbolise, amongst other things, religion (the image of hands folded in prayer recurs regularly) and the unease of the I-figure with her own physicality. Moreover, again many of the scenes seem to take place during the I-figure's youth, at which the I-figure – just like Van den Broeck earlier – looks with a certain alienation. 'That could be me on this photo, a child with a crate on its back.'

Like the other two poets discussed Deckwitz also chooses in a later anthology for a broader perspective. The focus of *De blanke gave* (The White Gift, 2015) is on images of water and the sea as a metaphor for the literal and figurative flows that occur all over the world these days. At one time the Western and non-Western world were strictly separated from each other geographically, but the refugee crisis has made the misery of people in search of greater prosperity in

Europe acutely tangible. Naturally, the Mediterranean Sea plays a crucial role in the current migration flows. 'We stuffed a whole continent / into a container. // There are two ships bobbing / there with bunches of lifeboats.' But past and present seem to flow into each other too, partly because of the unheard-of environmental upheaval we are experiencing due to climate change. In one of the poems, three 'ice mummies from the First World War' come out from under the melting ice of a glacier. But besides disasters, in this anthology flowing water also creates ties between people, as we see in a poem in which the I-figure looks to others for a sense of security in a melting world. 'When I left the hut there were people / I crept close to, with some I meant it. / I don't know what was thawing, so much had died in me.' In several 'water psalms' containing dystopic images of a flooded world, the anthology also describes how flexibly people cope with changed environmental situations. So, this anthology, which is more political and to a certain extent more sombre than its two predecessors, shows too how rapprochement can develop from a political crisis.

New Romanticism

What is interesting about young poets like Van den Broeck, Vanhauwaert and Deckwitz is that while they distance themselves from the avant-gardism of the twentieth century, they also present themselves as new Romantics. Contemporary young Dutch-speaking poets are not afraid of expressing emotions and combine a focus on the I-perspective with a sense of community, while placing people in broader social and environmental systems, as was customary in the early nineteenth century. The result is work that does well on stage and appeals to a diverse group of both younger and older poetry readers. Although at first glance the disappearance of the culture of polemical poetry has resulted in a loss of turbulence, that loss is compensated by many other things: a greater diversity of poets and increasing interest from the public, which no longer needs to feel excluded from the poetical wrangling that used sometimes to dominate. The end of the traditional progressive narrative heralds a dynamic period in Dutch-language poetry. ▩

Translated by Lindsay Edwards

Two Poems

By Charlotte Van den Broeck

Specialist Poulterer

Women make broth of themselves in the bath
until their insides simmer out in the form of a child.

This is how we are born: without a shell,
without the reassurance that one day we will find

a mouth so like our own
that we will speak through it.

We too will end up splay-legged
in the tub with clucking breath

and the nervous tic of a wobbling head
on a groggy body

while the water runs away in circles,
a tiny swirling tornado
that won't even make the weather report.

Speciaalzaak Poelier

Vrouwen trekken bouillon van zichzelf in het badwater
tot hun binnenste in de vorm van een kind uit hen kookt.

Zo worden wij geboren: zonder schelp,
zonder de geruststelling dat we op een dag een mond

zullen vinden, die zo sterk op onze eigen mond
lijkt dat we ermee gaan spreken.

Ook wij zullen uiteindelijk in kikkerzit,
met klokkende adem en de tic nerveux

van een kop op een verdwaasd lichaam
in de badkuip achterblijven,

terwijl het water in cirkels wegdraait,
kleine kolkende tornado,
die niet eens het weerbericht zal halen.

From: *Kameleon* (Chameleon), de Arbeiderspers, Amsterdam, 2015
Translated by David Colmer

Lethe

A stroke away from if and later, a touch does not
evoke expectation of connection, that fallacy belongs
to another generation, always the same metaphor:

all those boxes with all those kinds of cereal in the supermarket
mild desperation packed in a taxonomy of preference
the taming repetition

all movement begins with resistance, push back
until you realise that everything you wanted and did not want
and everything you will want is just an impulse

what is cherished is locked away behind passwords
and out of reach of the polyps of this or that desire
jittering up or down, storm or roars of laughter

as required, distance means haste
for a lover on speed dial in another city
in the space between two tones

the stubborn trembling hope that something will open in the silence
a siren singing glue, finally a lullaby
a meaningless paradox that points the way

to a boat ride and a ramshackle moon
from here the drowsy compass indicates a bed
a possible course

to drink from a river and forget
and all at once it seems so simple, subdued
the thirst for nothingness, raise the glass

Lethe

Een armslag naar als en straks, van een aanraking
wordt geen verbinding verwacht, die dwaling
hoort niet bij deze generatie, steeds dezelfde metafoor:

al die dozen met al die soorten ontbijtgranen in de supermarkt
kleine wanhoop in een taxonomie van voorkeuren verpakt
de herhaling, ze maakt tam

alle beweging begint met weerstand, duw terug
tot je beseft dat alles wat je wilde en niet wilde
en alles wat je zal willen maar een opstoot is

wat dierbaar is, ligt veilig achter wachtwoorden besloten
en buiten bereik van de poliepen van een of ander verlangen
dat op en neer danst al naargelang

storm of schaterlach, afstand is haast
voor een minnaar op sneltoets in een andere stad
in de ruimte tussen twee kiestonen

trilt de starre hoop dat iets zich in de stilte zal openen
een sirene die lijm zingt, eindelijk een slaaplied
een zinloze paradox die richting wijst

op een boottochtje en een gammele maan van hier
duidt de kompasnaald suf gedraaid een bedding aan
een mogelijk verloop

om van een rivier te drinken en te vergeten
het lijkt zo simpel opeens, ingetogen
de dorst naar niets, hoog het glas

From: *Nachtroer* (Night Stirring), de Arbeiderspers, Amsterdam, 2017
Translated by David Colmer

Two Poems

By Maud Vanhauwaert

when you cross the intersection someone else has got red
if you are heavy burdened
you mostly bow your head

look back far enough, you'll look forward again
you can tell it was a selfie
from an arm that's outstretched

to cheer or shout for help there's only one gesture
when someone taps you on the right shoulder
they're often standing on your left

you can smile to words like ravioli, overseas and grief
it won't be the corners of your mouth
that let the truth come out

a light is something you can dim
but you cannot slightly jump off a cliff

a wet finger tests the wind, asks a question or points the way
sex is going against each other, tomorrow
an excuse for today

your shadow sticks to you however fast you run
when people count to ten it's best to hide
and if you don't know where, do it in the daytime

in Marrakesh, on Jemaa El-Fnaa Square

als je oversteekt is het voor iemand anders rood
als je veel met je meetrekt
is het normaal dat je gebogen loopt

kijk ver genoeg achterom en je kijkt weer naar voren
dat je een foto zelf nam
zie je aan de vooruitgestoken arm

bij juichen en om hulp roepen hoort hetzelfde gebaar
je rechterschouder wordt getikt
als er iemand links van je staat

glimlachen kan je op woorden als spaghetti, pierewiet en verdriet
het is niet aan de mondhoeken
dat je de waarheid ziet

zoals je het licht kan dimmen
zo kan je niet een beetje
van een brug af springen

een natte vinger wijst, voelt aan de wind of stelt een vraag
seks is tegen elkaar ingaan, morgen
het excuus van vandaag

je schaduw blijft aan je plakken hoe snel je ook rent
als men tot tien telt verstop je je best
en overdag gaat dat bijzonder goed

op het Djeema El Fna-plein, in Marrakech

From: *Ik ben mogelijk* (I Am Possible), Querido, Amsterdam, 2011
Translated by David Colmer

I am unguarded and the old gent teases
the tangles from my hair. He has a lump
on his head shaped like a doorknob.
When he tells me things I see that his
lump swells a little. Like an air sac a
taut swollen air sac or no, a frog a
big frog you can put your hand on
like a doorknob that wobbles yes, like a
soft doorknob. 'Don't worry, it's not
malignant,' the man says and his lump
throbs a little, beating, almost like a
heart_

Ik ben onbewaakt en de oude heer trekt
de nesten uit mijn haar. Hij heeft een
knobbel op zijn hoofd in de vorm van een
deurknop. Terwijl hij vertelt zie ik dat
zijn knobbel een beetje zwelt. Als een
longblaasje een strak gespannen longblaasje of nee als een kikker een dikke
kikker waarop je je hand kunt leggen als
op een deurknop die meegeeft ja, als
een weke deurknop. 'Wees gerust, het is
goedaardig' zegt de man en zijn knobbel
bonkt een beetje, klopt, als een hart_

From: *Wij zijn evenwijdig_* (We Are Parallel_), Querido, Amsterdam, 2014
Translated by David Colmer

Two Poems

By Ellen Deckwitz

I get to know the previous ones better and better,
they are repeated. Their hands form
bowls too big for my breasts, there's a draught
between my bent back and the hollow
of their lap. They still defend themselves
with the spirit which floats behind
like a gas cloud. It's all right

like that. Let me fall
through the mattress, back
into dreams. Let me

attack memories, change them
into previous bodies as they move hesitantly
from birthmark to birthmark. I am content
with a foot

that misses mine under the table,
to stare past a shoulder at the ceiling.
To see it lacks cracks.

De eerderen leer ik steeds beter kennen,
men herhaalt ze. Hun handen vormen
te grote kommen voor mijn borsten, het tocht
tussen mijn gekromde rug en de holte
van hun schoot. Ze verdedigen zich nog
met de geest die er als een gaswolk
achteraan zweeft. Het is goed

zo. Laat me door
het matras vallen, terug
de dromen in. Laat me

herinneringen aantasten, veranderen
in eerdere lijven terwijl ze aarzelend van moedervlek
naar moedervlek trekken. Ik ben tevreden
met een voet

die de mijne onder de tafel mist,
om langs een schouder naar het plafond te staren.
Zien dat het barstjes ontbeert.

From: *De steen vreest mij* (The Stone Fears Me), Nijgh & van Ditmar, Amsterdam, 2011
Translated by Paul Vincent

Fifth Water Psalm

We were pumping hard
and saw the tips of the roofs emerging
beneath waves.

The oil slick shifted because of the high tide
from the Mexican gulf to the Amazon

and as the water sank descended
on the tree tops like a veil
of a stylish next-of-kin.

In New Orleans they were tinkling hard again,
fingers flew so high the keys
seemed made of magma.

There was also a proliferation of coral
and bamboo, as a result of which in Yemen
they shot some superfluous pandas, the ugly

frescos proved waterproof too. An excess
of St John's wort and valerian blossomed
by the doorstep, we pruned like crazy.

The ocean did not want to swallow up the coast
and even with the necessary back up
had little talent for spewing pearls.

     It bleated a bit about manoeuvrability
     and other legends. My own kilner jar full of remorse,

     while the factories were still working,
     the remaining children sailed happily on.

Vijfde waterpsalm

We waren flink aan het malen
en zagen de dakpunten onder golven
opkomen.

De olievlek verhuisde door het hoogtij
van Mexico's baai naar de Amazone

en tijdens het zakken van het water
op de boomtoppen gedaald als een voile
van een stijlvolle nabestaande.

In New Orleans werd weer flink gepingeld,
vingers vlogen zo hoog op dat de toetsen
van magma leken.

Ook ontstond er een wildgroei aan koraal
en bamboe waardoor ze in Jemen wat
overtollige panda's afknalden, ook de lelijke

fresco's bleken waterproof. Een overschot
aan sint-janskruid en valeriaan bloeide
naast de stoep, we snoeiden ons een ongeluk.

De oceaan wilde de kust niet opslokken
en had zelfs met de nodige steuntjes in de rug
weinig aanleg voor parels braken.

> Zo mekkerde hij wat over wendbaarheid
> en andere legendes. Mijn eigen weckfles vol wroeging,
>
> terwijl de fabrieken het nog steeds deden,
> de kinderen die resteerden zeilden blij.

From: *De steen vreest mij* (The Stone Fears Me), Nijgh & van Ditmar, Amsterdam, 2011
Translated by Paul Vincent

Intimacy Without Borders

The Photographs of Bertien van Manen

Can you call it magic? A photograph by Bertien van Manen pulls viewers into an unknown environment from where it doesn't immediately release them. The borderline between seeing and experiencing more or less dissolves in her photos. They don't really show a definite subject, but rather an atmosphere, an impression. Showing is already saying too much, for the voice of the photographer is so intimate. She takes us by surprise. In a quiet, unemphatic way, she tells a story that has many dimensions, all elusively fanning out.

Bertien van Manen takes her photographs during stays in faraway countries. There she settles within the hospitality of families who have become her friends. In this way she connects the foreign with the familiar and this is perhaps why as a viewer one feels so welcome and included and free to look behind the everyday facade without feeling like a voyeur.

These photographs often lack a dominant focus and the casual composition is supported by colourful accents that are too subtle to be immediately obvious. They require patient viewing. No wonder then that it took some time before the photographs of this photographer reached the art museum public. It had to get accustomed to the power of intimacy and to a genre that may be called documentary but revolves more around something like the portrayal of humanity. These days Van Manen's photographs are regularly exhibited in art museums all over the world. It is hard to think of a relevant institute that has not shown her work. The Museum of Modern Art in New York, for example, exhibited her work in 2005 and the Stedelijk Museum in Amsterdam has shown it on more than one occasion. While her work has been shown regularly since the 1990s, before then she photographed just as devotedly, though her subjects presented themselves primarily within the national borders and often within the theme of women's lib. From this engaged angle she made several supplements for the weekly *Vrij Nederland*, among which, as early as 1982, a supplement about *Women in Poland*. Also in 1982, commissioned by the Rijksmuseum, she shot a documentary series about the women's movement together with Catrien Ariëns. See *Zelfportret. Vrouwenbeweging in de jaren tachtig* (Self-Portrait. The Women's Movement in the 1980s; published by Feministische Uitgeverij Sara, Amsterdam).

Belgrade Boy,
Give Me Your Image, 2006

An eye that never sleeps

In recent years her free and poetic photographs have been collected in several
books. A noticeable example of Van Manen's intensely human working method
is the book *Give Me Your Image* which appeared in 2006. It is, as so often, a collection of photographs taken within families, average families, living in various
countries. The theme this time is the portrait and the place it has been given
in the living room. Sometimes such a photo has been framed and hung in a
nice spot, other times it has been stuck in the corner of a painting or ended up
between two vases. It presumably depicts a family member, who went away or
died in war. They are often lauded people who, in a standard photograph by a
professional photographer, have been raised above the rest of the family. The
soldier in uniform, the beau garçon with his blond hair, destined perhaps to become an actor, the glamorous photo of the beautiful daughter, the successful
images of a seaside holiday, the old photo of a captain wearing swastika insig-
nia. We see several generations, several forms of material well-being, but we
see especially the feelings that have been preserved through the photographs.
We suspect a tie with a lover or a child, possibly cut off by distance or time; we
feel the pride, the loss, the promise, the expectation, the deep sorrow. They
are so recognisable, those photos that have accreted in the interior. That we

are allowed to see all this is through the mediation of the photographer. The reason we don't feel uncomfortable at these harrowing sentiments that the re-photographing has exposed, are her optics: we see the photos in a domestic context. The objects and furniture around it get as much attention as the portrait itself. Besides, in many cases the image dissolves into visual complexity. Your gaze goes to and fro: from the photographed portrait to where it is located in the room. It requires you look well and attentively, and repeatedly. The photo-in-the-photo creates confusion regarding the rules of perspective. We seem to be dealing with cubist shifts. At what distance has the re-photographed photo been placed in the whole? Only when we have figured this out does the cubist illusion melt away and do we see the reality of the double photograph fully.

The photographer took her photos for *Give Me Your Image* in cities like Madrid, Chisinau, Rome, Budapest, Sofia, Munich, Vilnius, Stockholm, Novokuznetsk, Vienna, Belgrade, Toulouse, Paris, Prague, Athens, a geographic diversity that shows it is an understatement to say that this Amsterdam-based photographer travels. She is an unstoppable traveller; her whole oeuvre is rooted in her travelling which she does at a pleasantly slow pace. Only when she stays somewhere for an extended period can she be sure of a bond of confidence with her host family. Then the photographic distance disappears and the pressing of the button becomes part of a shared domesticity. Not a single photograph gives the impression that it has come about after lengthy preparations. The work has the freshness of snapshots, they are direct and to the point. She herself talks about coincidence, which is a modest explanation for an eye that never sleeps.

Sofia Red Lady,
Give Me Your Image, 2006

Balance and respect

Bertien van Manen was born in 1942 and started travelling when her children were grown. Her unquenchable thirst for the foreign she had up till then been able to satisfy with photos of women who had come to Amsterdam from a different culture, like the wives of guest labourers. They appeared in so-called women's magazines and were collected in her book *Vrouwen te gast* (Women Who Are Guests, 1979). Photography had come naturally to her. She was bitten by the bug when, as a young woman, she was a photographers' model herself and became fascinated by the other side of the camera. She always uses easy-to-handle, analogue cameras – she likes to be ready to shoot without her equipment visibly interfering. At first, she told in an interview, she didn't know *what* she had actually come to photograph, in that distant country. One doesn't have to hit the mark every time, of course, but she went to Istanbul three times, for example, without ever figuring out what she wanted to tell. She didn't go a fourth time. By contrast, her visits to China have yielded an endless stream of images. She started going there regularly, long before the mass invasion of western visitors to the country. The book *East Wind West Wind* (2001) shows her ability to look behind the doors of average Chinese people, letting unadorned lives and human sincerity speak for itself with a fruitful lack of embarrassment. Whether her eye falls on a grimy cupboard or a bed on which a couple in love has eagerly thrown itself, nothing is passed off as more beautiful than it is, while the photographs are at the same time models of balance and respect. It's as if the composition is only an afterthought and spontaneity is the rule. Only later does one notice that many of the interiors are dilapidated and not very aesthetic. Had it actually been all that pleasant to be a guest there for that long? Or is lack of comfort what drives a real encounter in a foreign place?

Weifang Travelling, *East Wind, West Wind*, 2001

'Let's sit down before we go'

Selecting photographs is clearly done with a most critical eye. Van Manen is a perfectionist and lots of material stays out of sight when she is in doubt, as the public was made aware when it viewed the formerly unused photographs of *Let's Sit Down Before We Go*, an exhibition the Foam Photography Museum in Amsterdam programmed in 2011. The photographs in the exhibition and the book with the same title were chosen and put in order by the English photographer Stephen Gill. They comprised a fascinating series of images that Van Manen produced between 1991 and 2009 in countries like Russia, Moldova, Kazakhstan, Uzbekistan, Ukraine, Tatarstan and Georgia. The title is a Russian saying when one sets out on a long journey. It turned out to be a brilliant idea by Gill to finally give these sidelined images the stage that they deserve. Is there just a bit more 'craziness' in this series than in Van Manen's usual selections? There would be nothing strange about that: you would want to treat your temporary friends, who are opening up their lives to you, with the utmost courtesy. But when you leaf back through her books you see that this isn't really so.

What surprises again at Foam is the format of the exhibited prints, which is very modest. Given the current museum practice of large prints, the subdued seize of these images places them beyond categorisation and while it does justice to the intimacy of the content, it doesn't make it easy for the viewer. For a first look is not enough and one has to be prepared to adjust one's antenna several times.

Bertien Van Manen's signature style came into full flowering with the phenomenal project *A Hundred Summers, A Hundred Winters* which was concluded in 1994 with an extraordinary book. The photographs were taken in Russia and embrace a side of Russian society that wasn't known to us in the West. Intuition and love for the people are the guiding principle. Colourful, messy kitchens are alternated with a magisterial shot from above of a rural funeral with a little orchestra leading a loosely formed procession around an open casket being carried high, followed by the cover which is carried separately. And then there are the small groups, three or four young people, with their piercing look into the camera. Their interaction depends on a tension of which we have no knowledge but which we can feel: these young people are ready to vigorously devote themselves to the adventure called life.

The individual photos never come with a title (the project itself has a name) and are therefore not bound to a specific meaning and welcome every projection from the viewer, something which contributes to the mystical ability of this oeuvre. The success of a photo depends on a multitude of conditions, social intelligence, curiosity, persistent visits, unwavering attention, lucky coincidence, a working camera. But all of this would lead to little if it wasn't backed up by Van Manen's superior sensitivity for image. With this something mysterious happens to time. It can't be denied that there is a defining moment but 'moment' in this case should be seen as enduring time, not as time brought to a halt but as prolonged mobility, an unstoppable form of life.

Novokuznetsk Funeral, *A Hundred Summers, A Hundred Winters*, 1994

Bely Yar Communal Kitchen, *A Hundred Summers, A Hundred Winters*, 1994

Kishinev, *A Hundred Summers, A Hundred Winters*, 1994

Propelled by sorrow

In more recent years the imagery has taken a different turn. The social aspect has become subservient to nature. When, in 2014, the long-running exhibition *Moonshine* was also concluded with a book – a project for which Van Manen had returned many times to the American Appalachians to stay among the male and female miners there, a project that shows kinship with *A Hundred Summers,*

A Hundred Winters – it was followed by the enchanting *Beyond Maps and Atlases* published in 2015. The title comes from a poem by Seamus Heaney (the poem 'Herbal', from the collection *Human Chain*) and the photographs came into being in Ireland, an 'elsewhere world' which Bertien van Manen was seeking during the years that she mourned the death of her husband. The churning white-blue sea, the soft-green grassland hidden in mist, a nearly deserted beach, the lonely house; all are metaphors for a soul adrift. They already existed in our collective memory, these photographs. But like a poet taking existing words and turning them into unique panoramas, Van Manen uses these images for an epic of the soul, her soul and those of others. This is what she wrote about it, in September 2015: 'At first, working in Ireland, I wasn't sure what I was looking for. My husband had died. I dispensed with the people and reflected on the atmosphere. I was guided by a feeling and a search, a longing for some kind of meaning in a place of myth and legends. There was mystery and endlessness at the edge of a land beyond which there is nothing but a vast expanse.'

You have to be a true artist, to be able to translate your personal grief into a universal language. Where earlier far-reaching empathy with others was a motif, the Irish project completely let go of that. Propelled by grief the photographer reached the unencumbered core, perhaps the highest achievable intertwinement of art and life. It is not an upbeat story; it unmistakably exudes a desperate and ominous atmosphere. It does indeed take the hand of a master to be able to derive from soft-coloured vistas something which in its elusiveness can be called magic. ■

www.bertienvanmanen.nl

Moonshine, 2014

Translated by Pleuke Boyce

Sonic Imaginings, Creative Mementos

The Musical Instruments Museum in Brussels

[ELISABETH SALVERDA]

'De la musique avant toute chose [...] encore et toujours!' – Verlaine, 1882

'It does not matter if at first it seems to some people more like a cactus than a rose' – Varèse, 1959

The 'Musée instrumental du conservatoire royal de musique de Bruxelles' first opened its doors 140 years ago, in 1878, a year after it was founded by its first curator and cataloguer Victor-Charles Mahillon (1824-1924). Opening on Thursday afternoons between 1 and 3 pm, the museum's collection was formed from instruments collected by two prominent musicologists.

In 1876, Raja Sir Sourindro Mohun Tagore (1840-1914),[1] eminent musicologist, composer and patron of the arts, had gifted 98 rare classical Indian instruments to King Leopold II (1835-1909) along with several books and manuscripts on music, musical theories, systems and notations, in Bengali, Sanskrit and English. As Mahillon stated in his application for the post of keeper of instruments at the Royal Conservatory of Brussels,

> the Indian collection...is the richest of all those in Europe [...] I would be happy...to assume responsibility for its classification, catalogue and conservation with all the care a precious collection such as this one demands [...] I would be sufficiently rewarded for my efforts in curating a collection of such profound interest to the musical world.[2]

Tagore's collection, together with the 82 instruments, 'exactly half of which were extra-European', of the celebrated musicologist François-Joseph Fétis (1784-1871) acquired by the Belgian government in 1872, formed the basis of the museum. Persuaded that no collection could be complete 'without [.] making comparisons amongst *all* possible sound objects', Mahillon massively expanded the scope of the collection, amassing 600 instruments in the first three years alone.

Mahillon, an acoustician, musician, musical instrument maker, and collector, had published a study on musical acoustics in 1874 (*Les Éléments d'acoustique musicale et instrumentale*). He also published a detailed and wide-

ranging inventory of the 3,300 instruments which had entered the Brussels musical instrument collection by 1913: *Catalogue descriptif et analytique du musée instrumental du conservatoire royal de musique de Bruxelles* (5 vol., Ghent, Brussels, 1880-1922 [reprinted 1972]). Mahillon ordered the instruments 'by mode of sound activation', in a taxonomy noted for having the potential to describe any instrument then in existence. Here, the four-fold scientific classification of instruments based on their material components and acoustic factors (vibrations through air, strings, membranes, or solids) found in the ancient Indian treatises described by Tagore will have been of significant influence.[3]

While clearly fascinated by musical instruments of all shapes and sizes and impressed by the ingenuity of their makers, Mahillon's perspective on many unfamiliar ones remains a barometer of his time. In the context of late nineteenth-century Belgian colonial expansion, and following in the tradition of the earlier cabinets of curiosities, he believed that 'where civilization has remained at a standstill [.] in Africa one can find the origin of all our instruments in an entirely primitive state'. While some of his contemporaries refused to study 'uncivilised' instruments, Mahillon argued they should rightfully be displayed for their acoustic value in a musical instruments museum, and not, for example, in the Royal Museum for Central Africa (RMCA) in Tervuren.

Back from the brink

At one point the collection was scattered over fifteen locations, but having survived decades of uncertainty the Musical Instruments Museum (MIM) is now a leading cultural attraction. Since 2000, over two million people have visited the MIM in the Mont des Arts/Kunstberg museum quarter with its prominent views over the city. The MIM is housed in two adjacent buildings: one of imposing white stone and neoclassical design built in 1774 by French architect Gilles-Barnabé Guimard when Brussels was still part of the Austrian Netherlands; the other a decorative art-nouveau facade in glass and black wrought iron built in 1899 by Belgian architect Paul Saintenoy. A dedicated exhibition, *Art Nouveau*, tells the story of the latter's original use as an Old England luxury department store, complete with photos and architectural plans.

Among the museum's founding principles was the aim to preserve and develop research on instruments of all kinds, and to provide music students with the opportunity to study early instruments. Today, as one of three currently open Royal Museums for Art and History (RMAH), with close to 10,000 instruments and open six days a week, the federal scientific institution regularly features students from the Royal Conservatory of Brussels in its own Wednesday lunchtime concert series. In a dedicated play area, children can explore the sound and workings of instruments such as the harp, piano, theremin, chimes, xylophones and talking drums, and multiple groups of excited primary school pupils in fluorescent bibs are often seen in the MIM's four themed galleries: *Keyboards*, *Traditional Instruments*, *Western Art Music*, and *Musicus Mechanicus*.

Over 1,200 instruments from all over the world – both originals and replicas – are on display, with others either out on loan, in storage for safekeeping, or being restored in the conservation workshop on the sixth floor, where instrument makers and researchers may request to examine them, and where conservators supervise students from University College Ghent's faculty of Musical Instrument Making. With an 'Instrument of the Month' feature, the MIM's trilingual website is an invaluable online resource. In addition, the museum participates in several free online catalogues, such as Carmentis, EUROPEANA, and the MIMO project, an inventory with sound recordings of multiple

Old England (detail)

A Ruckers keyboard depicted in: *El Oído* (*Hearing*), 1617 - 1618.
Oil on panel, 64 x 109.5 cm.
Museo del Prado, Madrid. Jan Brueghel the Elder (1568-1625)

musical instrument museum collections which is available in ten languages, while the extensive archive of the MIM's own reference library is currently being digitised.

In October 2017, the MIM hosted the fourth conference in a four-part series on WoodMusICK (WOODen MUSical Instrument Conservation and Knowledge) supported by the COST programme (European Cooperation in Science and Technology). The conference brought together researchers from different but related disciplines, including acousticians, organologists and instrument makers, conservators and curators, but also chemists, wood, material and mechanical scientists and engineers, often but not exclusively working in museum contexts. New publications at the MIM include an impressive tome of research, *The Golden Age of Flemish Harpsichord Making: a Study of the MIM's Ruckers Instruments* (2017), under the direction of the MIM's keyboard instrument curator Pascale Vandervellen. A multi-disciplinary and international project, the study brought together over thirty researchers from both cultural and academic institutions to examine the history, construction, alteration and restoration of the eighteen instruments in the MIM collection 'considered at the time of their acquisition to be made in the Ruckers workshop'.

Harpsichords and virginals made by the Ruckers family, active in Antwerp across four generations between c. 1580-1680, came to be held in such high esteem that counterfeit production became organised on a large scale. They are depicted on many Old Master paintings, such as *El Oído / Hearing*, painted by Jan Brueghel the Elder (1568-1625) in 1617-18, and currently displayed at the Prado Museum in Madrid as one of a set of paintings on the five senses by

Brueghel and Peter Paul Rubens (1577-1640). *El Oído / Hearing* presents an ode to music via hearing, communicated in images: an idyllic scene portrays a singing Venus at centre stage, surrounded by musical instruments, scores and birds, and in the background a group of merry musicians. Paintings within the painting show dancers and players in the act of listening, further symbolising the presence and enjoyment of music throughout history.

Turning now to the MIM's collections, we note that these are similarly filled with illustrations of sound and music on vases, prints, tapestries, paintings, and descriptions of instrument making and musical styles, testifying to musical experience as a timeless pursuit. The MIM offers a survey of an extraordinary creative array, from the oldest instrument, an Egyptian shoulder-harp circa 1500 BCE, via small Yucatan drums and whistles circa 600-900 CE, a 1930s Finnish bugle made from birch bark, to one of its newer additions, the 2014 electronic *Linnstrument*, an 'expressive MIDI controller with polyphonic touch sensing' resembling 'a musical iPad'. I can do no more than present a few unique highlights of invention and restoration related to music and mechanics and leave you to discover your own favourites.

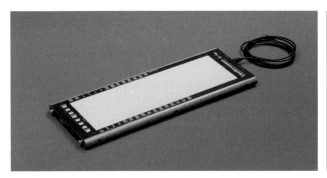

Linnstrument, 2014

IPEM studios, 1960s-70s

Infinite possibilities

The *Musicus Mechanicus* gallery showcases mechanical, electrical and electronic instruments, many of which relate to short-lived quirks and novel special effects. Charting the history of music technology, the collection ranges from automated music-boxes via the first amplifiers in the 1920s to the original 1960s-1970s sequencing equipment of the Institute of Psychoacoustics and Electronic Music (IPEM) in Ghent. One experimental endeavour which came into the collection under Victor-Charles Mahillon in 1876 is the *Componium*, an orchestrion built by the inventor of the metronome, Diederich Nicolaus Winkel (1777-1826), in Amsterdam in 1821. With nine organ stops for different timbral registers (3 flute, piccolo, violin, salicional, gamba, quintadena and trumpets), a tambourine and a triangle, the concept of the *Componium* was really an automated one-organ band. No longer housed in its original cabinet, it is possible to view how mechanical receivers are designed to read music 'data' from two large wooden cylinders, perforated paper rolls or cardboard books. The infor-

The *Componium* by
Diederich Nicolaus Winkel,
Amsterdam 1821

mation coded on the different inputs sets the machine in motion, creating musical output. As well as being able to play recognisable songs, the *Componium* had another 'shuffle' setting: it could play and compose or compute a practically infinite[4] and entirely unpredictable range of musical sounds. The two cylinders could be programmed to turn randomly, which would create different combinations of input data. A precursor to live coding perhaps, it required the turn of a crank to function. It didn't catch on, but composers such as Edgard Varèse (1883-1965), Pierre Boulez (1925-2016), Karlheinz Stockhausen (1928-2007) or György Ligeti (1923-2006) might have approved; Ligeti, after all, wrote *Poème Symphonique* for 100 metronomes in 1962, exploiting another invention of Winkel's.

The *Keyboards* exhibition explores all types of instruments operated via a keyed interface, from six-pedal pianos via synthesizers, keyed oboes, clarinets and harps to American composer Cecil Effinger's 1955 *Musical Typewriter* with notes and other musical script instead of letters. A rare hybrid instrument on display here is the only remaining original 'luthéal' mechanism in the world, a grand piano effects system built in 1919 by Belgian organ builder Georges Cloetens (1871-1949). Like the *Componium*, it has organ-like stops for creating different timbres. By lowering materials such as felt or metal onto or close to the piano strings, as well as its original piano setting, the 'luthéal' can imitate the sound of a lute with octave harmonic; a harpsichord; or a cimbalom (a hammered dulcimer) through combining the lute and harpsichord registers. Up to 18 combinations across the range of the keyboard are made possible since the bass and treble sections can be set to different effects. French composer Maurice Ravel (1875-1937) was the first to write music for the device, at around the same time that American composer Henry Cowell (1897-1965) was explor-

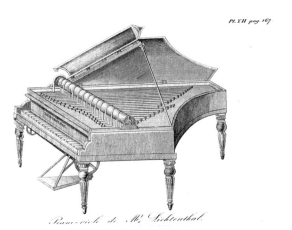

Pl. XII pag 167

Piano-viole de Mr. Lichtenthal.

Engraving of the *Piano-Viole*,
La Belgique Industrielle (1835)

ing the range of sounds which could be produced by playing a piano's strings instead of its keys. Installed in a 1910 Pleyel, Wolff, Lyon & Cie grand piano at the MIM, the system was restored to playing condition in 1979 by Dutch violinist Theo Olof and piano technician Evert Snel. Olof's research into the meaning of the score indication of Ravel's 1924 *Tzigane, Rhapsodie de concert pour violon et luthéal* had led him to discover the device in the MIM's instrument reserves. With their restoration of a long-forgotten instrument, Olof and Snel revived Ravel's intended sound palette, providing new insight into an essential component of his composition, where the registers are used to contrasting effect. Several recordings of Ravel's *Tzigane* have now been made using the luthéal at the MIM, and it has also been the source of inspiration for new compositions. For those unable to access the instrument itself, high-quality samples of its special sound can be procured from www.realsamples.net.

Another unique hybrid now restored to playable condition at the MIM concerns an invention on permanent loan from the Royal Palace of Brussels since 2014. Once belonging to King Leopold I, the *Piano-Viole* is a mechanically bowed, pedal-operated keyboard instrument invented in 1830 by the renowned Brussels piano maker Herman Lichtenthal (1795-1853). It has a unique belt-bow mechanism that can be traced back to one of three recorded Leonardo da Vinci drawings of bowed keyboard designs[5] for the *Viola Organista* circa 1490. A surprising invention, the *Piano-Viole* in fact belongs to a larger tradition of bowed keyboards, over 200 of which were built in the last 400 years. With a six-octave range (F-F), each string (one per note) can be bowed individually by a corresponding vertically turning leather belt-bow; the pedal crankshaft, assisted by a flywheel, operates a cylinder pulley above the string level on which all 73 bows are mounted. Resembling a grand piano in appearance, a distinctive semi-circular protrusion in its lid covers the cylindrical contraption when closed and resembles the hump of a dromedary camel.

Discovered at the palace in 2006 in a state of disrepair, restoration of the instrument has not been straightforward. With only two imprecise drawings, an 1830 patent description and varying reviews from the time to go on, and little left of the original mechanism, a process of reinvention, research and exploration of how the instrument might have worked and sounded began. This involved dozens of experiments regarding sound quality, consistency, dynamic and tonal potential, focussing on mechanism prototypes and interaction of different materials such as types of leather, strings, their advantages and disadvantages. An initial and promising result was demonstrated at the MIM in October 2017, and future events related to the *Piano-Viole* can be expected.

Listening to light

Alongside its permanent collections, the MIM also hosts temporary installations and exhibitions related to music and sound. In 2017, Overtoon, a platform for sound art, presented an exhibition in Brussels exploring the act of listening, *Où sont les sons? Where Are Sounds?*. As part of the exhibition the MIM exhibited a sound work, *Heliophone*, on its tenth-floor rooftop terrace. Curator Nicole Gingras states that various sound works in the show 'suggest that it is not only possible to hear a sound but also to see it, touch it, be pervaded by it'. *Heliophone*, a work by one of Overtoon's founders, Brussels-based artist and researcher into light Aernoudt Jacobs (b. 1968), is a photo-acoustic installation which transforms energy from the sun's rays into sound without recourse to electronic amplification: translating visible to audible. The constantly undulating tone which visitors were able to hear on the restaurant terrace and also via a speaker on the fifth floor indicated the fluctuating intensity of the light from the sun. Taking us back to the 1880s, Jacobs's installation employs the effect discovered by Alexander Graham Bell (1847-1922) while investigating the transmission of sound over long distances. Sunlight is focussed onto one point

Heliophone by sonic artist and researcher Aernoudt Jacobs
on the roof of the MIM

Toots Thielemans as a young boy

by means of a parabolic lens, and a rotating disc chops the light into small fragments, transforming them into sound waves via a photo-acoustic cell. Victor-Charles Mahillon would definitely have been intrigued.

Beyond the preoccupations and times of their curators, musical instrument museums such as the MIM in Brussels are testament to the creativity and skill of sound and music makers, allowing us to learn about and imagine the musical and sonic environments of past times – here and elsewhere – while maintaining their relevance for future generations the world over. Alongside the preservation of strange and ancient instruments, there is also an ongoing stream of new acquisitions: most recently, the instruments used and collected by the world-famous Belgian musician Toots Thielemans (1922-2016), tribute to a life lived in song. It is hard to think of a better place than the MIM for these musical legacies. ▨

NOTES

1   An elder relative of the poet, philosopher and winner of the Nobel Prize for Literature in 1913, Rabindranath Tagore (1861-1941), Raja Sir Sourindro Mohun Tagore attained some notable firsts: in 1884, he was the first Bengali to be knighted by Queen Victoria, for whom he wrote songs; in 1875 and 1895 he received honorary doctorates in Music from the University of Pennsylvania and the University of Oxford, respectively; and he set up the first Bengal Academy of Music. Interested in Western music, S.M. Tagore learnt to play the piano to pursue comparative musicological study. He published more than 68 works of and on music, and donated collections of instruments to dozens of museums worldwide, including the Royal College of Music in London, which honours him annually with a Tagore gold medal award, and the Metropolitan Museum of Art in New York.

2   Archives générales du Royaume (AGR), *Fonds* conservatorium, Dossier 552, in: Vandervellen, 2013. My translation.

3   Mahillon's framework was developed in 1914 by musicologists Curt Sachs (1881-1959) and Erich Moritz von Hornbostel (1877-1935) into their eponymous system still used today. While 'electrophone' was later added as a category, the H-S system cannot accommodate many hybrid instruments or extra features. Classification issues in museums, such as attributions to makers, also often arise with recycled instruments or restoration projects.

4   For a more recent foray into infinite musical installations, see Jem Finer's Longplayer project: http://www.independent.co.uk/news/business/analysis-and-features/jem-finer-from-here-to-almost-eternity-5368800.html

5   Manual bow, wheel bow, belt bow. Examples of the wheel bow can be seen on instruments such as the hurdy-gurdy, and the 2012 *Viola Organista* after Leonardo da Vinci by Polish instrument maker Sławomir Zubryzicki, featured by Björk on her 2015 album *Vulnicura*.

FURTHER READING

Faure, Eugène Gressin-Dumoulin, Benoît Valerius, *La Belgique Industrielle, Compte-Rendu de l'Exposition des Produits de l'Industrie en 1835*. Hauman, 1836.

Pierre Gevaert, Michel Terlinck, Elisabeth Salverda, 'Restoring the *Piano-Viole*: an Adventure in Sound', paper presented at the WOODMusICK conference at the MIM, 6 October 2017.

Nazir Ali Jairazbhoy, 'The Beginnings of Organology and Ethnomusicology in the West: V. Mahillon, A. Ellis and S.M. Tagore', *Selected Writings in Ethnomusicology, Volume 8: Issues in Organology* (1990), pp. 67-81.

Margaret Kartomi, 'The Classifications of Musical Instruments: Changing Trends in Research from the Late Nineteenth Century, with Special Reference to the 1990s', *Ethnomusicology* 45 (2) (2001), pp. 283-314.

Barry Lloyd, 'A Designer's Guide to Bowed Keyboard Instruments', *The Galpin Society Journal* 56 (2003), pp. 152-174.

Pascale Vandervellen, 'Histoire d'un joyau muséal: le mim'. *Brusselse Cahiers Bruxellois, Revue d'histoire urbaine / Tijdschrift voor stadsgeschiedenis: Promenades musicales / Muzikale wandelingen* (2013).

Pascale Vandervellen, *The Golden Age of Flemish Harpsichord Making: a Study of the MIM's Ruckers Instruments*. Musical Instruments Museum, Brussels (ed. 2017).

Stéphanie Weisser, 'Des palais des maharadjas à l'*Old England* de Bruxelles. Les instruments indiens du mim'. *Brusselse Cahiers Bruxellois, Revue d'histoire urbaine / Tijdschrift voor stadsgeschiedenis: Promenades musicales / Muzikale wandelingen* (2013).

Stéphanie Weisser and Maarten Quanten, 'Rethinking Musical Instrument Classification: Towards a Modular Approach to the Hornbostel-Sachs System'. *Yearbook for Traditional Music*, Vol. 43 (2011), pp. 122-146.

Saskia Willaert, 'The Growth of an "Exotic" Collection. African Instruments in the Musical Instruments Museum, Brussels (1877-1913)', Annual Meeting of the CIMCIM 2011 / Rencontre annuelle du CIMCIM 2011 (2012), pp. 61-71.

WEBSITES

www.aernoudtjacobs.info/heliophone.html
www.europeana.eu/portal/en/exhibitions/music-and-mechanics
www.metmuseum.org/blogs/of-note/2014/raja-tagore
www.mim.be
www.mim.be/the-golden-age-of-flemish-harpsichord-making
www.mimo-international.com/MIMO
www.museodelprado.es/en/the-collection/art-work/hearing

Writer in Service to the Underdog

On the Oeuvre of Chris De Stoop

[TOMAS VANHESTE]

'They want us out of here.' Chris de Stoop (1958) committed his brother's ex-clamation to paper in his book *Dit is mijn hof* (This Is My Farm, 2015). His entire oeuvre can be read as an attempt to give a literary journalistic voice to people for whom society has left no space: farmers like his brother who watch the advance of industry and new nature reserves around them and feel stifled by a forest of rules and regulations; psychiatric patients hidden away in woods and used as guinea pigs for the wildest experiments; illegal immigrants seen as con men and profiteers who should be forcibly deported.

De Stoop continually takes the part of the underdog. In his first book, *Ze zijn zo lief, meneer* (They Are So Sweet, Sir, 1992), that means trafficked women. A quarter of a century after its publication, the book still makes a deep im-pression, providing insight into the world of gangs operating internationally to recruit women as 'dancers', saddling them with debt for the journey to the west and then forcing them into prostitution and abusing them. After extensive digging and taking on various roles as an undercover journalist, from randy, drunken customer to pimp in search of merchandise, the reporter succeeds in exposing a worldwide network of women traffickers. *Ze zijn zo lief, meneer* con-tains uncomfortable revelations on the role of police inspectors and officials in the Netherlands and Belgium, who turn a blind eye in exchange for sexual and financial favours. It led to outrage and the appointment of a parliamentary research committee into women trafficking.

His second book, *Haal de was maar binnen* (Just Bring the Laundry In, 1996), is no less cutting. It is an indictment of the way in which illegal immigrants are portrayed and treated in Europe. De Stoop shows how in Germany, the Nether-lands and Belgium special patrols, prisons and transport systems are set up to track down and deport illegal immigrants.

Moral blueprint

However disconcerting De Stoop's many stories may be, there is also some-thing formulaic about his style of *J'accuse*. He sees pure injustice, not moral complexity. When the city of Cologne wants to deport a Roma woman because

she has not responded to an interview invitation she never received, the mayor reacts to the social protest against that decision 'with all the classic arguments of governments in Europe,' De Stoop writes. 'The deportation served as a deterrent to stop the "unrestrained surge" and "abuse of the right to asylum". The false refugees must be removed to protect the genuine ones. If illegal immigrants were not dealt with, it would damage social support for the integration of legal foreigners.'

In De Stoop's view the mayor's response is first and foremost an attempt to restore his reputation. The author does not indicate whether he believes those classic arguments might possibly have some basis, resolutely portraying the ministers responsible for asylum policy and those who execute that policy as ogres, not people confronted with a thorny task.

The Antwerp professor in *Dit is mijn hof* receives similar treatment, having done a deal with the devil in De Stoop's eyes to permit expansion of the port in exchange for the creation of new nature reserves, requiring farmers to give way. He speaks 'hurriedly and agitatedly, as if the devil is at his heels' and has a 'nervous laugh'.

Dit is mijn hof is a probing, personal book. The tragedy of De Stoop's brother who took over the farm from his parents and later committed suicide plays out in the background. De Stoop does not say so explicitly, but it is implied that a sense of having to leave played a role in the mixture of factors which led to his brother's act of desperation. In beautiful language De Stoop interweaves his brother's death, the destruction of his birthplace and his mother's decline into a narrative. But moving as the book is, we are left with the impression that the author's personal involvement clouds his view. His rage is focussed on 'the greens'. Previously farmers and nature lovers had joined forces in fighting the expansion of the Port of Antwerp, but in the eyes of De Stoop 'the greens' have sold their souls, suspending their resistance to the advance of the port in exchange for 'nature compensation', new nature reserves which flood or bulldoze old farmland.

De Stoop prefers to overlook the fact that the romantic farmland of his youth has long been lost. In his reply to the question of whether it is a problem that farmland should make way for new nature reserves, the professor he derides touches on a truth: 'Admit it, we are talking about over-fertilised cornfields and flat potato fields, with pesticide-filled canals in between.'

Curiosity and indignation

In his latest work *Ex-reporter* (2016), a collection of his best journalistic reportages, De Stoop says farewell to the field he worked in for decades as a journalist of the biggest Flemish weekly paper *Knack*. He describes the development in journalism which he rejects as follows: 'The media increasingly wanted to surf the waves of public opinion rather than swim against the current, which seemed wrong to me. When we constantly try to please everyone, we become lap dogs rather than guard dogs.'

In the prologue De Stoop also provides some insight into himself. On his journalistic career he writes, 'Indignation could be a motivation, but I am mainly driven by curiosity about human relationships and social processes. Relationships of trust, empathy, a critical reflex as a sixth sense, those were my primary tools.'

De Stoop's work undeniably springs from a combination of curiosity and indignation, but in my view he judges the balance between these forces a little too favourably. Indignation has the upper hand, certainly when he focusses on those in power, but also in his attack on contemporary journalism. Do today's quality newspapers really exhibit less depth and are they less inclined to play the guard dog than they were a few decades ago?

But curiosity wins out in the best of his work, where his viewpoint is not crystal clear but more nuanced, as in *Zij kwamen uit het oosten* (They Came from the East, 2003). In contrast with most of De Stoop's writing, this is a work of fiction. An author who ten years previously had written a book about trafficking of women now tells the story of an Albanian who, after much wandering, ends up as a sex worker in Antwerp. 'No one enters into dialogue with sex workers,' she says, 'but everyone wants to rescue victims. They are seen as passive, naive, weak creatures who should be protected and even controlled, as children who cannot look after themselves.'

We can also read it as criticism of early De Stoop. The writer does not spare himself. In Antwerp's Schipperskwartier, a brothel owner bitterly accuses him: 'Ten years ago, after that famous book of yours, there was one raid after another.' The sarcasm with which she calls him a 'knight' dents the image of the 'undaunted hero who had infiltrated one of the most dangerous criminal gangs in the world'. Self-doubt sets in. How honest was he really in his journalistic drive to expose the truth? 'Suddenly he saw himself: someone who played the role of a quiet, reliable interlocutor with a soft voice, a loyal look in his eye and an understanding smile,' the writer observes.

Ze kwamen uit het oosten is a hall of mirrors. It is scarcely possible to distinguish fact from fiction, culprit from victim or good from evil. We are left with moral confusion which sets us thinking rather than moral certainties which close down the discussion.

Equally ambiguous is *Vrede zij met u, zuster* (Peace Be With You, Sister, 2010), the story of a young Belgian woman who blows herself up in a failed suicide attack in Iraq. At the same time it is a group portrait of a circle of young people in Brussels who feel attracted to jihad. The writer does not judge, nor does he unfold a sociological theory as to the roots of terrorism. In the stories of these young people a multitude of more or less coincidental experiences might be seen to have nudged them in the direction of this path: psychological factors such as the inability to have children; school failure and frustrated social ambitions; discrimination against Muslims in the labour market; the sectarian character of Salafism; the distressing pain of the population in the Middle East; the self-image of jihadists as idealists fighting an occupation and injustice.

A soft voice, a loyal look in his eye

De Stoop tells their stories as if he is inside their heads. Initially the way these jihadists constantly murmur 'Peace be with you' is jarring. The reader laughs about their medieval belief in evil spirits and is surprised by the disconcerting oversimplification of their worldview. But thanks to De Stoop's great empathy you gradually begin to understand how they see the world. At times you catch yourself almost feeling sorry for those poor wretches who become terrorists.

In Vrede zij met u, zuster De Stoop again shows his ability to break through into parallel universes, worlds with which we normally have little contact. When it comes to people with power, sometimes he cannot refrain from judgement. Far stronger and more fascinating is the work in which he explores the perceptions of people for whom society has already decided on its judgement. The great strength of such work shows that his soft voice, the loyal look in his eye and his understanding smile are much more than just the attitude of a skilled journalist: they form the expression of a fertile curiosity as to motivation and an honest empathy for those scrabbling to make a living in this world. ▪

www.chrisdestoop.be

Translated by Anna Asbury

An Extract from *Peace Be With You, Sister*

By Chris De Stoop

The Parting

Hurricane Katrina raged across America like a nemesis. Like a biblical flood that engulfed the city of New Orleans and drowned a few thousand poor blacks. And the diabolical Bush, who had used the money intended for the levees for the war in Iraq, could no longer escape his punishment. The flood was the curse of Allah, some brothers in Sint-Joost-ten-Node felt, not without schadenfreude.

In Brussels it was oppressively hot. Dark clouds scudded eastwards over the European capital. Muriel and Issam had loaded up the Mercedes and were ready to leave.

On 1 September they went for the last time to Monceau and Charleroi, where they drew money from the bank. The area was still plagued by high unemployment, but looked noticeably better than five years before, when Charleroi had the reputation of being a hotbed of corruption.

In the renovated mine buildings of Monceau there was now a rehabilitation centre for junkies, delinquents and the unemployed. The slag heap of the Four Domains behind her parents' house, where Muriel had once slid through the coal dust on a sleigh, was now dubbed a paradise for nature lovers. There were guides who led groups to the top at weekends. Look, a rare kind of toad. And what a view over the black land of Charleroi...

The last visit to Muriel's family had once again degenerated into a conflict. She could no longer restore the bonds of the womb. What was not visible and scarcely nameable, what had great significance in her life, she could not share with her parents. Jean and Liliane could not understand that their daughter concerned herself with dead texts and talked of things from fourteen centuries ago as if it were yesterday. Nonsense.

When Issam and Muriel got out of the white Mercedes in the avenue de l'Europe, there were stared at by the inhabitants of the cité as if they were extra-terrestrial beings. He in his white djellaba and prayer cap, she in her black niqab and gloves. Muriel had phoned her mother in advance to say that they would be popping in unexpectedly.

- It's hot today. Aren't you boiling under a burka? Her father asked for a joke.

Jeannine, the neighbour with whom Muriel had played and stayed over with so often as a little girl, was in the living room at that moment. Muriel hugged her and asked how her children and grandchildren were. She took her veil off. Her wavy hair fell a long way down her back.

But when Issam saw Jeannine, he went through the house to the back garden. He stood there stock still. His lips moved as if he were praying.

- He mustn't be with strange women, said Muriel's mother.
- Oh, said Jeannine. Will he stay outside the whole time then?
- If he shakes hands with you he'll have to wash. You're unclean.

When Jeannine left in a huff – she didn't feel at all unclean, on the contrary, she had clean hands – Issam came back in. He sat down and said almost nothing. He read his Koran.

Liliane laid the table for four people. Issam asked again if men and women could eat separately. Jean's first impulse was to throw him out of the house right away, but he controlled himself. When Issam went into the kitchen to eat with Jean, he wanted to say his prayers first. Then he cleaned his plate with his napkin, as if it were dirty or contaminated. Jean got two Jupilers from the fridge and put them provocatively on the table. Issam asked if they could leave the beers. Jean still said nothing. Only when he wanted to watch the news after the meal and Issam took hold of the remote to switch off the TV, did he blow his top.

- If that's how you want it, you can stay in Brussels, he said to his daughter.

After a flaming row, they left the house.

Her father would not have anything more to do with her. He wouldn't have a fanatic like Issam laying down the law to him in his own home. In his view his daughter was letting herself be brainwashed by that weirdo in his tent dress. He thought the last straw was that he obviously wanted to convert him and his wife too.

Muriel had given her parents two books on the kingdom of the dead. *Before You Are Sorry*, a book in which Harun Yahya, the standard-bearer of the creationists, threatened those who did not quickly renounce their sins with hell and damnation. And *The Journey of the Soul After Death* by her favourite Salafist author Ibn Qayyim, which described the terrors that awaited one in the period between one's death and the Day of Judgement.

She was obviously very preoccupied with dying. In the past she had already told her parents that later as a Muslim she wanted to be buried in Muslim soil, wrapped in a white shroud.

- She's not our daughter Muriel anymore, Jean and Liliane said to each other after that last visit of hers. This is someone else.

They had put the two books in the sideboard cupboard and would never read them.

From *Vrede zij met u, zuster* (Peace Be With You, Sister),
Uitgeverij De Bezige Bij, Amsterdam, 2010

Translated by Paul Vincent

An Extract from *This Is My Farm*

By Chris De Stoop

There we stand then, my brother and I, in the late afternoon, deep in the mud, blue with cold, calling the cows, 'come, come, come', while behind us bullets suddenly start ricocheting off the roof of the stall. Instinctively we duck and look around. Sodden fields and meadows extend ahead of us to the horizon, surrounded by over-full canals. The only unusual thing we see is a bulldozer on the far side of the meadow behind the fence.

The older cows allow themselves to be rounded up with no trouble. They respond to nicknames like Stamper, Stickhorn or Whitehead and have previously experienced a winter in the warm stall. They plunge good-naturedly through the gate to the yard, past the long, fresh maize pit, the bitter-sweet smell of which hangs in the air like wet steam. They waggle their way, twisting their fat behinds, growling with pleasure, blindly to the stall, straight to the manger to eat hay.

The seven young heifers, with their orange chips still shiny in their ears, refuse to go to the gate even when we use the stick, so that they only went into the meadow in September, together with the mating bull. We shoo them along waving our arms, shout and rage, slip over and get soaked. At the last moment they keep turning round and charge past missing us by a whisker. Lowing loudly, they scatter in all directions. And since it has been established since childhood that I am the quickest and my brother the strongest, it is always my job to chase them.

The wind is getting up, I jump on the grass tufts at the side of a puddle, lose my balance and fall flat on my face in the mud. Exhausted, for half a minute I look at the great areas of grey and black that slide over each other above me. How often have we done this together? I always loved driving the herd in and out of the stall with my brother. In exchange every couple of years I am given the hind quarters. Not of the best cow, which is worth too much, but the worst. I bought a freezer for it and sometimes eat cow for months on end until I'm sick of it. Which happens all the more quickly if I knew the cow in question well.

Finally we succeed by completely opening the wire round the meadow somewhere else so driving the heifers to the yard by a roundabout route – a well-tried diversionary tactic. My brother walks ahead of the animals with a pitchfork of hay in order to lure them into the stall. When the last one is in we hurriedly slide the bolt in. Dead tired, we lean against the wall, the bottom of which is black with muck. We are gleaming with sweat and dirt.

Although I stopped smoking twenty years ago, I roll a cigarette, together with him. A thin one, as he is careful with his tobacco and watches me carefully. We smoke and cough without saying a word.

All the livestock is now in from the field and only the bulldozer remains outside in the rain, which gradually turns to sleet. Inside it is pleasant among the

Hedwigepolder © Michiel Hendryckx

steaming cows' bodies. But we no longer talk as we used to with satisfaction at the whole operation, we do not endlessly rake up how tricky it was and how wild they were and how lucky we were to get the animals back in the stall. No.

'Farming is almost finished,' says my brother for the umpteenth time, with on his face a mixture of fright and rancour. 'They want to get rid of us.'

'Not for a long while yet.'

We fall silent again and look round the stall, in which the decay is gradually becoming apparent in the crooked piping and rusty drinking troughs. The cows have lain down, close together, with their heavy heads resting on each other's bellies. They look back at us with eyes shining. Their breath is visible as clouds of steam. The young heifers are still restless. Sometimes they can't stand the itch and they rub themselves against the walls. Sometimes they arch their backs and lift their tails to piss and shit. It splashes up in our faces.

'Good girls,' I say in a forced voice, to appease him. 'A nice, self-contained and healthy dairy cow business, what more could a farmer want?'

'They've got the shits,' he says, 'And the farm's not working any more.'

From *Dit is mijn hof* (This is My Farm),
Uitgeverij De Bezige Bij, Amsterdam, 2015

Translated by Paul Vincent

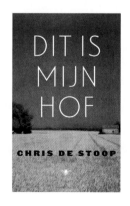

Losing Terrain Yet Thriving

The Position and Status of Afrikaans Anno 2018 in South Africa

[ANNE-MARIE BEUKES]

'It is a frequently asked question whether and why languages should be maintained. In a global human heritage perspective, languages are as unique as biological species and linguistic diversity should therefore be maintained in the same spirit as biological diversity.'
Pekka Sammallahti

Afrikaans, a language that originated at the southernmost tip of the African continent, finds itself in a new eco-dynamic habitat as one of South Africa's eleven official languages. South Africa's language dispensation is an intricate one where the forces of a 'free language market' offer little protection for indigenous minority languages, i.e. languages other than English. Such a highly diverse language environment requires effective language management in order to create and maintain sufficient space for indigenous languages to flourish. Over the past two decades of democracy precious little has been done to support South Africa's linguistic diversity, resulting in encroaching habitat loss for indigenous languages across most societal domains, including Afrikaans.

Although Afrikaans is South Africa's third most-spoken home language (after Zulu and Xhosa) and has been operating in a non-dominant juxtaposition with the nine other official indigenous languages since democracy in 1994, its position and de facto status are largely undervalued. Moreover, the language remains stigmatised in certain quarters owing to its association with the previous apartheid regime notwithstanding its inclusive profile with the majority of its speakers (both first and additional speakers) being non-white. Afrikaans is clearly at a crossroads, at a point where significant domain loss is impacting the vitality of the language and hence its status and position in society.

The road ahead for Afrikaans will largely be determined by coordinates such as the contributions of *language activists* on the one hand, and *organisations* involved in developmental work in Afrikaans communities and schools on the other hand. Activist groups such as AfriForum and Gelyke Kanse are engaging in legal action and court cases in an effort to turn around the English-only language policies that have recently been adopted by historical Afrikaans universities. The development work done by the very popular Afrikaans arts festivals such as the US Woordfees and the Klein Karoo Nasionale Kultuurfees, and also

the Stigting vir Bemagtiging deur Afrikaans and the Afrikaanse Taal- en Kul-
tuurvereniging, among others, is promoting the much-needed reconciliation
in the historically divided Afrikaans speech community. The success of these
respective initiatives will depend on the extent to which the umbrella body, the
Afrikaanse Taalraad (ATR), is able to create the necessary synergy between
seemingly divergent approaches to prevent Afrikaans proverbially being led
down the garden path.

Domain loss

An important domain loss that highlights the ground that Afrikaans stands to
lose was the #AfrikaansMustFall campaign mounted at the University of Pretoria in February 2016 by students demonstrating against the use of Afrikaans
as a medium of instruction in higher education. It has since become clear that
university managements at historically Afrikaans universities prefer the use of
English as a language of learning and teaching because it affords wider access
to students across the board. As a consequence, Afrikaans has been eliminated
from two historically Afrikaans universities, i.e. the Free State University and
the University of Pretoria, and from the University of South Africa (historically
a bilingual university). English has now become the sole language of learning
across all university campuses except the Potchefstroom campus of the North
West University and a few undergraduate modules at Stellenbosch University.

Sadly, the only remaining options for Stellenbosch students who prefer studying through the medium of Afrikaans are 'course outlines in Afrikaans, Afrikaans tutorials and the freedom to ask questions in Afrikaans and submit assignments and tests in Afrikaans. Afrikaans, which functioned for decades as an asset and as a language earmarked for constructive development, is increasingly viewed as troublesome, a stumbling block in the achievement of transformation objectives' (Visagie 2017). Judging by a poll conducted at Stellenbosch University in 2016, where two-thirds of Afrikaans students indicated a preference to be taught through the medium of English, it is just a matter of time before Stellenbosch University terminates the use of Afrikaans as a language of teaching and learning.

Type	Afrikaans		English		Bilingual		Total	
Year	2004	2016	2004	2016	2004	2016	2004	2016
Universities	0	0	7	10.67	4	0.33	11	11
Universities of Technology	0	0	5	5	0	0	5	5
Comprehensives	0	0	3	6	3	0	6	6
Total	0	0	15	21.67	7	0.33	22	22

Language dispensation at South African higher education institutions subsequent to a rationalisation process (2004) and change in language policies at historically Afrikaans universities (2016)

I have cautioned elsewhere that the debate on the status and future of Afrikaans in higher education 'should be understood against the backdrop of the reality that very few of the languages spoken in the world are in fact used in institutions of secondary and higher learning' (Beukes 2010: 210). An undisputed achievement of Afrikaans is that it is the only African language and one of only a few other modern languages (such as Catalan, Hebrew, Hindi, Indonesian) that developed in the course of the twentieth century to function as a fully-fledged language of science and as a lingua academica for teaching purposes. The domain loss that Afrikaans is suffering is clear from the statistics regarding journal articles published in Afrikaans in the period 1990 to 2002: the number of articles dropped from 14% to 5%.

Year	Afrikaans		English		Total
	N	%	N	%	
1990	912	13.8	5,705	86.2	6,617
1994	590	8.6	6,301	91.4	6,891
1998	408	6.1	6,235	93.9	6,643
2002	183	3.2	5,554	96.8	5,737

Number of journal articles 1990 to 2002 – Mouton (2005: 372)

Encroaching habitat loss is also taking place at primary and secondary school level as a result of the anglicisation of higher education. It is estimated that about 750,000 Afrikaans learners are currently still part of the public school system (Giliomee 2016), but Afrikaans parents are increasingly opting for English-medium schools as a function of the drastic domain loss of Afrikaans in higher education, as well as the 'common sense' choice for future access to the global economy. This state of affairs will most certainly impact negatively on the demand for Afrikaans-speaking teachers and their training in the future.

Thriving language festivals

In contrast to the domain loss that Afrikaans is suffering in education it is burgeoning in various other domains. This is a function of its loss of status as a 'public' language since 1994, but at the same time it points to a strong language vitality. A case in point is the phenomenal rise and thriving of Afrikaans language festivals these past two decades. The first festival, the Klein Karoo Nasionale Kunstefees (KKNK) held annually in the small Karoo town of Oudtshoorn since 1995, boasts significant increases in ticket sales from 30,314 in its first year to 135,000 in 2017. Another example is the Stellenbosch University's Woordfees with record sales in 2016, an increase of 27.8% since 2015.

If production is used as an indicator, trends in book publication since the 1990s indicate that Afrikaans is the strongest literary language in South Africa (Galloway 2002). In particular, as far as fiction and children's books are concerned, some 75% to 80% are produced in Afrikaans (Stassen 2015). When bearing in mind that first-language speakers of Afrikaans account for about 14% of South Africa's population of 55 million people the fact that 40 of the top 100 books sold in South Africa in 2013 were Afrikaans books is a significant measure of language vitality.

Language	Poetry	Theatre	Fiction	Total
Afrikaans	283	53	2,464	2,800
English	302	127	545	974
Multi-lingual	34	20	109	163
Bantu languages	342	283	635	1,260

Trends in book publication in SA (Galloway 2002)

Language vitality

At the dawn of democracy, former President Nelson Mandela at a meeting with Afrikaans organisations acknowledged the value of Afrikaans as a language of science: 'The argument for retaining, protecting and fostering Afrikaans is certainly a national concern rather than sectional. It is a South African language which, according to all standards, has produced significant achievements in

terms of its developing into a language of science, academia and intellectual expression' (my translation; Mandela 1995). Against the backdrop of the clear signs of language vitality, it is to be hoped that constructive language activism coupled with the Afrikaans speech community's 'language capital' (i.e. organisations and bodies such as the Afrikaanse Taalraad, the SA Academy for Science and Arts, the Commission for the Promotion and Protection of the Rights of Cultural, Religious and Linguistic Communities, etc.) will in future facilitate in enlarging the language's footprint and secure its future position and status. ■

FURTHER READING

A-M. Beukes, '"Opening the Doors of Education": Language Policy at the University of Johannesburg'. *Language Matters* 41 (2) (2010), pp. 193-213.

F. Galloway, 'Statistical Trends in South African Book Publishing during the 1990s'. *Alternation* (9) 1 (2002), pp. 204-225.

H. Giliomee, ''n Afrikaanse toekomsvisie'. Paper at SA Akademie vir Wetenskap en Kuns se Jaarvergadering, Stellenbosch, 2016.

N. Mandela, 'Introductory remarks by President Nelson Mandela at a meeting with Afrikaans organisations, Cape Town', 15 May 1996. Available at: www.mandela.gov.za/mandela_speeches/1996/960515_afrbus.htm

P. Sammallahti, 'Ethnic Groups, Language Maintenance and Ethnic Identity', 2005, p. 9. Available at: www.palmenia.helsinki.fi/congress/bilingual2005/presentations/Sammallahti.pdf

N. Stassen, 'Afrikaans 90: Afrikaanse boeke maak deure oop'. Maroela Media, 4 August 2015. Available at: maroelamedia.co.za/afrikaans/afrikaans-90-afrikaanse-boeke-maak-deure-oop

A. Visagie, 'A vision for Afrikaans'. University Seminar, 1 June 2016. Available at: www.litnet.co.za/a-vision-for-afrikaans/

Adriaen Brouwer, *The Smokers*, c. 1636, oil on panel, 46.4 x 36.8 cm,
Metropolitan Museum of Modern Art, New York

Architecture

The Benedictine Monk Who Showed Us How to Build
Dom Hans van der Laan

Dom Hans van der Laan's (1904-1991) architectural realisations are limited. As a teacher, this peculiar Dutch Benedictine monk advised his students on all kinds of projects, but his own main achievements are four convents and a house. He did not even have a proper architectural office, but worked from his own personal abbey cell. Nevertheless, Van der Laan is recognised as one of the most significant architects of the twentieth century.

Thanks to prominent architectural photographers like Frans de la Cousine, Friederike von Rauch, Hélène Binet and David Grandorge, images of his buildings are widely disseminated and have become part of architecture's collective memory. St. Benedictusberg Abbey in Vaals (The Netherlands, 1960-1982) and Roosenberg Abbey in Waasmunster (Flanders, 1975) are pilgrimage sites, intensely frequented by travelling architects and visitors who indulge in its elementary and austere architecture. As a contemporary Gesamtkunstwerk, these abbeys provide an aesthetic experience through purity of form.

St. Benedictusberg Abbey and Roosenberg Abbey can be considered as examples of the fundamental house, where each space has its designated function. With all the furniture and objects equally designed by Van der Laan, every action becomes part of a ritual. Movement from one space to another is orchestrated as an intense and contemplative experience, as if one is travelling outside of time and space. This effect is achieved through the use of classical architectural themes: series of colonnades and repetitive window openings, distinct rhythms of thick walls and austere building blocks with a rough materiality, a grey colour palette and minimum detailing. The series of openings create a changing light play, which is the only ornamentation. The composition of these classical themes is utterly modern. There is no symmetry and, despite the heaviness of the walls, the space seems to float because of the dynamic compositions.

Van der Laan's uniqueness goes beyond the experience of his architecture. The Benedictine monk regards his own realisations as 'specimens', practical testing fields that serve as a tangible and concrete background for his architectural doctrine. The abbeys are composed through a mathematical framework that is embedded within a larger philosophy of perception and space. In 1977, Van der Laan described this framework in *Architectonic Space, Fifteen Lessons on the Disposition of the Human Habitat*, both a manifesto and a design manual on how to build.

Van der Laan's starting points are the correlations between nature and architecture, inside and outside, mass and space, open and closed. Then he proceeds from classical systematics such as symmetry and eurhythmy to the scales of walls, houses and cities. Everything is linked through Van der Laan's systematic proportional series of the *Plastic Number*, the ratio 3 : 4.

Through this, he wants to create an order that directly relates to our abstract rational understanding of space. For Dom van der Laan, architecture has to create an order, a measurable and intelligible 'inside' within an unknowable 'outside'. Architecture makes the chaos of nature readable and understandable. The movement from the outside to the inside of a building is also a slow mental process of interiorization. This process of understanding, of creating an order, is closely linked to human cognition. On an intuitive level, we are constantly relating and assessing everything around us, constantly defining our position. We are measuring, counting and rounding up to parameters that we can rationally understand and name clearly. Architecture's main function is to be expressive through its order, and as such it imitates the process of cognition itself.

Likewise, architecture needs to mediate between intuition and rational understanding. One needs to be able to relate to architecture through its human scale and clarity. A house facilitates this process of counting and measuring in the best possible manner. Through a clear hierarchical order of whole numbers, everything in the house is interrelated; from the smallest building stone to the rhythm of the galleries and window series, to the overall spaces, the building site, and eventually the city.

With his theories on space, Dom van der Laan follows the classical tradition of building with numeric proportions. Series of robust columns and elementary window rows are organised according to repetitive bay rhythms. Spaces interrelate hierarchically through numeric proportions, such as 1:2, 2:3, 3:4...

However, the dynamics that are so typical of Van der Laan's architecture, are not simply the result of this proportional system as such. For Van der Laan, that system is merely an instrument, like the keys of a piano. He realises these highly unusual dynamics by the way in which he uses his tool to make compositions: interlacing spaces with one another into one narrative, like he is making music. The series of columns in Van der Laan's buildings all have different rhythms that create a spatial dialogue. Window frames, open porticos and doors are not placed following any central axe. They are carefully positioned near corners and always shifted towards each other, creating diagonal and continuous perspectives through successive spaces. This architecture is built as in-between space: the buildings come alive through the interchange between the material of their surfaces and the light.

Within a world of abundant imagery that overcharges our senses, Van der Laan's architecture inspires today's architects through its elementary stillness and austere simplicity.

CAROLINE VOET

www.vanderlaanstichting.nl/en/home

Caroline Voet. *Dom Hans van der Laan. A House for the Mind. A Design Manual on Roosenberg Abbey*, Flanders Architecture Institute, Antwerp, 2017, 224 p.

Fashion

The Successful Balance Between the Commercial and the Creative
Dries Van Noten

Born in 1958, fashion designer Dries Van Noten has passed the milestone of a hundred fashion shows and is celebrating the event with a two-part book. This monumental publication renders the universe of the designer with photographs and video stills. Anyone wishing to familiarise themselves with his style, would do best to view the images from his 100th collection. The show was an anthology of Van Noten's oeuvre: young and old models displayed simple, smartly cut pieces that formed a feast of colours, prints and embroideries. Urban sounds could be heard in the background, a dash of Louis Armstrong, a pinch of David Bowie, a little Pina Bausch and the music from Pedro Almodóvar films. This soundtrack demonstrates the wide range of sources that inspired this Belgian designer. The discerning viewer can spot hints of other cultures. Still the presence of ethnic influences is not as explicit as in collections from a few years back.

At the time Van Noten made much more literal references to kimonos, saris, or Moroccan traditional attire. It is much more difficult to do that in the current politically sensitive climate. A Peruvian sweater with an alpaca motif (the alpaca is a South American mountain llama, which is kept as a pet in the Andes) was subject to major criticism on his Instagram account. Van Noten is quoted as saying in an interview with *The Business of Fashion*: 'If you follow that logic I should only be allowed to be inspired by Belgian folklore'. Nonetheless, he toned down his explicit cultural influences. But his pieces still travel all around the world before they end up on the store racks. A shirt can be dyed in Asia, embroidered in India, dyed again in Africa and sewn together in Belgium.

Still, having been born and raised in Antwerp, Van Noten is no globetrotter. A fascination for other cultures may have stemmed from early childhood. His parents owned a boutique called Nusson's in Essen (a small town north of Antwerp) and later Van Noten Couture in Antwerp itself. As a young boy he travelled with his father to foreign countries

to buy collections. His love of beautiful pieces was inculcated at a tender age and by the time he was twelve he started organising his own in-store fashion shows.

Van Noten is profoundly influenced by the commercial way of looking at fashion. Unlike such fellow contemporaries as Walter Van Beirendonck and Martin Margiela, he would never try to convey big messages with his collections. 'There is no room for political ambition in the world of fashion, even if the objects are inspired by current events', he is once quoted as saying in an interview. And so for him the success of a piece can be directly gauged to how well it sells. Having said that, he still is a supporter of slower fashion. For example, in contrast to many of his competitors Van Noten does not make collections between seasons. One should not expect the very latest trends from this Antwerp man, even though French fashion genius Jean-Paul Gaultier once praised him as someone supremely able to sense what is hanging in the air at any given moment.

The successful quest to find the balance between the commercial and the creative has not done Van Noten any harm. He went to study at the Antwerp fashion academy in 1977. While studying, he already worked for five commercial companies and was assistant buyer in the designer boutique owned by Linda Loppa, a former student of the academy. Together with his contemporaries Ann Demeulemeester, Marina Yee, Walter Van Beiren-

donck, Dirk Van Saene, Dirk Bikkembergs and Martin Margiela, later dubbed the Antwerp 'Six + 1', he scoured hip punk parties and performances. To this day, there are still glimmers of those rebellious influences in his designs. His teachers at the academy also left their mark on him. A Van Noten dress is hardly ever sexy in an explicit way. Many of his hemlines remain chastely below the knee. The influence of the academy's woman director Mary Prijot is clearly present, who disapproved of tight dresses and short skirts.

The designer's early years as a student have also left an indelible mark. Van Noten attended a Jesuit college where priests strode the corridors. The designer duly graduated from the fashion academy with a collection that displayed religious influences. The natural world is another recurrent source of inspiration. Botanical prints can be found in practically every collection for women. His house, *Hof van Ringen* (Court of Rings), a late classicist mansion, is surrounded by a spacious yard with various animals. That mix of modestly cut fabric, distinctive prints, ethnic elements and shades of punk influences make up the fashion designer's trademark look.

Nowadays Van Noten can safely be called the head of a modest empire. He owns boutiques in several countries and his accessories for men and women have a large following. Another remarkable aspect of his success is his having financed every step of the way himself. He opened a small store in Antwerp in 1985, when still a fledgling designer; four years later he had made enough money to buy the *Modepaleis* (Fashion Palace). Van Noten's store is still housed in the gorgeous building on Nationalestraat in Antwerp. The purchase was a symbolic act. After all, the store was located right across from *'t Meuleken*, his grandfather John Van Noten's store, who made his living as a tailor. His great competitor and father-in-law Guillaume Arts, also used to own a store in the *Modepaleis*.

'My greatest goal is to ensure that selecting clothing is an act of self-esteem', the designer once said, aptly summing up his entire oeuvre. In the meantime, Van Noten is steadily building up his brand. Having published a book after his fiftieth collection, he has now added a second volume. The man from Antwerp is content, but like a true fashion mogul he is looking forward: 'I'm not too keen

on doing another 100 shows, but I certainly have enough ideas for the future'.

CHARLOTTE VAN HACHT
Translated by Scott Rollins

Dries Van Noten, Tim Blanks and Susannah Frankel, *Collections 1-100*, Lannoo, Tielt, 2017, 912 p. (ISBN 978 94 0144 61 36). Also available in separate volumes: *Collections 1-50* and *Collections 51-100*.

Film

An Inverted Orpheus and Eurydice
Le Fidèle by Michael Roskam

When, after a Porsche Supercup contest, Gino (Matthias Schoenaerts) sees Bénédicte (Adèle Exarchopoulos) getting out of her racing car in the pits, his interest is immediately aroused. She – nicknamed Bibi – puts her life on the line on the racing circuit; he – nicknamed Gigi – does the same when he carries out armed robberies with his gang of thieves. Both are aware of the risks of their profession. Both are addicted to the kick. But then they fall in love.

Following *Bullhead* (*Rundskop*) (2011) and *The Drop* (2014), *Racer and the Jailbird* (*Le Fidèle*) is Michael Roskam's third feature film and is similarly set in a criminal milieu. Roskam uses this world as an arena to link together paradoxical elements – innocence, crime, vulnerability, brutishness, feelings and lies – in modern *film noir* productions that are striking for their painterly authenticity and complex, raw and realistic character studies.

While in *Bullhead* the accent was on the absence of love, and *The Drop*, according to Roskam, was a 'desperate search for innocence', in interviews he has called *Racer and the Jailbird* 'my melodramatic fantasy of love and death; of Eros and Thanatos' – which according to Freud are the most fundamental urges. Roskam sees absolute love as a paradoxical tension between desire and surrender; the feeling of being confined that goes with attachment: 'Like a dog that lies on the threshold with its head outside'.

What he had in mind was an amour noir, his own back-to-front variant of the classic *film noir*. To the online magazine *The Italian Rêve*, Roskam said, on this topic: 'Where mostly, love affairs are like a satellite around the crime story, I wanted this [to be] different... This is a love story where crime was the satellite'. In this regard, Roskam took inspiration, loosely, from the Haemers gang, which carried out a series of spectacular robberies around Brussels in the 1980s and 1990s, as well as kidnapping the former Prime Minister Paul Vanden Boeynants and succeeding in escapes from prison several times. *Racer and the Jailbird* also includes a spectacular robbery involving a shipping container; it elicits a boyish admiration, without the violence used being glamorised as is usual in American action films. This brute force is more sickening than anything else.

Shortly after they first meet, Bibi – who thinks that Gigi is in the car trade and commands him not to bring any flowers – asks what his biggest secret is. With utter honesty he answers: 'I'm a gangster. I rob banks'. This sounds so absurd to her that she has to laugh out loud. However, it gradually becomes clear to her that his answer was no joke. Gigi the gangster is a wild animal that wants to be tamed by love. Their life together only has any chance of surviving if Gigi abandons his illegal activities: if he leaves the underworld for the upper world. Bibi does all she can to get him out of it; *Racer and the Jailbird* is an inverted Orpheus and Eurydice. But it is also a tragedy with an ambiguous ending, but more about that below. (Spoiler alert: the rest of this article contains details of how the story ends.)

The excesses from which *Racer and the Jailbird* suffers detract from the richness of its story: it too often emphasises what we already understand. Gigi surrenders again and again: to the police, to Bibi's world – which to him is the equivalent of prison. The adage 'no flowers' is so good at typifying Bibi's tough, independent personality that Roskam's scenarists Thomas Bidegain and Noé Debré (who also worked on Jacques Audiard's Golden Palm winner *Dheepan*) could not resist the temptation to use it so often that it becomes ridiculous. The same applies to the frequent presence of dogs, usually on a leash or in a cage. Gigi is afraid of them, Bibi isn't.

While she thinks a pit bull is a fine dog, he sees it as a killing machine. It's a question of perspective that's determined by the experiences they grew up with: she as the carefree daughter of a rich family, he in juvenile institutions after his violent father had abandoned him.

'Would you follow me anywhere?' Gigi asks Bibi early on in the film over breakfast in her flat. 'Yes, of course,' she says and asks him the same. 'Yes, of course,' he answers. But then he reflects for a moment: 'No, it depends. Whether you looked behind you or not.' A sentence that is as crucial as it is casual, and which refers to the fidelity in the title. They can only be together if they dare to trust each other blindly.

Just as in the Greek myth, fate steps in. Once Gigi has ended up in prison, Bibi turns out to be terminally ill. She manages to arrange with a powerful Albanian underworld boss for Gigi to be freed after her death and to be shipped off to the city of their dreams, Buenos Aires. But Gigi does not wait for his ship: he slips through the Albanians' fingers and races to Bibi's grave in a superbly filmed drive through the mists of early morning Brussels. In the meantime we hear him – as a voice-over – asking Bibi, long ago, for her deepest secret too. To which she answers: 'I'm immortal'. Perhaps that's also why she said 'no flowers' – an answer that probably made him laugh just as much at the time as she did at his answer.

But which of them is it that looks back? Bibi at Gigi by arranging his destination following her death? Or him, as he races to her grave? Is this why the miracle of her resurrection in Buenos Aires does not happen? Or do they still meet again in the Elysian Fields? Roskam leaves it open: we do not see what happens to Gigi when he vanishes from view in the cemetery. This ambiguity perfectly fits the paradoxes that Roskam's work is founded on. And it challenges the viewers to figure out how far they would dare to put their faith in a mythical miracle themselves.

KARIN WOLFS
Translated by Gregory Ball

The Italian Rêve, 'Interview with Michaël R. Roskam: Torn Between Love and Noir', Valentina Carraro, 17 September 2017.

History

The Elites Consistently Charted a New Course
A Concise History of the Netherlands

James Kennedy's history of the Netherlands was not written for a Dutch public. It is part of a series published by Cambridge University Press, which includes concise histories of Spain, Brazil, Finland, Bosnia, Bolivia and many other countries.

Kennedy is an appealing choice for a project such as this. He is a popular historian and valued participant in the public debate. He is also 'an outsider': an American of Dutch origin, who grew up in the Calvinist Orange City, Iowa. He became a professor of contemporary history at VU University Amsterdam in 2003, and is now dean of University College Utrecht. His doctoral thesis, *Building New Babylon*, dealt with the cultural history of the Netherlands in the 1960s. All of that means he is able to view that history from an international perspective, perhaps less focussed on the historical discourse within the country itself, with all its hobbyhorses and pet topics. That discourse has become very lively of late, and has even taken on a strong political tint. So a little distance can do no harm.

The book is redolent with a spirit of solidity and restraint. Its very conciseness already makes it remarkable, covering the whole gamut from *homo heidelbergensis* up to and including Geert Wilders in around 400 pages.

Kennedy concentrates on the political, economic and social history of the Netherlands. He is especially sparing in his treatment of culture, and out of necessity he leaves out large swathes of the country's Asiatic history. But he does include the Caribbean territories, because a contemporary history of the Netherlands cannot ignore slavery. Kennedy rightly devotes attention to Tula, the leader of the Curaçao Slave Revolt of 1795, and to the poor Ghanaian Jacobus Capitein, the first black student to obtain a doctorate at Leiden University, in 1742 – though in fact there is some doubt as to whether he really did so.

The structure of the book betrays the fact that Kennedy's own expertise is in modern Dutch history, and he is particularly at home when discussing developments after 1870. He expresses little by way of any specific Christian opinions. Kennedy has said in earlier interviews that, whilst he knew that history was under God's leadership, as the course of that history is uncertain a Christian historian needs to adopt a modest stance.

Solid and restrained, then: the book could even be called strikingly traditional. As we know, history is 'one damned thing after another', and that's how it is interpreted in this book, too. Condensing the span of Dutch history into 380 pages is without doubt a very considerable feat. Almost everyone is there, almost every familiar figure makes an appearance, though they are rarely accorded more than a single line, with the exception of the stadtholder King William III, Johan van Oldenbarnevelt and William the Silent. The need for conciseness means that Kennedy allows virtually no distraction, embellishment or coloration. There is no space for 'experience'. Kennedy almost never allows any Dutch person to appear 'in person', with a snappy quote, a charming diary entry or a personal note. The book is as nutritious and dry as a ship's biscuit.

There is in reality also nothing particularly original in Kennedy's interpretation of the history and his pointing out of the longer haul. He starts from the perspective that the Netherlands is indisputably an exceptional country, which is wrongly ignored by international and domestic historians alike as a little country with a strange language. The factors which make the country great are the familiar ones. The country's maritime location, cut through by rivers, forced the Dutch to collaborate. They accordingly developed an above-average 'ability to create' and 'ability to adapt', and the country's geographical position also awakened a spirit of commercialism. Dutch history is also characterised by a remarkably lively culture, religious diversity and centuries-old tradition of tolerance or, to use a nice term introduced by Kennedy, 'everyday ecumenism'.

In the nineteenth century, the Netherlands was reborn as a unitary state, with a strong self-image, and even a sense of moral superiority. This positive self-image has taken an emphatic tumble in recent decades, however, and Kennedy too speaks of an identity crisis. But, he goes on, the historic achievement of the Dutch is still inspiring. Despite the many fractures and minorities, the country has survived and even flourished; it has been engaged with globalisation and immigration from the start, and has absorbed all of that with a high degree of stability.

That sounds dull, but it is precisely in its dullness that the Netherlands can offer an example to other countries. For Kennedy, the origin of this success lies deep in the Middle Ages. There was a lack of centralised authority in the Netherlands even during the Roman era. Power was shared. The nobility and the Church were relatively weak; there was an independent farming community, and towns everywhere flourished from the twelfth century onwards. The Dutch also had a number of other political entities, such as the water authorities and the Hanseatic League. All later attempts at centralisation, or the introduction of a unitary culture by the Burgundians and Hapsburgs, met with resistance. It was only after the period of French rule that this decentralised state structure came to an end, but public life remained fragmented, divided into 'pillars' and separate communities. But that fragmentation in turn formed the basis for a stable democratic system, in which the elites have always managed to chart a new course in time, so that revolutions have rarely led to actual bloodletting.

It is all true, though that opinion could have been voiced more sharply. In his treatment of slavery, for example, Kennedy comments that the Dutch disapproved of slavery, but found it very easy to put aside their moral reservations – the slave trade was simply too lucrative. Is that also an example of 'ability to create and to adapt', or is it merely ruthless opportunism? Is the slave trade also an example of 'innovation'?

KOEN KLEIJN
Translated by Julian Ross

James C. Kennedy, *A Concise History of the Netherlands*, Cambridge University Press, 2017, 502 p.

What the United States Learnt from the Netherlands

John Lothrop Motley's History of the Dutch Revolt

A little more than thirty years ago, Simon Schama caused a commotion with his book *The Embarrassment of Riches*. While this history of the Dutch Golden Age flew off the bookshelves and provided pleasurable hours of reading, the professionals grumbled and began sharpening their knives. Nicely written, nicely put together, they agreed, but ... A storm of criticism ensued which has not yet abated.

Schama was not the first Anglo-Saxon historian to put forward a controversial view of Dutch history – not the last, either: James Kennedy also belongs in that group – and thereby spark off debate and research. He was preceded by a man who in a sense deserves the honour of having laid the foundation for Dutch political historiography, not so much because he wrote it himself as because he prompted his critics to do so. The man in question is John Lothrop Motley (1814-1877), a name which is all but forgotten today. Jaap Verheul, a lecturer and researcher in cultural history at Utrecht University, has written a book about him: *De Atlantische pelgrim. John Lothrop Motley en de Amerikaanse ontdekking van Nederland* (The Atlantic pilgrim. John Lothrop Motley and the American discovery of the Netherlands).

Together with men such as Prescott, Carlyle, Bancroft, Renan and Macaulay, Motley could be slotted into the group of 'great popularisers of history'. After a number of failed attempts as a novelist and a stranded diplomatic career, Motley turned to the study of the Dutch Republic, and in particular its beginnings. The first impulse for this came from the works of Goethe and Schiller, who published heroic tales of the Dutch struggle for freedom in the years surrounding the French Revolution. Those stories found wide appeal. But there is another reason, and a more important one: the American desire in the years after the Declaration of Independence to find a tradition for its own history. According to the dominant picture in the US at the time, such a tradition could not possibly be found in the Netherlands. Thanks to Washington Irving's famous satirical history of New York, the Dutch were seen as a nation of pipe-smoking,

gin-guzzling dimwits who were constantly battling through wind and weather and who lived in what one US ambassador called a 'decayed and decaying nation'. Partly thanks to Goethe and Schiller, Motley took a completely different view of this.

After years of study and a lengthy stay in Europe (Dresden, Brussels, The Hague), he published *The Rise of the Dutch Republic* in 1856. In this book he more or less presented Dutch history, and in particular the struggle of the Dutch against the Spanish, as the model that the United States had also followed – itself also a republic which had developed into a federation following a struggle for freedom, in this case against the British. In doing so, he was providing a country which had just shaken itself free with a historical example. The picture that Motley paints of the Netherlands – and in particular its 'father', William of Orange – is thus as illustrious as the image that he portrays of its enemy – Spain, led by Philip II – is deeply dull. The contrast not only worked, but caught on, all the more because Motley had done his homework very well and possessed a skilful pen. On both sides of the Atlantic, but especially in the US, his book garnered great success, received critical acclaim and sold well. The latter was not unimportant because Motley, who came from a well-to-do Boston family, had invested just about his last cent in the project. Ultimately, the investment paid off: *The Rise of the Dutch Republic* not only provided its author with an affluent lifestyle, but also earned him prestige. Suddenly Motley was a 'famous American'.

In the Netherlands, the book was received with mixed feelings. That was not surprising: in earlier decades, Dutch and Belgian historians had followed the nineteenth-century fashion by accessing lots of archive material and using it as a basis to produce a fair number of detailed studies. What had not yet been produced, however, was an overview, let alone a vision of the history of the fatherland. And then suddenly an unknown American appeared and put the key moment of that past on the international map with a few large brushstrokes. That could do nothing other than rankle.

The sharpest criticism of Motley's book came from the man regarded as the Dutch version of Leopold von Ranke, the greatest German historiographer of the nineteenth century: Robert Fruin. A year after the publication of *The Rise of the Dutch*

Republic Fruin, who at that time was a teacher in Leiden, published a tract on the years 1588-1598. It appeared as an appendix to the annual report of his school, the Stedelijk Gymnasium, and went virtually unnoticed.

But that soon changed. In 1859 and 1860, Fruin placed a discussion of several books about the Dutch Revolt in the journal *De Gids*. In reality, this discussion was a fierce criticism of Motley's work. Motley described events in an appealing way, Fruin conceded, but fell seriously short when it came to analysis. The main reason for this was that he placed all the emphasis on freedom and ignored state formation – the absolute topic of the moment in the nationalistic Europe of the nineteenth century. Partly because of these articles, a year later Fruin was appointed a professor in Leiden and published a series of works which formed the basis for classical Dutch political historiography.

What makes Jaap Verheul's book so readable is the good mix it offers of biography and historiographical context. But there is more than that. It is also important because Motley, as Verheul illustrates persuasively, was a more important figure than people realise. While he provided American history with a tradition, he also forced Dutch historiography to formulate a vision. Those are two large birds with one stone.

CHRIS VAN DER HEIJDEN
Translated by Julian Ross

Jaap Verheul, *De Atlantische pelgrim. John Lothrop Motley en de Amerikaanse ontdekking van Nederland* (The Atlantic pilgrim. John Lothrop Motley and the American discovery of the Netherlands), Boom, Amsterdam, 2017.

From Ghent to South Korea
Ghent University at 200

Ghent University is celebrating its 200th anniversary in 2017/2018. Together with its sister university in Liège and stakeholders within and outwith the university, the anniversary will be used to mark the position and significance of the university in the twenty-first century. But it also offers a perfect opportunity to commemorate the history of the old university. A brief exhibition has been held, a book has been written and a website has been created documenting the 'memory' of the university community.

How are universities born? In the case of Ghent University, it was tied in with matters of statehood. In 1817, William I became the new king of the United Kingdom of the Netherlands. To bring together his newly acquired territories in a sense of a shared culture, he needed to invest in language and education. On 25 September 1816, the king proclaimed a higher education law which created six state universities throughout the kingdom. One of the southern universities was in Ghent. The two others were in Leuven – where the medieval university had been abolished in 1797 – and Liège. Partly due to the policy used to appoint professors, the new universities became the tools of an enlightened politics which sought to promote Dutch as a language of unity. Among the well-known figures who either taught or studied in Ghent between 1817 and 1830 were the Dutch statesman Johan Rudolf Thorbecke and the Ghent psychiatrist Joseph Guislain.

After the Belgian Revolution (1830), which saw present-day Belgium separate from the Netherlands, Ghent, like Liège, once again became the seat of a state university. Henceforth, however, the language of teaching and science was French. Free universities were established by private initiative in Leuven and Brussels. The two state universities consequently found themselves ranged against a Catholic (Leuven) and a liberal (Brussels) counterpart. Until the university expansion in the 1960s, these four institutions held each other in balance. Despite the wave of secularisation, ideological oppositions still played a role in Flemish university life.

These ideological oppositions arose shortly after 1830. In areas such as care and education, the early liberal governments increasingly found themselves facing a militant, ultramontane Church. The state university in Ghent fell victim to this polarisation; in the 1850s the university found itself at the heart of the clerical struggle that ensued from a number of headline-making disputes about the rationality of its teaching. The number of students fell to 291. The then newly formed – but still in existence today – student society *'t Zal wel Gaan* was even the subject of a papal excommunication order, an edict that was received as if it were a trophy.

The 1880s ushered in a new period. A dynamic chief administrator took the helm at the university, and a period of expansion followed, with new buildings erected, new disciplines added, more scientific and specialist teaching and research. Until the First World War, student numbers continued to rise. Many of them came from abroad to study at the engineering department, which enjoyed international renown at that time. During the First World War, several students from Ghent went to the Front, where eighty-two of them lost their lives. In the meantime, the German Occupier, supported by a group of radical Flemish nationalists, seized the initiative to found a Dutch-language university in Ghent, the *Vlaamsche Hoogeschool*, which operated between 1916 and 1918. Also known as the Von Bissing University, it functioned for barely two academic years and numbered no more than a few hundred students. But its symbolic significance was considerable. The controversy surrounding the 'collaboration university' meant it was unable to recapture its pre-war glory days in 1918. The whole interwar period was dominated by the question of the language of education. The university community divided. A 'Flemish front' of students and professors was created to oppose the long-standing *Gand français*. A new law passed on 5 April 1930 transformed the French-speaking *Université de Gand* into the Dutch-speaking *Rijksuniversiteit Gent*. The first rector of the first Dutch-speaking university in Belgium was the art historian August Vermeylen. Other successes followed. In 1938, the pharmacologist Corneel Heymans won the Nobel Prize for Medicine. At around the same time, the architect Henry Van De Velde designed a new university library in the form of a tower, which would become the *Boekentoren*. In keeping with its function as a symbol of science and knowledge, it was built at the highest point in the city. In 1940, the new library proved to be an ideal spot for the German occupying forces to position a lookout post with gun emplacement.

The Second World War was followed by a period in which Ghent University, like many others, became a mass institution. It democratised, expanded and opened new campuses in other towns and cities. Big Science became the norm in the university's research: large, interdisciplinary research groups whose peer-reviewed research sought to attract national and European research funds. The first student accommodation appeared in the townscape in the 1960s, the university's response to the massive increase in student numbers; in 1940 there were 1,782 students; in 1970 this had risen to 11,486, and in 2000 to 21,387. 1969 and 1978 were the peak years of student revolt and protest.

The status of the university changed in 1991, when it was transformed from the State University of Ghent into Ghent University, an independent institution with its own legal personality and autonomy. New, more structural changes followed in the 2000s. The academic programmes of University College Ghent and Ghent University were brought together in the *Associatie UGent*. At European level, the teaching activities were harmonised by bringing in Bachelor and Master programmes to replace the old *licenties* and *kandidaturen*. Further afield, Ghent University opened an overseas campus in South Korea. Meanwhile, the student population continued to grow, reaching 35,424 in the 2016/2017 academic year. Their social profile has become more varied and contains more women, but there is still a predominance of white students.

This highlights one of the objectives of the present management team, namely raising the number of students with a migration background entering higher education. A socially minded, engaged

Matheus Ignatius van Bree, *The Solemn Inauguration of Ghent University by the Prince of Orange in the Throne Room of the Town Hall on 9 October 1817*, 1817-1830, oil on panel, 65 x 52 cm, Rijksmuseum, Amsterdam

university that is open to everyone: that is the direction on which the university, in its anniversary year, is looking to embark.

RUBEN MANTELS
Translated by Julian Ross

www.UGentMemorie.be

Gita Deneckere, *Uit de ivoren toren. 200 jaar Universiteit Gent* (From the Ivory Tower. 200 Years of Ghent University), Tijdsbeeld & Pièce montée N.V. Publicaties, Ghent, 2017, 352 p. Patrick De Rynck, Agnes Goyvaerts et al., *200 jaar UGent in 200 objecten (Ghent University. 200 Years in 200 Objects)*, Hannibal, Veurne, 2017, 240 p.

Literature

A Reynard for Our Time

Animal tales are among the most ancient, widespread and enduringly popular forms of storytelling. Their range is enormous – from the Bible and its seductive snake in Paradise, the Greek myths of their gods in animal disguise and the many Indian tales that made it into Aesop's fables, through the South East Asian adventures of the mercurial mouse deer Kancil to the Arctic with its Inuit folktales of men as salmon spirit and the stories of Anansi the Spider from Africa.

In Low Countries literature, one animal tale stands out in particular: Reynard the Fox, a brilliant contribution to the genre, which originated in the medieval Latin epic *Ysengrimus* (1150) by Master Nivardus of Ghent, translated into French as the *Roman de Renart* in 1170, then also into Dutch around 1250. Of its Flemish author not much is known beyond his name, 'William who made Madocke'. But his comedy has delighted readers down the centuries, for its literary qualities and its portrayal of Reynard as a cunning trickster who again and again outwits his enemies and escapes the punishments they have in store for him. With its Machiavellian intrigue and mischievous humour, this was a fox for his time. The tale was written down, copied and edited in the monasteries; told, retold and performed at court and in popular theatre; translated into many English, German and other versions, printed in early chapbooks; widely disseminated across northern Europe; and it has continued to inspire new versions until today, such as Louis Paul Boon's *Wapenbroeders* (Comrades in Arms; 1955), and Italo Calvino's 'Giovanuzza the Fox', included in his wonderful collection of *Italian Folktales* of 1956.

Ranking fourth in the authoritative Canon of Dutch Literature of 2002, Reynard's satire continues to flourish, and so does Reynard scholarship. In 2017, an online series of Reynard talks was included in the open access course on Dutch medieval literature at Antwerp University. *Tiecelyn*, the lively e-platform of the Belgian Reynaert Society, provides Reynard lovers with news of scholarly and other activities. And the International Reynard Society offers biennial scholarly conferences, while its multilingual yearbook *Reinardus* is published by John Benjamins in Amsterdam.

Here, the long history of Anglo-Dutch connections provides an obvious context for further investigation. For the Madocke riddle discussed by Alexia Lagast and Cor Hendriks, for example, there is the intriguing question what link there could have been between Reynard's Flemish author and the 'William Madocke' listed on the parish priest name board in the Welsh village church of Manorbier on the Pembrokeshire coast.

Reynard's future, meanwhile, is central to the new North Sea Crossings Project, funded from 2017 by the National Lottery, which aims to bring Reynard as Fantastic Mister Fox to British schools and children through a programme of cultural heritage education in new and imaginative ways.

For this project a four-way partnership has been established, between, first, Bristol University professor Ad Putter with his cutting-edge scholarship in medieval English and European literature, witness his recent edition of *The Works of the Gawain Poet* (Penguin, 2014); then secondly, the Bodleian Library in Oxford with its incredible riches in documentary heritage, texts, book history and the iconography of the Fox; thirdly, Aardman, the Bristol-based Animation Studio, with its technological wizardry in animation and its world-famous comedies, from *Wallace and Gromit* (1985) through

Chicken Run (2000), *Creature Comforts* (1989) and *Shaun the Sheep* (2015) to its prehistoric caveman film *Early Man*, released in January 2018; and finally, the Oxford-based creative education organisation Flash of Splendour, which is taking these animal tales to reach out and go beyond reading, using innovative pedagogical approaches and new media in creative workshops for primary and secondary schools and in particular for children with special educational needs.

Marshalling the expertise of its four partners to produce an innovative, virtual and animated Fox for British children of any age, the project will culminate in 2020 in a programme of events around Reynard the Fox, including the publication of two books on Reynard (one for children, one academic); an exhibition in the Bodleian; a Reynard the Fox Day, school workshops, film festivals and of course Aardman's animation of Fantastic Mister Fox. All this a tribute to the enduring fascination of this Fox, with its wicked sense of humour, forever young.

REINIER SALVERDA

Reynard the Fox and Other Mediaeval Netherlandish Secular Literature. Edited and introduced by E. Colledge. Translated by Professor Adriaan J. Barnouw and E. Colledge. Leyden / London / New York, 1967.

Cor Hendriks, *Richard Deacon, Master of Disinformation*, 2016. Pdf available at: robscholtemuseum.nl.

Alexia Lagast, 'A la recherche de l'œuvre perdue: kritische status quaestionis van het onderzoek naar de Madoc', in *Millennium* 24 (2010), vol.1, pp. 19-33.

Aardman – https://www.aardman.com

Bodleian Libraries – https://bodleian.ox.ac.uk

Bristol University, Professor Ad Putter – www.research-information.bristol.ac.uk

Dutch medieval literature online at Antwerp University – www.moocmnl.kantl.be

Flash of Splendour – www.flashofsplendourarts.com

International Reynard Society – www.rose.uzh.ch/de/forschung/reynard_society.html

Tiecelyn – www.reynaertgenootschap.be

Alone on the North Sea Coast
Adriaan Roland Holst

Adriaan Roland Holst (1888-1976) set himself a truly formidable task when in 1932 he embarked on *Een Winter aan Zee* (*A Winter by the Sea*), published five years later, in 1937. It comprises sixty-three lyric poems, each eight lines long, each obeying the rhyming scheme *abacbdcd*, each in iambic trimeters. The sequence – but this is very much a *singular* work – is divided into ten sections, to the nature of which the poet supplied a brief, illuminating, though personally reticent 'explanation', included here as afterword. That the work has profound autobiographical roots there can be little doubting, with the first person regularly present, and noticeable in both the first and last poems. It gives us a man alone on the North Sea coast, bereft of the woman he has loved (and still loves?): she has gone to an unspecified city he believes to be corrupt and corrupting. The voice we hear – surmounting all ingenuities of language and metrics and all unflinching interior analyses – is one of agonised individuality. The speaker finds comfort however in the thought of his countless emotional predecessors, members of humanity throughout the ages abandoned, isolated, yet determined to understand their fate.

It is enormously to the translator's credit that this voice prevails – and stays with us – even as he himself wrestles with fashioning from Roland Holst's virtuosic scheme and verse-forms an English-language artefact – mostly in contemporary English, though there are echoes of the Elizabethans on whom translator Roger Kuin is an expert. Yet – and opposite the English text the original is placed in photographed manuscript – he is consistently and scrupulously faithful to a Dutch itself often extremely intricately wrought. Now and again there are sacrifices of fidelity of language to fidelity to Roland Holst's elaborate poetic ingenuities, but these seem unimportant beside the creation of a work that can stand up as a whole, a monument to intensity of feeling and artistic ambition.

Perhaps, as with so many works from the 1920s and 1930s, readers fare better after absorbing the writer's 'explanation': Eliot's *Waste Land* (1922) set an enormous precedent, and, as there, Roland Holst invites us to recall the ancient and the mythological. He studied at Oxford University when young, and from that time on was a great admirer of W.B. Yeats, sharing 'The Fascination of What's Difficult', the need for classical and Celtic analogues to key situations and characters, and an obsession with the woman Helen of Troy who, Janus-headed, stalks *A Winter by the Sea*. The poet's own loved one continually brings Helen to our imaginative attention; she was 'impassioned beauty incarnate' when he loved her beside the North Sea. She represented for him then the 'City of the World', a platonic *Sancta Civitas*. This she subsequently betrayed by moving to a modern city of worldly values, where, 'tarnished' as likely as not, she 'now wanders, old and embittered, and recognized by no one.' The reason for this cruel fate lies in the terrifying paradox that, through her very beauty, she (like Helen of Troy before her) brought about that first city's destruction. 'Who shall perceive the sense / of emptiness and ages? / Where towers stood battled, tense? / burning, she too can mark / mere fullness of time's pages.' The parallel with Yeats ('When Helen lived' etc.) scarcely needs further comment.

Of the ten sections five are 'groups' of poems – sections I, III, VI, VIII and X – and five – sections II, IV, V, VII and IX – are 'series'. In a 'group' the poems are numbered and should be taken as separate entities, even if themes and images link them; in a 'series' the poems, unnumbered, fol-low on one from another, and, read consecutively, have cumulative effect. Section I establishes the woman loved by the poet and the North Sea setting of their passion, Section II introduces and imposes on us the tragic, destructive, analogous figure of Helen. In Section III humanity stretching back to antiquity is apostrophised; Section IV is a beautiful, disquieting 'intermezzo' of only two poems, showing today's world under threat from 'alien powers' envoy'. Section V (a 'series') brings us back to the woman herself, recalled in her disappearance, Section VI (a 'group') reveals consequent developments in the poet's own psyche. Section VII is another intermezzo, dealing again with hostility to the world from without; Section VIII is arguably the most personal of all – or, rather, *supra*-personal since the lovers are depicted as inspirited by characters from the past. Section IX 'sings the beloved's departure' while not foregoing sombre recognition of her avatars; Section X (a 'group') attempts not so much resolution as lyrical reconciliation to loss as being inextricable from experience.

Every so often the writer – not for nothing was he called 'The Prince of Poets' – rises to solemn musical heights, and his translator with him:

> *Where did the time go? How*
> *long has it been snowing?*
> *A mirror's silence now*
> *holds this room hostage, no*
> *more sign of life is going*
> *through. What if she were lying*
> *– alone, as I am so*
> *alone – somewhere and dying.*

PAUL BINDING

A. Roland Holst, *A Winter by the Sea*, translated into verse by Roger Kuin. Ian Jackson, Berkeley, 2017 (limited edition of 250 copies), 148 p. (ISBN 978 1 944769 58 1).

A Piercing Eye Alert to Every Detail
Charlotte Brontë's Brussels Legacy

It's easy to think of novels set in London, Paris or New York, but no one has ever written the great Brussels novel. The city's most famous writer, judging from the number of plaques dotted around

Adriaan Roland Holst (1888-1976)
Picture taken by the Dutch poet Lucebert
© Het geheugen van Nederland

the city, is the French exile Victor Hugo. Other than that, there isn't much for Waterstones bookshop to shelve under the heading Brussels fiction.

Unless of course you count Charlotte Brontë's *Villette* (1853). The novel is set in a fictional city, so it isn't strictly a Brussels novel, but it is clearly based on the city where Charlotte studied and later taught in 1842-1843.

Many Brontë experts have described Charlotte's impressions of Belgium, but few have considered what the Belgians thought of Charlotte. The Brussels-based writer and translator Helen MacEwan now fills this gap with her second carefully researched Brontë book: *Through Belgian Eyes: Charlotte Brontë's Troubled Brussels Legacy*.

In the course of fourteen chapters, MacEwan builds up a detailed portrait of life in Brussels during the 1840s. She draws on a wide range of sources, including old newspaper articles, travel pieces and archive prints to create a rich panorama of Brussels life.

MacEwan is a sharp observer who charts the urban transformation of Brussels in the nineteenth century. She describes the new boulevards and grand museums that were intended to turn Brussels into a mini Paris. But she also describes the depressing destruction in 1909 of the famous Pensionnat Heger that formed the setting for Charlotte's *Villette*.

MacEwan has dug deeply in French and Dutch sources to find out every possible nugget linked to Charlotte Brontë's stay in Brussels. She has even translated a *De Standaard* article by Kristien Hemmerechts in which the Flemish writer forgives Charlotte for her unflattering description of the Flemish. 'Whatever she may have said, it is thrilling that this great English author wrote about "us",' Hemmerechts said.

While MacEwan's book is rooted in nineteenth-century Brussels, the author realises the Brontë story has a modern resonance. In a chapter on the immigrant experience in Brussels, she unearths a book on migrants in Brussels by historian Sophie De Schaepdrijver which unexpectedly cites Lucy Snowe's experience in the city as an example of a young immigrant woman finding her place in a foreign city.

The book is dotted with other unexpected observations that might seem odd in a book about Char-

The Pensionnat Heger in Brussels

lotte Brontë. Who would have thought there was any connection between the author of *Villette* and the Brussels comic book writer François Schuiten? But MacEwan has found it in the buried section of the Rue Isabelle, close to the site of the Pensionnat, where Schuiten locates a passage to a fictional 'obscure city'.

The author's determination to uncover every last Brontë crumb is evident in the chapter titled *The Brontës in Africa and Charlotte in the Congo*. It seems a puzzling title, since the Brontës never set foot in the Congo, which moreover was only acquired by King Leopold II in 1885. But MacEwan has uncovered a 1956 article, *Les Brontës en Afrique*, by the author Marie Gevers, in which she reflects on the Brontës during a trip to the Belgian Congo.

But it is the love affair, real or imagined, between Charlotte and her teacher Constantin Heger that brings most people to the Isabella Quarter in Brussels. MacEwan's book doesn't try to resolve the nature of Charlotte's 'hopeless romantic love'. But her forensic examination of Charlotte's letters to Heger prove that it was a complex infatuation that we will probably never properly understand.

Not many writers have succeeded in producing an authentic portrait of Brussels. Most authors, from Baudelaire to Bill Bryson, have contributed nothing much more than another caustic essay in Brussels bashing. But MacEwan shows that Charlotte Brontë, while often critical, was alive to every detail in the city, from the distinctive pistolet rolls to the dreary daily routine in a Catholic girls' school.

Like her subject, MacEwan has a piercing eye that is alert to every detail of Brussels urban life. Her detailed and nuanced book deserves to be read by anyone interested in Charlotte Brontë or the city she wrote about in such a compelling way.

MacEwan cites several newspaper articles in which eminent Belgian writers and critics have urged the city to put up a memorial to the Brontës.

Their efforts have so far failed to convince the authorities, but we at least have MacEwan's rich and readable book to remind us of an extraordinary moment in European literary history.

DEREK BLYTH

Helen MacEwan, *Through Belgian Eyes: Charlotte Brontë's Troubled Brussels Legacy*, Sussex Academic Press, Eastbourne, 2017, 312 p.

A Soldier at a Typewriter
Alfred Birney's Novel about Java

Alfred Birney's (1951) book *De tolk van Java* (The Interpreter from Java) makes its readers shiver. It is a novel about a traumatised father, Arend, who murdered dozens of people in Indonesia during the war, a war which for him simply continued within the family he subsequently began in the Netherlands. That war only ends for Arend's son, the first-person narrator of the novel, with his father's death. 'I won't fight anymore, this is where it ends', states the final sentence of this rich novel about identity, trauma, racism (in Indonesia, in the Netherlands and in the Dutch army), the Japanese occupation of Indonesia, the bloody battle of the Dutch against Indonesian independence, a father who abuses his children and the boarding-school life which begins for the narrator and the four other children from the family when they are sent away from home. The reader will find no sweet nostalgia here (that is a 'lie', writes the father, and the narrator wants nothing to do with it either) or a description of childhood paradise, as is often the case in famous Dutch literature about Indonesia.

Birney has lived with this theme for years, but his novel came along at the right moment: in 2016, the year in which *De tolk van Java* was published, the Netherlands saw the reopening and deepening of a discussion of war crimes committed by the Dutch army, which was tasked with restoring the colonial administration in Indonesia after 1945, and about the government which did not wish to accept independence. Until then the official version had stated that the main issue had been incidental 'excesses' (rape, robbery and plundering), rather than structural war crimes, covered up by the colonial administration, the Dutch government and the military judiciary. After new research it can no longer be denied that the Dutch army was responsible for systematic war crimes.

De tolk van Java begins with a sentence about Arend which stretches over more than a page, describing what he saw and heard, stating who he betrayed, and that he was tortured and helped the Allies. These are stories which Arend always told his son, his son who hates him, who sees him as a mass murderer and who accuses him of largely ruining his life. Arend raises his children as he himself was raised: harshly and with liberal use of his fists, confirmed in his path by his traumatic war experiences. He always sleeps with a knife within reach, even taking it with him in his bicycle pannier when he goes into town, and one day he pursues one of his suspected enemies in The Hague carrying it.

Birney makes his father the central character and his identity is far from unambiguous: born in Java as the illegitimate son of an Indo-European father, who refuses to acknowledge him, and a Chinese mother, he is the only one in his family to identify with the Netherlands. While his fellow soldiers keep pin-ups on their walls, above his bed hangs a portrait of the queen of the Netherlands. Due to the turbulent events in Indonesia, Arend regularly changes sides and doubts his choices: together with Indonesian friends he fights the Japanese occupiers, but after 1945 he sides with the Dutch against his compatriots. Indonesia is not his country, he says: as an illegitimate child he has been humiliated by the 'Indo' (Dutch-Indonesian) people and as an Indo boy he found himself caught between the Dutch and the Indonesians. His son doubts his principles and suspects that Arend simply always took the side of the strongest party. Just before his departure for the Netherlands, Arend plans to change his name to Noland, in order 'to distance himself from colonially tinted Indo-Europeans and similarly white Indonesian Dutch people'. It is a name which speaks volumes for his hybrid identity, and one which also has predictive power, as he will never feel at home in the Netherlands either. His intended paradise turns out to be a country riddled with racism.

When I say that Birney's novel makes me shiver, it is an allusion to a pronouncement by a member of the Dutch House of Representatives, who in 1860 after the publication of Multatuli's then controversial novel *Max Havelaar* said that 'recently, a certain chill has gone through this country, caused by a book'. Birney makes various references to this classic of Dutch literature: in his mother's new friend's pantry the narrator finds 'the sea chest from my father's passage to the Netherlands'. He continues: 'I opened the chest and saw all sorts of paperwork inside: books, piles of papers, letters, photos and files.' This is reminiscent of another package, which also came from Indonesia, 'Scarfman's package' from *Max Havelaar*. Droogstoppel, one of the narrators from that book, says, 'There I found treatises and essays', followed by a list of subjects. While large parts of the 'Package' are woven into *Max Havelaar*, parts of the father's manuscript are published in *De tolk van Java*.

In his manuscript, which he tried in vain to publish, Arend describes his youth and the period up until his forced departure to the Netherlands. Forced, because he was blacklisted by Sukarno, the first president of the independent republic of Indonesia, a country in which he was now unsafe because he had murdered countless Indonesian freedom fighters. This message is central to the novel and the narrator confronts his mother, who has very little interest in Indonesia, and his brother with its content, raises questions and provides commentary. One part, almost 200 pages, in which Arend recounts the events from 17 August 1945, the day on which Sukarno announced independence, until he leaves Indonesia on a ship bound for the Netherlands, is included without interruption or commentary from the narrator. It consists of sometimes detailed descriptions of horrific crimes – on the side of the Indonesian freedom fighters too. For that reason, and because it is written from the perspective of the Dutch army, the losers, it can be compared with the atrocities in Curzio Malaparte's 1944 novel *Kaputt*. Malaparte, too, opted for the perspective of the losing party.

Those responsible for the Dutch war crimes in Indonesia have never been prosecuted and the Dutch government will have to adopt a new position with respect to that period. While historical research leaves no room for doubt, Birney presents a more complicated and less straightforward take on the entire issue – that is the task of literature. Questions of whether Arend wrote the truth and whether his memories are correct pervade throughout the book and in the discussion between the brothers. Here, too, Multatuli offers a clue, as the question is not whether all the details are true, but what effect the book has on readers. After the story of Saïjah and Adinda in *Max Havelaar*, Multatuli writes, 'But I know *more*. I know, *and I can prove*, that there were *many* Adindas and *many* Saïjahs, and that *what is fiction in particular is truth in general.*'

But *De tolk van Java* is more than a contemporary *Max Havelaar* or a Dutch version of Malaparte's *Kaputt*. Birney has now published fifteen novels, essays and anthologies and this may well be his most important book, in which he impressively unites all the themes of his previous work. It is only fair that he has won two Dutch literary prizes for it.

JAAP GRAVE
Translated by Anna Asbury

Alfred Birney, *De tolk van Java*, De Geus, Breda/Amsterdam, 2016. The English translation, *The Interpreter from Java*, is to be published by Head of Zeus, London.

Music

Turning Windmills and Exploding Ships
Popular Music from the Low Countries

Writing about music is like dancing about architecture: that well-known witticism attributed to various celebrities is generally used by musicians to put music journalism and criticism into perspective. Or to brush them aside, as in the case of singer-songwriter Elvis Costello, who in no uncertain terms added '*It's a stupid thing to do.*' Fortunately, those words did not prevent Lutgard Mutsaers and Gert Keunen from compiling *Made in the Low Countries*: a fascinating book in the Global Popular Music Series at Routledge, a prestigious publishing house that specialises in academic books and periodicals.

Or were the comments by Costello and co. still in the back of the compilers' minds when they contacted academics from Flanders and the Netherlands to contribute to this reader? For *Made in the Low Countries*' main focus is not on the music as such but rather on the broader context in which it is made, historical and social developments seen alongside sociological and economic processes. That is what the Global Popular Music Series sets out to do: in its statement of intent the study of local music is first and foremost characterised as an 'immensely precious key to understand different cultures and economies'.

In *Made in the Low Countries*, André Nuchelmans's piece 'Upstart among the Arts. The Rise of Rock into the Dutch Subsidy System' is an example of how the attitude of the Dutch authorities has fundamentally changed with regard to pop (musicians): from '"Get a job" was the message at the social security window' in the early 1970s to 'a club circuit unique in the world' in the 1980s and later on.

Cultural sociologist Gert Keunen's contribution starts from a clash between the ideal son-in-law Jonathan Vandenbroeck (Milow) and the somewhat more caustic Tom Barman (from the rock band dEUS) to describe how a new 'zone' has arisen in the Flemish (music) media and concert and festival sector. In between the two classical poles Mainstream/Commercial and Underground/Alternative, there is now the 'Alternative Mainstream', that combines artistic credibility and 'authenticity' with a mass audience – without selling out to 'commercialism'.

This distant, academic approach doesn't work to the advantage of all the articles included in *Made in the Low Countries*. Whereas Nuchelmans's and Keunen's well-written and lively contributions are nimbly able to lead the reader through rather dry institutional information – and in passing still present a good picture of the music worlds of the Netherlands and Flanders, respectively – other authors get stuck in the jargon of reports and statistics. At such moments this book, with hardly any illustrations and a graphic design that at best can be termed 'respectable', is a hard nut to crack.

Even so, the reader does pick up some interesting information from the drier articles as well. For instance, in 'From Thrash to Cash: Forging and Legitimizing Dutch Metal' we learn how the heavy metal genre, despite a lack of artistic recognition, was still able to get government grants for the export of Dutch music. Viewed in that light, it comes as no surprise that precisely in that country, in Eindhoven in 2013, 'the world's first 3-year training degree in metal music production called Metal Factory' came into being.

Riveting from beginning to end are the articles in which the authors reveal apparently time-bound phenomena to be crucial phases in pop history, without reverting to 'those were the good old days' or the exoticism of 'how crazy we were back then.' Two examples.

In his piece about pirate broadcasters who introduced commercial radio to the Netherlands from ships in the North Sea, Ger Tillekens does not withhold the juicy details (a bomb attack on a ship by a rival broadcaster!). But more importantly is the convincing manner in which he demonstrates that the focus on youth and appeal to targeted groups around such a broadcaster partly shaped the social upheavals of the 1960s. Moreover, the influence of those long-gone pirate radio stations continues to be felt in today's media landscape – if even only because the highly personal presentation style of that era's disc jockeys is still in vogue today.

Something similar applies to 'This Must Be Belgium', in which Pedro De Bruyckere provides a historical context and traces the effects of the long-maligned New Beat genre (a form of 1980s electronic dance music). 'The craze cultivated DJ culture, foreshadowing the rise of superstar DJ's of the 1990s and beyond', writes De Bruyckere. Moreover the genre which he calls 'truly unique and born out of the love of music and dancing' created a fruitful breeding ground for further electronic music production and for a few years turned the eyes of the world to Belgium, 'that's been far more innovative than people give it credit for'.

The pieces on pirate radio and New Beat also show that *Made in the Low Countries* can hardly be considered a classical history of pop music in the Low Countries from 1955 to the present, and it doesn't offer a survey of the most important artists either (only the chapters on Herman Brood and Golden Earring qualify as such). Instead, the authors pay – sometimes a little too much – attention to specific partial aspects. That too appears to fit the bill of Routledge's Global Popular Music Series: 'uncovering the wealth of studies flourishing in so many countries [...] is by now no less urgent than considering the music itself'. Anyone writing the 'definitive' history of Belgian and Dutch popular music has little to fear from this book, but is certainly a treasure trove of information, also due to the reference section at the end of each article and an extensive 'Selected Biography' at the back.

Despite its somewhat fragmentary impression, there are some interesting themes running through *Made in the Low Countries*, such as the relationship of the music from the relatively small Low Countries to the overwhelming Anglo Saxon tradition, and the way in which music from Belgium/Flanders and the Netherlands expresses a regional/national identity (e.g. the insightful piece by Lutgard Mutsaers about the ultra-Dutch song 'The Windmill's Turning'). Those two themes often intertwine in this book, especially in the article by Geert Buelens about the language in which artists from the Low Countries sing. Dutch has never become an international pop song language and that is partly due to the morphology of the language itself – even according to those who have had the most success with it.

Still, it is possible for Flemish and Dutch artists to create masterpieces in their mother tongue, as proven by Raymond van het Groenewoud, born and bred in Brussels of Dutch parentage. He is interviewed by Geert Buelens at the end of this informative book. In that piece, which is well worth reading, the singer-songwriter is compared to Elvis Costello ('I don't really understand him [...] he comes across as academic', Van het Groenewoud responds) and Serge Gainsbourg. What Van het Groenewoud has to say about the latter, might possibly contain the key to making good music: 'He removed the pompous aspects of the genre he came out with. He just did what he felt like doing [...].'

And yes, that might even be *dancing about architecture*.

PIETER COUPÉ

Translated by Scott Rollins

Lutgard Mutsaers and Gert Keunen (eds), *Made in the Low Countries. Studies in Popular Music*, Routledge Global Popular Music Series, New York/London, 2018, 229 pp.
www.globalpopularmusic.net

More Than Ideal Grandchildren
The Jussen Brothers

The impressive success enjoyed by the Dutch piano brothers Jussen has many sources, aside from the fact of the quality of their playing. In some respects their careers resemble those of every young exceptionally gifted musician. Born in 1993, Lucas won the important *Rotterdamse Pianodriedaagse* in 2001 and three years later Arthur, who was born in 1996, was voted the young musical talent of the year in the Netherlands. That talent did not come from strangers: their father is percussionist in the Netherlands Radio Philharmonic Orchestra and their mother gives transverse flute lessons. The children, just like Janine Jansen, Lisa Jacobs, Noa Wildschut and other highly talented Dutch music child prodigies, went through the established contemporary channels of concources, concerts, interviews, debut CDs, media appearances, music awards, plus lessons from a foreign celebrity (in their case Maria-João Pires).

In the Jussen brothers' case, other influences were also factors, some of which were very Dutch while others much more archetypal. Two great talents in a single family just happens to attract more attention than one and elicits stronger sentiments than two people from different families. When their first CD was released with great fanfare in 2010, containing works by Beethoven and on which the brothers could be heard playing both separately and together, it provoked strong feelings among quite a few of those who bought the album (at the time I was working in a CD store) reminiscent of grandmothers watching their grandchildren shine in the local children's choir (I am not exaggerating). The thing that both reinforced as well as put those emotions into perspective, was the fact that despite their talent and entrance into the bigtime music world, the teenagers were able to maintain

The Jussen Brothers

a youthful candour and not get too big for their boots. Though it would appear Lucas and Arthur regularly receive fashion tips on how to dress, they still (along with their managers perhaps) succeed in giving the impression of just being themselves and not bothering with creating any image. Moreover, their musical star is rising at a time when classical music appears to be attracting a diminishing audience, most of whom would appear to be old people. (The latter was also true to a certain degree seventy years ago, but due to the ascent of youth culture and the changing relations between the older and younger generation, anything not directly geared to a young audience these days is sometimes made into a problem.)

In that context two extremely talented adolescents who excel at classical music are a godsend to the music industry. An added attraction for the business aspect is the brothers' apparently effortless willingness to go along with the current demand of presenting a smooth image in the media. Practically all their new CD releases (after Beethoven, CDs followed with Schubert, Mozart, French music, and most recently with music by Saint-Saëns, Poulenc and Fazil Say) were marked by guest performances in The World Keeps Turning, a very popular television programme in the Netherlands.

The Jussen brothers' repertory is partially made up of well-known works for two pianos and four hands, by such composers as Mozart, Fauré, Poulenc and Saint-Saëns. Despite that degree of predictability they cannot be considered narrow-minded pianists. They were invited by the Holland Festival, that programmes a great deal of contemporary music, to perform Stockhausen's *Mantra*. Furthermore, they were able to discuss their performance at length in a popular TV talk show in which the interviewer did not half-jokingly dismiss the music as difficult and elitist. The brothers considered it expressive music they believed in; that belief was something they wanted and were able to express, first on TV, afterwards in concert. And so it does not come as a complete surprise that Dutch contemporary composer Theo Loevendie (born in 1930) wrote a piece especially for them entitled *Together*.

The brothers' CDs exhibit a clear development: from a certain hesitation in the interpretation of

Beethoven to a resolute blend of robustness and refinement in the French compositions. And even though the albums are good, like so many artists, their playing is also more exciting in front of an audience than in a studio.

The brothers also have active solo careers. The older of the two is more fiery and classical. I have not yet heard them in recitals, but in piano concerts (for the time being they are limiting themselves to the iron repertoire) they both love to accentuate the expression of detail (the influence of Pires?) and appear to regard lyricism more important than architecture. When they play as soloists there is a slight deviation from the way in which they perform as a duo, where a certain degree of regularity is clear cut and inevitable but in which their familiarity with the classical repertoire enables them to give it more surprise and nuance.

The brothers' fame is starting to make international inroads. On a number of occasions, they have accompanied the members of the Dutch royal family on state visits. True, their first CD was released on the international label DGG, but only in the Netherlands. The fact this very quickly changed speaks volumes.

EMANUEL OVERBEEKE
Translated by Scott Rollins

arthurandlucasjussen.com

Politics

For the 'Ordinary' Dutch Citizen
The Third Government Led by Prime Minister Mark Rutte

General elections were held in the Netherlands on 15 March 2017; the new government took office on 26 October 2017. After more than 200 days of negotiation – the longest cabinet formation process ever in the Netherlands – Mark Rutte presented his third cabinet. It is a government with a completely different make-up from the previous two.

Mark Rutte himself is a member of the centre-right VVD party, which has been the largest party

Mark Rutte

in the Netherlands since 2010. And although the party lost seats at the most recent elections, it held onto that position. Mark Rutte is regarded as a master of the balancing act, someone who can work with everyone. And that would seem to be a logical conclusion if we look at the composition of his cabinets.

In 2010 he formed a government in coalition with the Christian Democrats. That government received the support of the anti-Islam PVV party led by Geert Wilders, though without them being members of the government. Wilders withdrew that support two years later, prompting another election and ushering in a coalition with the social democrats (PvdA). The new government was formed within a few weeks. As an alliance of the centre-right and the left, it had a totally different make-up from Rutte's first, conservative cabinet (Rutte I).

The coalition of the PvdA and VVD made it through a full term, with five years of give and take by both parties. When it came to the elections on 15 March 2017, it was the social democrats who had to swallow most of the bitter fruits of this collaboration, with the PvdA losing no fewer than 29 of its 38 seats.

This election result opened the way for a series of highly complex negotiations. Mark Rutte's VVD party remained in the driving seat. But Rutte was no longer willing to work with the party that came second, Geert Wilders's anti-Islam party, and attempts to forge a coalition with another of the election winners, the Greens (Groen Links) failed. For its part, the PvdA had lost too much to be willing to venture into government again. Forming the new government was thus a lengthy and complex challenge.

If the second Rutte government (Rutte II) was characterised by give and take between two parties, the arrangements for the Rutte III were set out on paper right down to the last detail. Ultimately, four parties managed to reach agreement: the centre-right VVD, the Christian Democratic Appeal (CDA), the social-liberal D66 and the small, religiously inspired Christian Union (CU), a party with social principles but also conservative ideas on intangible issues such as euthanasia.

Rutte I was a conservative, right-of-centre government; Rutte II was a government of the centre-right and left; and Rutte III is in reality a mix of everything. The *NRC Handelsblad* newspaper summarised the coalition agreement briefly as government of the individual and the community, from gender-neutral registration with the authorities to the obligation to sing the national anthem (the *Wilhelmus*) in the classroom; an attempt to unite two totally different political worlds: that of the cosmopolitan, individualistic city-dweller and the uncertain citizen of the provinces who attaches importance to his or her local community.

The new government describes itself as being above all for the 'ordinary' Dutch citizen: '(...) and above all the shared conviction that the groups in the middle, people with an ordinary salary and an ordinary home, owner-occupied or rented, should now start to see that the sacrifices they have made in recent years to overcome the crisis have not been for nothing. They deserve to get ahead. And, to be absolutely clear: that word "ordinary" is inclusive: it makes no difference where your roots lie, where you live, what you believe or what your station in life is.'

A government for everything and everyone, then, but still a government with the smallest possible majority in Parliament. Several MPs of the new coalition parties have been extremely critical of Prime Minister Rutte whilst in opposition in recent years. The leaders of the various coalition parties have therefore opted to continue sitting in Parliament and not to become ministers, the idea being that this will give them a better chance of controlling the critical colleagues in their own parties.

Whether Rutte III will manage to see out a full term is of course difficult to say. For the moment, however, the next national elections in the Netherlands are scheduled for 17 March 2021.

JORIS VAN DE KERKHOF
Translated by Julian Ross

Brussels, I Love You But You Make Me Cry

Minister Pascal Smet of Brussels recently learnt a lesson when, in an interview with the European news site Politico, he compared Brussels with a 'whore'. Anyone can gripe about Brussels – and a great deal of it goes on – but do not touch the residents' love for their city. That means a return to 'one for all'.

Of course the minister's comparison was entirely misplaced, but the core of his argument holds. Brussels is a city which simultaneously attracts and repulses. *Brussels, I love you but you make me cry.*

That's something the capital has in common with many capital cities. Talk to a rural Frenchman about Paris and he will mix equal measures of disdain and pride. The social, geographical and cultural gap between town and country is one of the deepest fault lines in western societies. Only now that 'country' occasionally gains the upper hand – take Brexit and Trump, for example – are we acutely aware of it.

Traditionally cities are beacons of freedom and progress. That's why conservative MPs have always viewed them with suspicion. And that's why Belgium in particular maintained an anti-urban spatial planning policy in previous centuries. People were permitted to live anywhere, but preferably not in the big, chaotic city. Besides freedom, the metropolis was also always associated with alienation and dilapidation.

Now Brussels does have a problem. The city really is dilapidated in some places. A fitting symbol is the still new pedestrian zone. From Gothenburg to Seville the trend for car-free city centres has

been a formidable success. In Brussels it is an improvised, filthy mess, and sadly also a choice arena for anyone looking to cause trouble.

Brussels is certainly not the only metropolis in the world where poverty, disadvantage and migration form a brew which sometimes boils over. What is unique is that social disadvantage is located in the old city centre. Brussels has no suburbs. The districts where migrants showed up and settled decades ago are the city centre. Brussels is in that sense less hypocritical than other world cities. Here you cannot avoid confrontation with poverty and multicultural challenges.

Not that that has brought a solution any closer. Brussels has been too monstrously disfigured in an institutional sense for that. The Brussels Capital Region numbers 1.2 million residents and as the capital of Belgium is officially bilingual, with the Dutch-speakers forming a protected minority. It is one of three regions of Belgium and consists of nineteen municipalities, with as many mayors and six police zones.

Not only are there far too many mandates in the region and municipalities for the scarce political talent; the 'powers' also hold one another locked in a desperate standstill. There is movement, but, in the international perspective of urban renaissance, it progresses frustratingly slowly.

Flanders and Wallonia have long taken little notice of all that. Even the people of Brussels often consider this surreal amateurism rather charming and 'quaint'. That is changing. The fact that the labyrinth of Brussels has proven an ideal hiding place for jihadi terrorists has shown many city residents the ugly side of their political improvisation act. Recently scandals of self-enrichment among the many political mandates have been added to the picture. Again, citizens have discovered that there are limits to political permissiveness.

So, who knows, perhaps that double shock will be the kiss this beautiful city needs to awaken her from her deep sleep. Although, to be honest, it is far from clear which prince will emerge from the ballot box in October 2018.

BART EECKHOUT
Translated by Anna Asbury

Science

A Bridge to the Future

In mid-October 2017 the first completely 3D-printed concrete bicycle bridge opened to the world near 's-Hertogenbosch in the Netherlands. This is an innovative first which illustrates the great potential of this new technology.

The eight-metre-long bridge is part of the new ring road at Gemert (southeast of 's-Hertogenbosch) and connects the N605 with the N272. It was not cast in situ, as is usual, in a formwork that is first constructed, then filled with concrete transported by concrete mixer trucks. The bridge was made in the experimental laboratory at Eindhoven University of Technology (TU/e), with a 3D printer which bears no resemblance to the sort of printer people have at home to print out text. It could be imagined as a small gantry crane with a computer-driven arm suspended from it, which pushes a thick substance like dense toothpaste from the opening while the print head closely follows a pattern. In this way the 3D printer layers the special concrete mortar in the specific form programmed by the software. The bridge consists of 800 sprayed layers and was assembled at the final location.

At TU/e people had been working for several years on the development of this 3D concrete printer. The research group 3D Concrete Printing (3DCP) started up at the end of 2014 as part of the Structural Design division of the Department of the Built Environment. Professor Theo Salet leads the research group in developing concrete prints into fully-fledged and broadly deployable technology for making components and buildings. The current result is the big 3D concrete printer with a print volume of 9 by 4.5 by 3 metres which can 'print out' the desired constructions thanks to a four-axle robot which applies the concrete in the right place and a mixer pump which delivers the right kind of concrete for the process.

This technology offers an unseen freedom, because it is possible to create components which cannot easily be achieved by traditional methods. Special shapes with a level of detail previously inconceivable are now feasible.

Complex components can be made more cheaply and quickly with the 3D technologies, which also allow for affordable customisation in any location. The use of robots means that any design can be produced uniquely every time with a new print instruction.

The technology saves on formwork construction and materials and on the concrete itself. That is good news for the environment. 'The printer uses far less concrete. And concrete leads to substantial CO_2 emissions. Reducing the quantity, along with the saving on formwork, therefore makes a serious contribution to the sustainability of a construction', Salet commented on Dutch television. Less material is needed, so there is less waste. It is also cheaper and quicker than the traditional building method, while requiring less preparation work.

TU/e has conducted several trials with printing concrete and is already dreaming of larger bridges, viaducts and other concrete constructions. Builders are considering the possibility of moving the 3D concrete printer to the construction site itself so that the desired products or parts can be made on location. Following the Netherlands' lead, people are also experimenting with printed concrete elsewhere in Europe, but in China they have advanced still further. There complete houses are built by 3D concrete printers. The walls of these houses are printed hollow, so that they can subsequently be filled with insulation and wiring.

Techniques for printing with pure metals or alloys, plastics, ceramic materials or food are well on their way. 3D printing is currently most commonly used for making prototypes, moulds, instruments and machines or machine components. The era of industrial digital production is drawing ever closer. It is already advancing rapidly in space travel and medicine. Prosthetic teeth and bones or heart valves can be printed in 3D. People are dreaming out loud about bio-printers for tissues. The company Melotte, situated in the Belgian province of

Limburg, is one of the world leaders in ground-breaking precision production.

In the future, mass-produced goods will make way for personalised products. Consumers will increasingly design, make, adapt and print their own products. That might lead to shifts in the economy. Some jobs will perish and new ones will come into being. The print technology is still in its infancy, but in combination with synthetic biology and nano-technology it will lead to a radical transformation in many design, production and logistical processes.

GEERDT MAGIELS
Translated by Anna Asbury

Theatre

At the Heart of Society
The Nation by Het Nationale Theater

Over the last two or three years theatre makers in the Low Countries have become increasingly involved in the cultural diversity debate. In their different ways, they take seriously their mission of manifesting 'the abstract and brief chronicles of the time', as Hamlet qualifies the travelling actors who come to shake up the Danish court. In 2017 Het Nationale Theater in The Hague came out with the urgently current production *The Nation*, a five-hour marathon conceived, written and directed by the multi-talented Eric de Vroedt (b. 1972).

The Nation, billed as "a topical theatre thriller about the frenzy of Dutch multicultural society", begins with an apparently everyday anecdote about the search for an eleven-year-old boy named Is-maël, who has disappeared without a trace after a short visit to a police station in The Hague. The search is woven into a tense web of intrigues and whole and half-truths, repeatedly inviting onlookers to revise their assumptions. In design and style, *The Nation* unfolds as a television serial on stage: image techniques, cliff-hangers and other methods from the Netflix box of tricks serve the topical story which De Vroedt aims to tell.

The innovative aspect of *The Nation* lies particularly in the surprising way in which the world of

the stage is combined with that of modern media. From the first instant Ismaël's disappearance provides the requisite suspense and holds the viewers' attention through six episodes. All those episodes start live on stage, with a short filmed sequel on colossal screens, where credits for the characters and theatre staff are projected on vast, dynamic panoramas of The Hague. Action resumes on stage, until once again the screens support, if not annex, the dramatic course of events. This varied structure provides the viewer with an unprecedented experience, treading a middle ground between conventional theatre and binge watching on the couch, taking in a favourite series from beginning to end in a single sitting.

In terms of content this offers the public a surprising perspective on the banality of traditional norms and values. The globalised world of the twenty-first century is a complex construct, and *The Nation* confrontationally exposes both the dubious motives which determine the power of big business and the ridiculous hypocrisy at the foundation of what we think of as political correctness. It is precisely these elements which disrupt relationships and get in the way of peaceful solutions in a heterogeneously composed society: that is the lesson the production teaches us. As the audience, we get to know a multitude of characters, from a malicious, corrupt project developer at one end of the spectrum to an unbearable salon socialist at the other, who converts to Islam and starts wearing a headscarf out of solidarity with the Muslim community.

If this modern morality play conjures up any emotion, then it is first and foremost indignation. According to a standard pattern of expectation, theatre with political content appears to conform to the philosophy of a left-wing avant-garde, but *The Nation* breaks through that thinking in the directions it takes, the affiliations it exhibits and the principles it reveals, showing us society in its complete – often surprising, disruptive – multifacetedness. 'Good' and 'bad' are effectively redefined. The duplicity of the main characters, both to the left and the right of the middle in varying distances, pulls the audience mercilessly from that kind of personal bubble.

The Nation is built around a cast of top actors, a mixture of players with a considerable record of

Photo Sanne Peper

service and young, promising talent successfully following in the footsteps of the old guard. But even this distinguished tableau cannot conceal some rough edges towards the end of the production. De Vroedt appears not to have entirely succeeded in weaving the ingredients of the intrigue he has built up into a coherent whole, the initial episodes having left quite some loose ends. In the end the public is somewhat disappointed by the rather abstract apotheosis, although the final part offers several interesting plot twists.

But aside from the odd critical note it can be said that enough remains standing to make *The Nation* an event of the kind one only sees once every few years. Eric de Vroedt, since 2018 the new artistic director of Het Nationale Theater, together with his team of actors and staff has created an unparalleled tour de force. Following on from an already respectable production series at Het Nationale Theater, thanks to De Vroedt, *The Nation* is a production which does not lean on the great repertoire of the past, but which adds an original, monumental classic to the theatre canon. A contemporary, if not hypermodern and hyper-topical creation which begins from an apparently minor incident in a disadvantaged district of The Hague, but which eventually shines a light on the complex global world we live in.

JOS NIJHOF
Translated by Anna Asbury

www.hnt.nl

1   The first three parts of The Nation are available in full on You-
    Tube.
    Episode 1: www.youtube.com/watch?v=6a_8LrP_YEY&t=940s
    Episode 2: www.youtube.com/watch?v=U3xR_6xQzwY
    Episode 3 www.youtube.com/watch?v=us4rmh9rFRc
    A brief 'encore' is also available on YouTube:
    Episode 7: www.youtube.com/watch?v=a7nu7TbY_2g

Visual Arts

Adriaen Brouwer Returns Home

Ask the average art-lover to name the most important seventeenth-century Flemish artists and it's quite likely that they will think of Rubens, Van Dyck and Jordaens. Adriaen Brouwer will rarely figure in the list, even though he undoubtedly belongs there. His contemporaries admired his work. Rubens, who was an inveterate collector, had no less than seventeen works by Brouwer. Rembrandt too had a sketchbook and several of his drawings. Van Dyck painted the master's portrait.

Very little is known with any certainty about Adriaen Brouwer. He was probably born in the Flemish town of Oudenaarde in about 1605-1606. He soon left his birthplace and moved to the Northern Netherlands via Antwerp. In 1625 he lived in Amsterdam and in 1626 in Haarlem, where he joined a local chamber of rhetoric. His name also appears in a deed concerning the sale of paintings. Some sources state that in that city Brouwer was apprenticed to Frans Hals or his younger brother Dirck. But there is no proof of this apart from a few similarities of style.

In 1631 Brouwer returned to Antwerp and joined the Guild of St Luke. His name often appeared in municipal documents, usually in connection with his debts. He also spent some time in prison. When he was released, he moved in with the well-known engraver Paulus Pontius, who worked for Rubens, Van Dyck, Jordaens and other artists. In the same period Brouwer also joined the chamber of rhetoric called *De Violieren*.

Adriaen Brouwer died in 1638, aged barely thirty-two. In spite of his short career, he established a solid reputation and his paintings were much in demand. This popularity only increased after his death. This is apparent from, among other things, the large number of copies and forgeries that were made of his work. Nowadays his paintings are to be found in the collections of several major museums. The largest collection is that of the Alte Pinakothek in Munich, which has nineteen works.

Brouwer was a genre painter. Such painters were very popular as from the sixteenth century thanks to Pieter Bruegel the Elder. In genre paint-

Adriaen Brouwer, *Feeling*, c. 1635, oil on panel, 24 x 20 cm, Collection Residenzgalerie, Salzburg (Austria)

ing, everyday things are depicted in a realistic manner. Adriaen Brouwer's paintings are populated by habitués of inns, drinking, smoking, gambling and fighting. What he portrayed especially was human vices, and his paintings in the main have a moralising tone. But above all he was brilliant at rendering such emotions as joy, pleasure and rage.

Brouwer cannot simply be called an imitator of Bruegel. He updated that sixteenth-century master's visual idiom, adapted the range of colours and introduced new subjects. The quality of his small, loosely painted scenes raised him to solitary heights and he had a considerable influence on the artistic development of the Northern and Southern Netherlands. He continued to gather followers until long after his death, including Adriaen van Ostade (1610-1685), Joos van Craesbeeck (1605-1606 to c. 1660) and particularly David Teniers II (1610-1661).

Even today, Brouwer retains his reputation as a cheerful pub-crawler. The subjects of most of his paintings certainly contribute to this, but his membership of several chambers of rhetoric also plays a part. In Flanders, a romanticised biography by the popular writer Felix Timmermans, published shortly after the Second World War, also reinforced this bohemian image. In Oudenaarde, his native town, he was absorbed into local folklore and a brown beer and certain annual festivities are among the things named after him. The town also has a statue in which the artist is holding a paint-

er's palette in one hand and a tankard of beer in the other. But is this an accurate portrayal? Anthony Van Dyck's portrait of the master in any case shows a completely different, much more conventional Adriaen Brouwer.

In late 2018, an ambitious exhibition of work by Adriaen Brouwer is being held in the local museum in Oudenaarde. It is more than thirty years since a retrospective of this sort was mounted (at the Alte Pinakothek in Munich). In Oudenaarde they want to assemble at least thirty works by Brouwer. They will be accompanied by about thirty-five paintings by his contemporaries. In addition to a thorough re-examination of his work, a technical study will be made of the materials he used in the paintings. The exhibition will be held in the renowned late-gothic town hall and will be laid out on the basis of five thematic clusters, each with one absolute masterpiece as its focus. These clusters will form the foundation for a portrayal of Brouwer's artistic personality. The town of Oudenaarde will receive works on loan from a great many international museums. Among those that can be admired will be *The Smokers* from the Metropolitan Museum in New York. This is the only painting in which Brouwer portrayed himself. He looks at the viewer in surprise, while smoking and drinking with his painter-friends. This is Brouwer bearing out his own reputation.

DIRK VAN ASSCHE
Translated by Gregory Ball

Adriaen Brouwer, *Master of Emotions* (curator: Katrien Lichtert), from 15 September to 16 December 2018 in Oudenaarde's historical town hall (MOU).

Drama with a Touch of Humour
Jan Steen at the Mauritshuis

Jan Steen (1626-1679) was one of the most productive and popular painters of the 'Golden Age' in the Netherlands. He worked for both the free market and wealthy collectors and is best known for his depictions of chaotic households, inn scenes, brothels, quack doctors and feast days including that of St Nicholas. What is less well known is that he also did serious history paintings show-

Jan Steen, *Lot and His Daughters*, 1665, oil on canvas,
86 x 68 cm, Collection Städtische Wessenberg-Galerie,
Constance (Germany).

ing stories from the Bible and classical antiquity. Most of them date from the end of his life, after he had moved to Haarlem. The Mauritshuis in The Hague has now devoted an exhibition to this relatively unfamiliar part of his oeuvre. The occasion was its acquisition in 2011 of the history painting *Moses and Pharaoh's Crown*, which is a fine complement to the other fourteen paintings by Steen in the Mauritshuis collection. This painting has now been joined by twenty more exceptional history paintings, mostly from abroad. The informative, superbly produced catalogue, with its numerous illustrations of details, discusses and reproduces many more of Steen's history paintings.

The stories from the Old Testament or classical antiquity that Steen chose to depict are full of excitement and drama. In the works exhibited, a colourful collection of lively and richly costumed figures express their state of mind through their body language and facial expressions. Two of the paintings show *The Wrath of Ahasuerus*. When Esther, the Jewish wife of the Persian king Ahasuerus, reveals during a banquet that his trusted aide Haman was working on plans to destroy the Jewish people, Ahasuerus explodes with fury. In the painting from Birmingham, he leaps up wide-eyed and with clenched fist, much to the alarm of his courtiers, while Haman tries to duck away with

his face in his hands. This violent action knocks the peacock pie off the table and this also symbolises the pride that comes before a fall, Haman's in this case. A porcelain dish is already lying shattered on the floor. In the version from Cleveland, the same moment is portrayed slightly differently. On the extreme right, a jester with a bauble and red slouch hat is looking at the viewer with a grin; a minor but telling motif, because in sixteenth-century literature and art it was the jester's mockery that was intended to highlight the relative nature of human deeds and emotions.

The scene showing Anthony and Cleopatra, taken from Pliny's *Naturalis Historia*, is also set at a banquet. The Egyptian queen Cleopatra had bet her lover, the Roman military leader Mark Anthony, that she could easily spend the astronomical sum of ten million sesterces on a single feast. The dishes that Cleopatra had had served during the banquet were not extravagantly expensive, so Mark Anthony was already thinking he had won. But during the dessert, Cleopatra took a particularly precious pearl from her earring, dissolved it in vinegar and drank the mixture in one gulp. Before she could repeat this stunt with the other earring, she was declared the winner. Steen and his clients were evidently fascinated by this wager, because we know of four works that he painted on this subject. In the work from Göttingen exhibited here, Anthony's amazement is portrayed splendidly. In one of the other versions Steen included a self-portrait. While looking towards the viewer, he laughs at such decadence and waste.

Another striking painting is *Lot and His Daughters*, a story from the book of Genesis. Following the destruction of Sodom and Gomorrah, when Lot's wife had been turned into a pillar of salt, his daughters were under the impression that they and their father were the only people left in the world. Since they saw it as their duty to produce offspring, they made Lot drunk so that they could have intercourse with him. In this painting, Lot is apparently enjoying it. With sublime self-mockery, Steen gives him his own broadly smiling face, which we know from his self-portraits; the jester's red slouch hat, symbolising idiocy, is lying on the floor in front of him. In this way Steen emphasises not only the stupidity of the daughters' misapprehension, but also implies that every man can fall victim to his own lecherousness. Inappropriate sexual desire is also the subject of *Amnon and Tamar*, from the book of 2 Samuel in the Bible. Amnon, King David's eldest son, was in love with Tamar, his half-sister. When he feigned illness and Tamar took cakes she had baked herself to his bedside, he sent everyone out of the room so that he could rape her. He later took a dislike to the girl and called a servant to send her away. However, the consequence of this was his death.

The drama and the passions that Steen depicted can be seen as expansions of situations from everyday life presented as if on a stage. His characters play their parts with violent gestures and dramatic facial expressions. It is striking that they are wearing turbans, old-fashioned trunk-hose and open sleeves with slits that look as if they have come out of the costume chest box. The figure who looks straight at the viewer from the painting, offering a comment, also reminds us of the stage practices of that era. The most appealing theme in theatre, literature and opera is still that which Steen incorporated into many of his history paintings: women as temptresses or as the victims of male desires, and men who are unable to control their passions or other emotions. But what distinguishes Steen's paintings from those of his fellow artists is his mockery of the idiotic behaviour of his main characters. This mockery and humour are expressed above all in the clownish minor characters, the commentator or laughing jester, or Steen's grinning self-portrait. In his work, these familiar stories become an entertaining farce. The painter appears to want to tell us that people act with stupidity and that their emotions are only fleeting; but what's more, it's better to laugh at human behaviour than cry.

Jan Steen was one of those people who put human life very much into perspective. The ease with which he was able to capture dramatic moments appealed not only to the public of his day, but still makes him an attractive artist to a modern public too.

ILJA VELDMAN
Translated by Gregory Ball

Jan Steen's Histories, at the Mauritshuis in The Hague, until 13 May 2018 (www.mauritshuis.nl)

The Catalogue of Rubens's Oeuvre
Fifty Years of Work in Antwerp

The year 1968, half a century ago, saw the publication of *The Ceiling Paintings for the Jesuit Church in Antwerp*, the first part of what should, by 2020, become the complete catalogue of Rubens's oeuvre: the *Corpus Rubenianum Ludwig Burchard*. How did this massive project, carried out in Antwerp, come into being?

As early as 1919, the Antwerp art historian and museum director Paul Buschmann expressed the wish that the Rubens House there, which it had been decided to restore, should have a Rubens documentation centre to cater to the needs of researchers. When the plans for restoration gradually took shape in the years that followed and were finally carried out, it became clear that the building would be too small to serve this purpose. So, for this documentation centre, which by then had been named the 'Rubenianum', those concerned started thinking about a separate building adjacent to the restored Rubens House. The dilapidated Kolveniershof, where Antwerp's archer's guild had once met and which adjoined Rubens's garden, was discovered by chance during the Second World War. This building turned out to be the perfect location for the Rubenianum. After the war, the city council purchased the building. However, it was only many years later, in 1975, that work was able to start on the restoration of the old Kolveniershof and a new wing to extend it. In the meantime, as from about 1950, an academic library had been installed in the Rubens House, specialising in the Flemish art of Rubens's day. The intention was that it would one day be housed in the Rubenianum.

One of the milestones in the history of the development of the Rubenianum was the purchase, in 1963, of the complete documentation collected by the German-British art historian Ludwig Burchard (1886-1960), who had dominated the field of *Rubensforschung* (research into Rubens) since the 1930s. The collection amounted to about 8,000 books and many tens of thousands of photos.

Thanks to a focussed purchasing policy, the Rubenianum has gradually been able to develop into an important research centre that is open to students, scholars and others with a specific interest in Rubens and the Flemish art of his era. It was

initially housed on the upper floor of the Smidt-Van Gelder Museum in Antwerp, but since 1981 it has been located in the modern accommodation that was built at the now restored Kolveniershof, which is used for conferences, talks and representational purposes.

The most important task of the Rubenianum is the encouragement of the study of Rubens, specifically by stimulating the publication of an oeuvre catalogue based on the documentation bequeathed by Burchard. Enabling this publication was one of the imperative conditions of the agreement made between the city council and Burchard's heirs in 1963. The city council entrusted this task to the then Nationaal Centrum voor de Plastische Kunsten van de 16de en de 17de Eeuw (National Centre for the Plastic Arts of the 16th and 17th Centuries), which is now called the Centrum Rubenianum. This centre was established in 1959 and since its foundation was headed first by the Ghent professor Roger-Adolf d'Hulst (1917-1996) and subsequently by the then director of the Rubens House, Frans Baudouin (1920-2005). They can justifiably be called the 'founding fathers' of the whole Corpus Rubenianum project.

To implement this ambitious enterprise, an appeal was made to several young and recently appointed members of the academic staff of the Rubenianum who had in the meantime had the opportunity to specialise in the study of Rubens. It goes without saying that this small group (initially only three people) could not manage this whole operation on its own. For this reason help was also sought from experienced foreign scholars who were familiar with the oeuvre of Rubens and his contemporaries. In this way, the publication of the Corpus Rubenianum Ludwig Burchard became an international project, the first part of which was able to be published in 1968, exactly fifty years ago. This publication was from the beginning planned as a major series, initially consisting of twenty-six parts (this has since increased to twenty-nine). Of these parts, a considerable number are divided into several volumes, so that the final number of separate books is estimated to reach more than fifty. Each part of the Corpus is devoted to a particular subject in Rubens's oeuvre and is edited by one or more art historians who, as its authors, are responsible for the content, with their names printed on the title page.

Each author starts out from the information assembled and interpreted by Burchard and the views he adopted, which must be made clear and evident in the text. But each author/editor must at the same time check Burchard's material against present knowledge. Where necessary, they must supplement and correct and also clearly explain their own points of view when they differ from those of Burchard. Forty-four volumes have so far been published. The same number of authors are (or were) currently involved in the project. They are of Belgian, Dutch, French, British, German, Austrian and American nationality.

The project was initially subsidised by the Belgian National Fund for Scientific Research, and later by its successor, the Research Foundation – Flanders. However, this financial backing came to an end shortly after the beginning of this century, and the years that followed were not easy for the project. As from 2010, however, work was able to continue with new zest. The Rubenianum Fund was set up under the wing of the King Baudouin Foundation, led energetically by the Belgian entrepreneur Thomas Leysen. This patron funding aims to support Rubens research in Antwerp and to make completion of the Corpus Rubenianum Ludwig Burchard possible by 2020. Thanks to this fundraising project, the Rubenianum Centre was able to establish a group of proper editorial staff so that the tempo of publication could be substantially increased, meaning that 2020 now appears to be a feasible deadline for the project.

HANS VLIEGHE
Translated by Gregory Ball

www.rubenianum.be/en

Contributors

Dirk Van Assche
Deputy Editor *Ons Erfdeel vzw*
dirkvanassche@onserfdeel.be

Lars Bernaerts
Professor of Dutch Literature at Ghent
University
lars.bernaerts@ugent.be

Anne-Marie Beukes
Professor at the Department of
Languages, Cultural Studies and
Applied Linguistics at the University of
Johannesburg
ambeukes@uj.ac.za

Paul Binding
Writer and Critic
paulbinding@yahoo.co.uk

Derek Blyth
Journalist
derekblyth@lycos.com

Till-Holger Borchert
Director Musea Brugge
till-holger.borchert@brugge.be

Eric Bracke
Art Critic
eric.mc.bracke@gmail.com

Hans Cools
Historian at KU Leuven
hans.cools@kuleuven.be

Pieter Coupé
Editorial Secretary *Ons Erfdeel vzw*
onserfdeel@onserfdeel.be

Lise Delabie
Critic
lise.delabie@gmail.com

Ann Demeester
Director
Frans Hals Museum | De Hallen
Haarlem
a.demeester@franshalsmuseum.nl

Luc Devoldere
Chief Editor *Ons Erfdeel vzw*
luc.devoldere@onserfdeel.be

Bart Eeckhout
Journalist
bart.eeckhout@demorgen.be

Jaap Grave
Academic Researcher and Critic
jaap.grave@gmx.de

Laurens Ham
Lecturer of Modern Dutch Literature at
Utrecht University
l.j.ham@uu.nl

Charlotte Van Hacht
Fashion Critic
charlottevanhacht@hotmail.com

Chris van der Heijden
Historian and Writer
chris.vanderheijden@hu.nl

Leen Huet
Art Historian and Writer
leen.huet@scarlet.be

Joris van de Kerkhof
Journalist
joris.van.de.kerkhof@nos.nl

Koen Kleijn
Art Historian and Writer
koenkleijn@gmail.com

Jorn Konijn
Architecture & Design Curator
jorn@thismustbetheplace.nl

Everhard Korthals Altes
Art Historian at Delft University
e.korthalsaltes@tudelft.nl

Pieter Leroy
Professor of Political Sciences of the
Environment at Nijmegen University
p.leroy@fm.ru.nl

Geerdt Magiels
Biologist and Philosopher
geerdt.magiels@telenet.be

Ruben Mantels
Historian and Researcher at
Ghent University
ruben.mantels@ugent.be

Jos Nijhof
Theatre Critic
nijhof@xs4all.nl

Emanuel Overbeeke
Music Critic
overbeekemanuel@gmail.com

Koen Peeters
Writer
koenrm.peeters@telenet.be

Tineke Reijnders
Critic
tineker@xs4all.nl

Eric Rinckhout
Art Critic
eric.rinckhout@gmail.com

Elisabeth Salverda

Piano Technician, Musician,
Researcher, Translator
elisabethdamai@gmail.com

Reinier Salverda

Honorary Professor of Dutch Language
and Literature (University College
London)
reiniersalverda@yahoo.co.uk

Gary Schwartz

Art Historian
gary.schwartz@xs4all.nl

Manfred Sellink

Director Royal Museum of Fine Arts
Antwerp
manfred.sellink@kmska.be

Anja K. Sevcik

Head of the Department of Baroque
Painting
Wallraf-Richartz-Museum & Fondation
Corboud
sevcik@wallraf.museum

Irina Sokolova

Curator of Dutch Paintings,
Hermitage Museum
i_sokolova@tele2.nl

Tomas Vanheste

Deputy Editor *Ons Erfdeel vzw*
t.vanheste@telenet.be

Ilja Veldman

Art Historian
ilja.veldman@gmail.com

Alejandro Vergara

Senior Curator of Flemish and
Northern European Paintings
Museo Nacional del Prado
alejandro.vergara@museodelprado.es

Gerdien Verschoor

Director CODART
gerdien.verschoor@codart.nl

Hans Vlieghe

Emeritus Professor of History of Art at
KU Leuven
hansvlieghe.artes@skynet.be

Caroline Voet

Architect
info@carolinevoet.be

Adriaan Waiboer

Head of Collections and Research
National Gallery of Ireland
awaiboer@ngi.ie

Mirjam Westen

Curator Contemporary Art at
Museum Arnhem and Critic
mirjam.westen@museumarnhem.nl

Karin Wolfs

Film Critic
mail@karinwolfs.nl

Yao-Fen You

Associate Curator of European Sculpture
& Decorative Arts
European Art
The Detroit Institute of Arts
yyou@dia.org

Ad Zuiderent

Poet and Critic
ad.zuiderent@xs4all.nl

Translators

Anna Asbury
Gregory Ball
Pleuke Boyce
David Colmer
Lindsay Edwards
Chris Emery
Scott Rollins
Julian Ross
Elisabeth Salverda
Paul Vincent
Laura Watkinson

Advisor on English usage
Elisabeth Salverda (United Kingdom)

Colophon

Institution

This twenty-sixth yearbook is published by the Flemish-Dutch cultural institution 'Ons Erfdeel vzw', with the support of the Dutch Ministry of Education, Culture and Science (The Hague), the Flemish Authorities (Brussels). In partnership with CODART.

CODART
International council
for curators
of Dutch and Flemish art

'Ons Erfdeel vzw' also publishes the Dutch-language periodical *Ons Erfdeel* and the French-language periodical *Septentrion. Arts, lettres et culture de Flandre et des Pays-Bas*, the bilingual yearbook *De Franse Nederlanden – Les Pays-Bas Français* and a series of books in several languages covering various aspects of the culture of the Low Countries.

The Board of Directors of 'Ons Erfdeel vzw'

President:
Herman Balthazar

Managing Director:
Luc Devoldere

Directors:
Bert De Graeve
Patrick Kindt
Hilde Laga
Mark Leysen
Marita Mathijsen
Frits van Oostrom
Danny De Raymaeker
Jan Schinkelshoek
Paul Schnabel
Adriaan van der Staay
Ludo Verhoeven

Address of the Editorial Board and the Administration

'Ons Erfdeel vzw', Murissonstraat 260,
8930 Rekkem, Flanders, Belgium
T +32 56 41 12 01, F +32 56 41 47 07
www.onserfdeel.be, www.onserfdeel.nl
thelowcountriesblog.onserfdeel.be
VAT BE 0410.723.635

Philippe Vanwalleghem *Head of Administration*
Dorothee Cappelle *Administrative Secretary*

Aims

With *The Low Countries,* a yearbook founded by Jozef Deleu (Chief Editor from 1993 until 2002), the editors and publisher aim to present to the world the culture and society of the Dutch-speaking area which embraces both the Netherlands and Flanders, the northern part of Belgium.

The articles in this yearbook survey the living, contemporary culture of the Low Countries as well as their cultural heritage. In its words and pictures *The Low Countries* provides information about literature and the arts, but also about broad social and historical developments in Flanders and the Netherlands.

The culture of Flanders and the Netherlands is not an isolated phenomenon; its development over the centuries has been one of continuous interaction with the outside world. In consequence the yearbook also pays due attention to the centuries-old continuing cultural interplay between the Low Countries and the world beyond their borders.

By drawing attention to the diversity, vitality and international dimension of the culture of Flanders and the Netherlands, *The Low Countries* hopes to contribute to a lively dialogue between them and other cultures.

ISSN 0779-5815
ISBN 978-90-79705-290
Statutory deposit no. D/2018/3006/1
NUR 612

Copyright © 2018 'Ons Erfdeel vzw' and SABAM Belgium 2018
Printed by die Keure, Bruges, Flanders, Belgium
Design by Stelvio D'Houst (die Keure)

Prices for the yearbook 2018, no. 26

Belgium € 37, The Netherlands € 39, Europe € 39

Other Countries: € 45
All prices inclusive of shipping costs

You can order this book from our webshop at www.onserfdeel.be and pay by credit card

As well as the yearbook
The Low Countries,
the Flemish-Dutch cultural
institution 'Ons Erfdeel vzw'
publishes a number of books
covering various aspects of
the culture of Flanders and
the Netherlands.

Wim Daniëls
Talking Dutch.
Illustrated; 80 pp.

J.A. Kossmann-Putto &
E.H. Kossmann
*The Low Countries.
History of the Northern
and Southern Netherlands.*
Illustrated; 64 pp.

Isabella Lanz &
Katie Verstockt,
*Contemporary Dance
in the Low Countries.*
Illustrated; 128 pp.

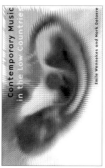

Mark Delaere &
Emile Wennekes,
*Contemporary Music in
the Low Countries.*
Illustrated; 128 pp.

*Standing Tall in Babel.
Languages in Europe.*
Sixteen European writers
about their mother tongues.
Hardcover; 144 pp.

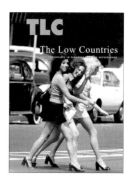

Between 1993 and 2017
twenty-five issues of the
yearbook *The Low Countries*
have been published.

Dutch language area	
French language area in Belgium	
Brussels bilingual area: Dutch and French	
German language area in Belgium	
Bilingual area: Dutch and Frisian	
◉	Capital city
•	Provincial capital
——	National frontier
......	Provincial Boundary

EUROPE

NORTH SEA

GRONINGEN
•Groningen
Leeuwarden
FRIESLAND
Assen
DRENTHE

NORTH HOLLAND
FLEVOLAND
Lelystad
•Zwolle
OVERIJSSEL
Haarlem
AMSTERDAM

The Hague
Utrecht
UTRECHT
SOUTH HOLLAND
GELDERLAND
Arnhem

ZEELAND
Middelburg
's-Hertogenbosch
NORTH BRABANT

LIMBURG

Antwerp
ANTWERP
Bruges•
EAST
WEST FLANDERS
Ghent
FLANDERS
FLEMISH BRABANT
BRUSSELS•
•Leuven
LIMBURG
Hasselt•
Maastricht

GERMANY

•Wavre
WALLOON BRABANT
HAINAUT
Mons•
Namur•
LIÈGE
Liège•

FRANCE

NAMUR

LUXEMBOURG

LUX.
Arlon

0   km   50

© Carto